Paulus

CW01662820

EWEN McGOWAN

# Salvaging the Pelican

*Confronting tragedy and adversity in the heart of Africa*

MEREO

Mereo Books

2nd Floor, 6-8 Dyer Street, Cirencester, Gloucestershire, GL7 2PF
An imprint of Memoirs Books. www.mereobooks.com
and www.memoirsbooks.co.uk

Salvaging the Pelican

ISBN: 978-1-86151-589-6

First published in Great Britain in 2023
by Mereo Books, an imprint of Memoirs Books.



The names of some characters have been changed.

A CIP catalogue record for this book is available from the British Library.


The address for Memoirs Books can be
found at www.mereobooks.com

Mereo Books Ltd. Reg. No. 12157152

Typeset in 11/17pt Plantin
by Wiltshire Associates.
Printed and bound in Great Britain

*TO KAREN AND KATE*

# Contents

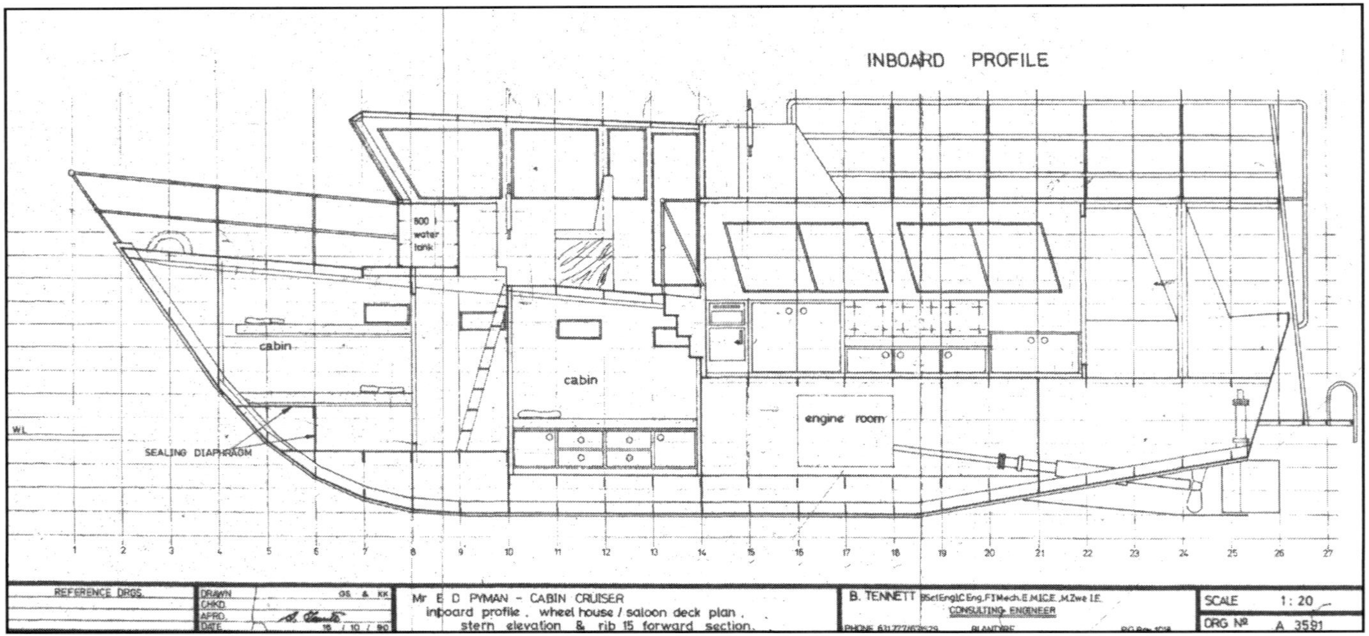
INBOARD PROFILE
800 l water tank
cabin
cabin
engine room
SEALING DIAPHRAGM
WL
1 2 3 4 5 6 7 8 9 10 11 12 13 14 15 16 17 18 19 20 21 22 23 24 25 26 27
REFERENCE DRGS.
DRAWN GS & KK
CHKD
APPD
DATE 15 / 10 / 90
Mr E D PYMAN - CABIN CRUISER
inboard profile, wheel house / saloon deck plan,
stern elevation & rib 15 forward section.
B. TENNETT
CONSULTING ENGINEER
SCALE 1 : 20
DRG Nº A 3591

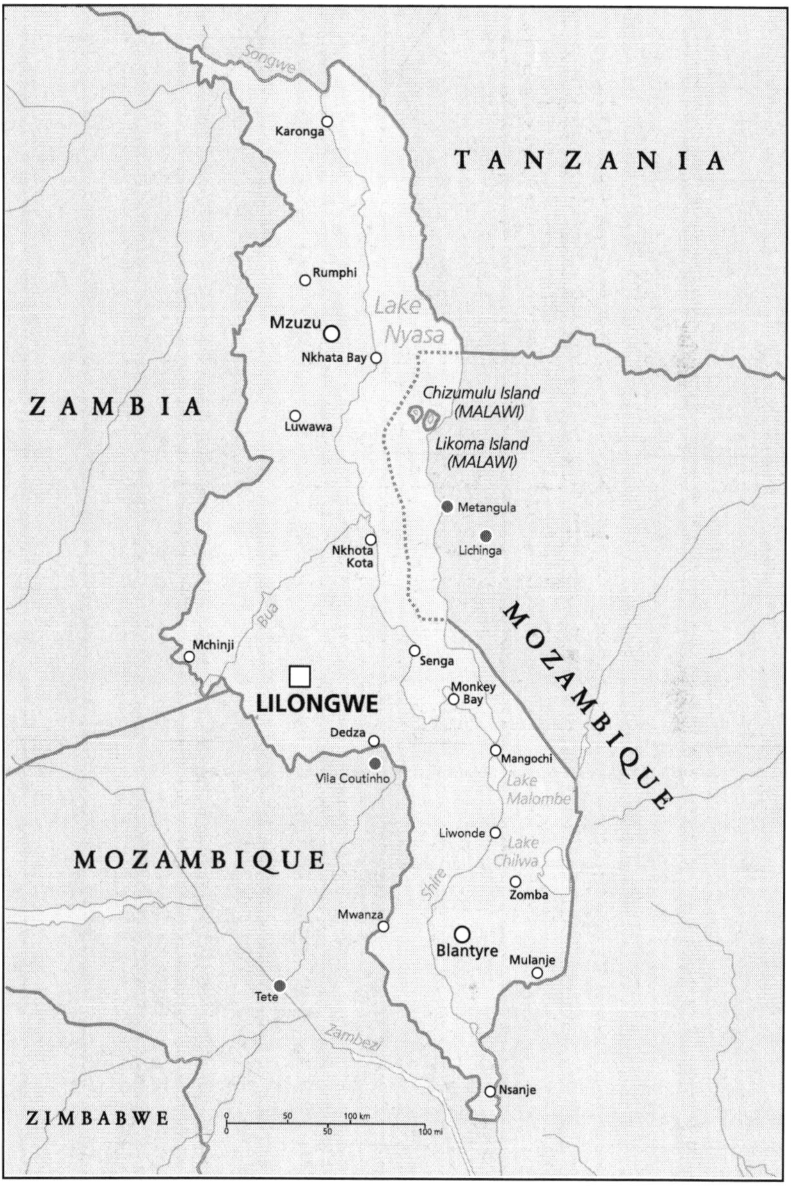

Songwe
Karonga
TANZANIA
Rumphi
Lake
Nyasa
Mzuzu
Nkhata Bay
ZAMBIA
Chizumulu Island
(MALAWI)
Likoma Island
(MALAWI)
Luwawa
Metangula
Lichinga
Nkhota
Kota
Bua
MOZAMBIQUE
Mchinji
Senga
LILONGWE
Monkey
Bay
Dedza
Mangochi
Vila Coutinho
Lake
Malombe
Liwonde
Lake
Chilwa
MOZAMBIQUE
Zomba
Shire
Mwanza
Blantyre
Mulanje
Tete
Zambezi
Nsanje
ZIMBABWE
0
50
100 km
0
50
100 mi

*The friends whom we have lost do not rest in the earth, they are buried in our hearts ... so that we should always be in their company.*

Alexandre Dumas, *The Count of Monte Cristo*

*When in the end the day came on which I was going away, I learned the strange learning that things can happen which we ourselves cannot possibly imagine, either beforehand, or at the time when they are taking place, or afterwards when we look back on them.*

Karen Blixen, *Out of Africa*

A large and majestic bird, the pelican is regarded as a symbol of bravery, kindness and self-sacrifice. The ancient Egyptians believed that it represented healing and renewal, possessing the ability to affirm safe passage in the underworld for someone who had died. It was also believed that pelicans would plunge into storms to save those in peril at sea.

# Prologue

The twilight drama has lots of onlookers. Not only our workers; it seems as if the entire nearby village is strung out around the shoreline of the little bay, the girls from the morning parade standing silently with the adults, all waiting and watching expectantly. The portside lean of the *Pelican* has increased yet further and is now so severe that Stephen and Anderson are struggling to keep themselves and the pump in place. I have Stephen's torch, flicking the beam between the pump, the hatch and the mooring lines, nervously looking for any signs of trouble, ready to shout out a warning if any of the lines snap.

Surely there could not be much water left in the rear compartment? I am beginning to doubt that the silted lake bed will ever release the *Pelican* from its cloying embrace when we feel an almost imperceptible shift in the decking. Then, in slow motion, the *Pelican* rolls to starboard and levels out as the stern rises out of the water. In unison Stephen and I roar '"Yeeees!' We shut the pump down and from out of the twilight come shouts of jubilation and we can see shadows in motion, the morning parade cavorting and splashing around, hollering out the universal high-pitched African yodel. Calisto's head appears at the hatch, the light from his head torch jumping across our faces and revealing huge grins all round.

So there are simple memories. Snapshots of our lives if you will. Those fleeting recollections that often seem to spring out of the blue accompanied by a crooked grimace or a quirky smile. A particular song from a bygone era will often do the trick, the spicy smell from something an old flame used to cook or perhaps the utterance of a particular phrase. Funny, sad, nostalgic, embarrassing, they dance around the edges of our inner self.

Then there are what I call vignettes. More entire than simple recollections, they are those adventures centred around intense experiences and streamed with full on sound and colour. Smiles and grimaces, sobs and sighs of despair and relief, the external expressions of whirring internal emotions. Almost surreal and yet so crystalline that it seems as if they happened perhaps only last week, or last month, rather than a decade or more ago. The images can roll one into another until they form a long line of links stretching over many years creating a chain of living narratives with the most profound of them framed in unexpected achievements or grim ordeals etched deep into our consciousness. Hard-fought triumphs that lift our spirit soaring high into cerulean skies and traumas that drive us far down into the dark, silent depths. Quite often it seems to me that the direction of our lives is determined by the smallest of margins. Crazy, sublime, frightening or devastating, these reminiscences are locked into the core of our memory vault and recalled at will – although the worst of them we would often dearly like to bury and be able to forget. And yet, whether these vignettes eventually turn out to be inspiring or destructive, they are an integral part of us, fashioning and defining us by shining a light onto the jumbled mosaic that is our very personal inner life. How we react to them inevitably tells us a lot about ourselves.

CHAPTER 1

# Concepts and Crocs

It's a hot, sultry day on the river and the *Pelican* is taking provisions on board. The 'boat' is fifty feet long and nearly nineteen tons of solid steel plating powered by twin diesel engines. That probably makes her more like a small ship or a large motor cruiser, but I tend to think of her as a boat. In my mind ships are the length of football pitches and filled with oil, stacked with containers or carrying hundreds of passengers, whilst motor cruisers conjure up images of fast, luxury craft owned by the rich, and although the *Pelican* is comfortable, she is certainly not fast or luxurious.

She is moored in the reeds alongside the eastern bank of the Shire River near a large trading centre called Liwonde in the Republic of Malawi, a small landlocked country in south-eastern Africa. Just downstream is a solid barrage across the river whose enormous gates are opened and closed to help control the great flow of water which originates from Lake Malawi some seventy kilometres upstream and from where it heads south until eventually it joins the massive Zambezi and heads east to the

Indian Ocean. It's a total journey of two thousand kilometres, substantially more than the distance we are intending to embark on with the *Pelican*. But then journeys can't be measured only in distance. Or time.

I first met my father-in-law to be, Don Pyman, in 1993. Just under six feet tall with an angular, wiry frame, a short white beard and penetrating light blue eyes, he had a ready smile and a loud guffawing laugh. Highly gregarious, he loved to engage in animated discussions where his passion and commitment in relation to a wide range of topics shone brightly but could at times also seem overbearing. Despite his deep-rooted principles and beliefs, he respected those who stood their ground and gave as good as they got. Frequently in the evenings family and friends would congregate in the drawing room of his house for sundowners. Dressed in light brown slacks, a check shirt and cravat with a small Browning pistol in his trouser pocket as life insurance against any violent intruders, he would sip on a whisky whilst the conversation whirred around the room. The Malawians working for him on the farm loved his interaction and hands-on approach. Rather like the medical mantra for teaching surgeons, he believed in watch me do this, now you have a go, now you show someone else how to do it. Scrupulously fair and even handed, he was quick with praise and equally quick with his Welsh temper – although everyone knew it was mainly bark with only a tiny bite. He had a delightful linguistic quirk. He spoke English without any real trace of an accent, but he spoke the local language, Chichewa, with a thick Welsh accent. I've often wanted to find a linguist or speech therapist who could explain this bizarre anomaly to me.

Early on in our acquaintance it became clear to me that Don had a persistent hankering centred around ships and the sea. His great-grandfather, George Pyman, was a fisherman based in West

Hartlepool on the north-east coast of England who first went to sea at the very youthful age of ten in the family coble, a small flat-bottomed, high-bowed fishing vessel developed on the north-east coast. The high bows enabled this small open boat to cope with the choppy seas and the flat bottom had the great advantage that it could be beached on a sandy or shale shore – often the only way to find safety on that highly exposed coastline. The coble was regarded as dangerous for the uninitiated sailor but fast and safe for those with experience. I imagine that George quickly became very experienced. By 1843, at the age of only twenty-one, he was working as the master of a brig collier – a two-masted, square-rigged wooden sailing ship with a displacement of over 450 tons and noted for its speed and manoeuvrability.

The construction in 1851 of that huge glass and iron showpiece known as Crystal Palace earmarked the real start of the industrial revolution, and George must have recognised the opportunity presented by the rapidly growing demand for coal. The marvellous phenomenon known as the steam engine was changing the world, with industrialization growing at an exponential rate, fuelled by the black stuff. George went into partnership with his brother-in-law and a businessman called Thomas Scurr. The firm grew until they owned a number of brig colliers, which were used to export coal to Europe and the Baltic region. The cost of a screw collier, the larger steamship version, was around eight times the cost of a brig collier, but by 1865 Pymans was able to launch its first steamship capable of carrying double the quantity of coal, around 650 tons. It was also much faster and more reliable than the brig colliers. From there on the company expanded rapidly and also became involved in the timber trade.

George and his wife, Elizabeth, had a typically large Victorian family of nine children. Having taken on responsibility at a young age, George clearly felt that his sons should do the same, so at the age of twenty-two his fifth child, John William, 'JW', was sent to another coal mining area, Penarth in South Wales. In 1874, with George's help and connections, young JW set up in business as a shipbroker and coal merchant under the banner of Pyman, Watson and Co in Cardiff. The following year JW married Sarah Emma Emerson and together they went one better than George. Sarah bore him ten children, one short of a football team, and Don's father, Sydney, number nine in the line-up, set up as a dairy farmer in Ross-on-Wye, where Don was born in 1920. The family firm of Pyman, Watson & Co continued in one form or another, run by his brothers and their heirs, until 1964, when the records show that it went into liquidation.

I know the area around Ross-on-Wye well as I used to go climbing and walking around there. Located on the northern edge of the Forest of Dean, an ancient woodland with great ecology, it is aptly called an area of outstanding natural beauty. My strongest memories are of climbs around Wintour's Leap, so named because during the English Civil War Sir John Wintour, a Royalist who was being hotly pursued by the Roundhead Parliamentary forces, apparently escaped them by leaping off the cliff on his steed and landing in the River Wye below. I can safely say that his chances of surviving such a leap without a parachute for him and his horse would have been nil.

Subsequently Sydney, his wife Millicent and their four children moved again, this time to a large country home just outside Paignton in Devon. Growing up in the countryside, Don developed a lifelong love for its flora and fauna. He and his older brother, Desmond, spent days on end exploring the woods, tracks, hedgerows, streams and fields around them. Eventually, however, these explorations had to be put on hold following the outbreak of the Second World War. Don signed up for the Air Force and was sent to Salisbury in Rhodesia, modern-day Zimbabwe, where they were training pilots to be sent back to fight the war in the skies over Europe. Don morphed from being a student pilot to a pilot instructor. I can imagine that his character – a no-nonsense, firm approach – would have seen him earmarked as a trainer from early on. Don rarely spoke about this time in his life, but the stresses involved in trying to train pilots up to a level where they would stand some sort of a chance in the crowded, lead filled skies of Europe, clearly took its toll on him. After all, the odds were not good. A fighter pilot's chances of surviving the war were less than fifty per cent. As the weeks passed Don and his fellow instructors would get news from back home, usually sober and grim, of pilots shot out of the sky. He developed ulcers, which were to plague him for the rest of his life.

Upon being demobbed, Don knew one thing for certain. He wanted to return to explore the countryside – the African bush. It was the heyday of the colonial era in Africa. White Mischief and all that. Don, though, had more important business in mind. First with the British Central Africa Company and later with the British Cotton Marketing Board, he was busy far out in the bush of Nyasaland (now Malawi) in an area known as the Lower Shire, growing crops and setting up cotton ginneries, exploring and tracking game. Eventually, however, even he tired of the very solitary existence and the furious heat and humidity. He moved upstream to the cooler Upper Shire and closer to civilization. With very little cash and a very big loan, he purchased a farm just outside the then capital of Zomba, where he would settle, marry, raise a family and remain, very contented for the most part, for the rest of his life.

There was, however, just the little matter of a vessel and the lake. In his late sixties Don felt the call of George and JW. A sort of hereditary tug at his heartstrings. A boat to explore the lake now sat at the top of his bucket list. It was something in a sense which he could not escape.

In his study he had hung a huge old oil painting. It's a truly Victorian portrait of JW dressed in a dark suit and set against a dark background. There's really only one area to look at because it's the only area of light – his face, collar and tie. He's probably in his mid sixties at the time, silver hair with a receding hairline and a matching silver moustache. A maroon tie complements his stiff white collar, with a pearl tiepin just below the knot. His slightly ruddy complexion is not that of a sailor who's spent a lifetime on deck in the sun and wind, but of a businessman running a shipping company who spends too much time sitting behind a desk and enjoys a tipple of port and wine. The look is stern and there are no laughter lines, just a couple of faint frown lines between his eyebrows. The look says that life generally, and portraits in particular, are no laughing matter. He has Don's light blue eyes, which stare out of the canvas and follow you à la Mona Lisa. Ever watchful, he conveys to me some deep inner sadness, as if he's harbouring a terrible secret or is party to a great tragedy. I can imagine Don sitting at his desk looking out of the window, JW on the wall behind, boring into his back. Perhaps he's reproachful and insistent and makes the hairs on the back of his neck stand on end. 'So what about it? You come from shipping stock. You've explored the land. Get on with you and explore the lake.' On the other hand he might just have that knowing look that says, 'Build a ship in the middle of Africa and sail around in it? Are you seventy or twenty? Are you delirious? Do you think you're David Livingstone?'

And that was the point. Malawi is a small landlocked country, but it has the seventh largest lake on the planet, 500 kilometres long, 80 kilometres wide at the widest point and around 700 metres deep at its deepest. The Colonials called it the Calendar

Lake because the measurements equate roughly to 365 miles long by 52 miles wide. Right on his doorstep, the lake provided Don an opportunity and an eloquent solution to the call of the sea. He was left with the tantalizing problem of finding a suitable craft to plonk on it. The answer lay in going the extra mile. Instead of scrabbling around to find and modify an existing boat, why not build one from scratch to your own design preferences?

Although Don conceived the idea of the *Pelican*, he had to work out how to put the thought into practice. He approached Basil, a long-time friend and a consulting engineer, and together they hatched a plan to build not one but two ships. One each. The design and drawings were purchased from Bruce Roberts International, an Australian firm based in Brisbane. 'Building your boat makes more sense than ever,' their brochure proclaimed. 'Save 65% to 75% basic cost.' Now that would have appealed to Don and Basil. Hugely. Design, do and create. Don hated wastage and excessive cost, the modern disease and frenzied obsession with buy and consume. They purchased the bare minimum in the way of drawings for less than one thousand dollars and Basil then tweaked things and put together the technical drawings for each craft. In May 1991 they approached Brown and Clapperton, a small local company that specialized in making steel windows and doorframes for houses, about putting together the steel superstructure. Located in Blantyre, the capital of the southern region of the country, the company was only an hour's drive from Don's farm and was almost on Basil's doorstep.

Although this was clearly well outside their normal remit, B&C was happy to take on the work, which would guarantee jobs for quite some time to come. It tackled the assembly of the steel superstructure fearlessly but very slowly. Don made weekly trips into town to check on the progress of his conception, which if not immaculate was, as far as the local populace standing outside the 'shipyard' gawking at it were concerned, verging on the miraculous.

Three long years passed but finally, many thousands of welding rods later, the hull was completed. Two reconditioned 4-litre Perkins diesel tractor engines were winched up and bolted into the engine compartment and the decking was then welded onto the hull. Almost overnight the whole project suddenly took on real shape and form. It's always surprised me how very much larger a hull looks out of the water, and Don's little ship truly dominated its surroundings. I've often subsequently wondered how many hundreds of litres of red oxide paint went into protecting all that steelwork from the elements.

Bolted on to a purpose-built trailer, she was towed a kilometre down the road to a small Italian engineering company. Progress was painfully slow, carried out between slack periods in the company's normal work schedule. Eventually, some two years later, all the engineering works – insertion and connection of the props, the steering gear and so forth – were completed, and the *Pelican* continued her quixotic journey towards some form of completion and water readiness. She was now trailered fifteen kilometres north of town to a Catholic Technical Training Institute. I remember watching the students staring in bemusement as they were handed the plans and charged with sorting out the electrics, gas and water connections, helping with the pumping system, all the woodwork and basically anything and everything else that the design drawings revealed or Don requested. If they succeeded in these various tasks their curricula vitae were guaranteed to have an interesting twist that would enable them to chat intimately and at length with prospective employers about the complexities and experience gained in fitting out a ship!

By the time the *Pelican* made her final journey on land, down the highway to the Shire River in November 1996, she had a full complement of vital statistics. She weighed in with a displacement just under nineteen tons, an overall length just over twelve metres, a beam of three and a half metres and a draft (the distance between the waterline and the bottom of the hull) of only one metre. She had a main cabin with a fridge and cooker, two double sleeping berths forward along with the heads, a wheelhouse and a top deck with a dual set of controls. It had taken five and a half long years from inception.

The launch, on a hot and sultry morning in mid-November 1996, provided its own bit of drama. The ancient mobile crane that had trailered the *Pelican* down to the Shire noisily reversed the trailer down to the edge of the river. The bolts and welds attaching the *Pelican* to the trailer were removed and the crane arm began to slowly winch the *Pelican* down into the water. Impatient with all these careful, fussy logistics and with sudden impetuousness, the *Pelican* launched herself, sliding off the trailer and pitching rapidly backwards into the river, pulling the crane over as she plashed into life. In a few seconds she converted Don's dream from a project into a reality, and in the water she was transformed, immediately taking on a new identity. You might, if you had that sort of curiously singular and bizarre mind that tries to make parallels between boats and people, say that she was neat and trim, a very pretty little ship with nice curves and the undeniable hint of quite possibly being rather lively. A Kylie Minogue rather than, say, a Pavarotti.

Don gave a short speech to the small assembly of friends and relatives. 'For many years I have had an ambition to own a ship in which I could cruise on Lake Malawi and the Shire River during my sunset years. This ambition has at long last been achieved.'

He gave a potted history of his family's proud shipping heritage, thanked all involved and could barely hide his excitement and impatience to step aboard.

In September 2003 a South African architect named John Fleming was a man on a mission. Driving from Johannesburg up to Metangula in northern Mozambique, a trip of around 2,500 kilometres, his 4x4 was loaded to the hilt, as was the double axle trailer he was pulling. With tight self-imposed timelines and the edgy impatience that is a noted hallmark of the Johannesburger, he had been pushing himself and the vehicle hard. As he was driving along the stretch of road that marked the boundary of my brother-in-law Stephen's farm, one of the trailer axles found all the joggling and bouncing around on the old road too much, and it snapped. Having inspected the problem and realising that he was not going anywhere further in a hurry, John barely had time to ponder his next move before Stephen drove by. Recognizing someone in an unhappy situation, he pulled over and made a plan. John stayed the night with Stephen and his wife, Tam. Over dinner, he explained to them what he was about. He worked for a Johannesburg-based company called Hugh Brown Holdings and he was heading up the company's Niassa Eco-Tourism Project, which was based in northern Mozambique in what is now Niassa Province, bordering the eastern side of Lake Malawi.

The project comprised two parts. Firstly, the company had obtained a concession from the Mozambican government on an enormous area of forestry reserve – possibly as big as fifty thousand hectares – directly inland of the little port and naval base called Metangula. They were putting in the road infrastructure and intended to build a luxury lodge for clients who were interested in game safaris and hunting. This was a seriously isolated part of the planet and had barely been touched by human habitation or the recent civil war.

John, however, was not involved to any meaningful degree in the lodge and safari project. His baby was putting together a concept on the lakeshore to attract ultra high net clientele from South Africa. In furtherance of this concept they were starting by rehabilitating an existing landing strip on the Metangula Peninsula so that prospective investors could be flown in by private plane. The intention was to put together enough backers so that they could build luxury apartments on the lakeshore together with a number of very exclusive private villas. The mega-rich could buy or rent a villa or an apartment, fly in with family, friends or a mistress or two and enjoy something unique and exclusive. Communications would be upgraded so that these clients could broker their multi-million dollar deals whilst lounging around an infinity pool enjoying the view, or perhaps motoring out onto the lake in a chartered cruiser, fishing, diving and exploring the coastline. Those feeling even more adventurous could venture inland to go on safari.

Over the ensuing months and years we all got to know John well. Alongside his amiable manner and clean good looks, he had a sharp eye and a mind that was deeply focused on his work. An architect by training, he was also a natural salesman with an infectious enthusiasm. His seemingly boundless energy appeared to be directed entirely towards driving 'his concept' forwards.

The mention of boats led to talk of the *Pelican*. John had noticed the motor vessel on previous trips when crossing the Shire River at the Liwonde barrage, but he had not known who owned it. Now he did. He immediately floated the idea of chartering the *Pelican*. It was just the thing to help promote the project. They could take backers out on it for sundowners and to inspect the glorious, rugged coastline. Stephen said he would put the idea to his father-in-law, who might well be amenable to the idea. After all, Don had built the *Pelican* specifically to explore the lake, so this might well be the opportunity to finally take his boat up into the lake and put her to use properly.

Less than twenty-four hours later, with the broken axle welded, John was flying up the road towards his concept. I surmise that he was musing that the broken axle had in fact not been all that irritating but rather pleasantly providential. Don, it turned out, was happy for the *Pelican* to take her next step in life, up into the lake.

It took seven months to get everything ready. Not only checking and provisioning the *Pelican*, but also obtaining the seaworthiness certificate from the government's Marine Department, insurance, Charter Agreement between Don and John Fleming and in particular all the necessary and critically important documentation to allow us to take the boat into Mozambique waters.

We had heard of a speedboat with white Malawi residents on board which recently had inadvertently drifted into Mozambican waters when their engine failed. The Mozambicans, in probably their only working Customs boat, were very excited when they found this boat, and were not inclined to accept the occupants' explanations for their presence without papers. They were surely spies (spying on what, you might reasonably ask) or guns and contraband smugglers. There was no sign of these items on board so they were clearly coming over to collect, and the failed engine story was just a cleverly planned ruse to try to fool the Mozambicans. But they were smarter than that and were not to be fooled. So they locked them up for a while to see if they could eke out a confession or two.

Eventually the diplomats got together and sorted it all out. Face-saving apologies were given by the supposed spies/smugglers and they returned safely back to Malawi to take up their posts as engineers and company directors.

Finally it was D Day: Sunday, 2nd May 2004. In the early morning five of us – Don, my wife Karen, my brother-in-law Stephen, Andrew Barr aka Drew, a very good family friend, and myself – squeeze into Don's Toyota Landcruiser and drive from the farm down the escarpment to Liwonde. We potter around doing last minute checks on the boat as the temperature and humidity quickly rise. There's no river breeze here. The *Pelican* is sheltered by tall grass and reeds that trap any wind and turn the riverbank into a heat sink.

I've already been down into the engine compartment and squeezed, pulled and cursed my way along the bottom of the hull between the port diesel tank, which is like an enormous radiator bolted to the side of the hull, and the port engine. It's claustrophobic and seriously dank down there and I need a head torch to do the inspection, plus a boiler suit to keep the grime off me. The suit adds hugely to my body temperature and the general feeling of being hemmed him. Within seconds I'm bathed in sweat and constantly running a sleeve over my forehead. There are no signs of any diesel or water leakage, so I struggle back up to the main cabin and lose the boiler suit as quickly as possible.

Walking forward and up the steps into the wheelhouse, I find Don sitting on the captain's swivel chair watching life on the river. There's never a dull moment. On the barrage there's an incessant stream of people and transport. Overloaded, teetering buses belching diesel fumes, cars crammed with people and goods, the occasional new 4x4 belonging to either a government official or an NGO (Non Government Organisation), the 'Lords of Poverty' as one author called them. A constant stream of bicycles, back racks loaded with charcoal, or perhaps live goats, or baskets filled with live chickens or sacks full of seasonal fruits and vegetables. Hundreds of pedestrians on personal errands or 'busyness.'

On selected areas of the riverbank the grass has been cut and trampled away and women and children are busy washing pots and pans and clothes, rubbing the latter furiously on large polished stones and then stepping into the river to rinse them out. Young children are helping with the washing or playing, boisterously skipping and splashing in the shallows. Fishermen in wooden pirogues – essentially chiselled-out tree trunks – float around on the river in their notoriously unstable craft, dropping bamboo sticks with hook and line attached into the murky depths in the hope of catching a fish or two. Unseen, probably on our side, which is much the quieter side of the river, there are crocodiles lurking in the grass, watchful and opportunistic. It's a typical river scene being replicated throughout most of the continent. Sporadically the water on the banks of one of these rivers will suddenly turn into a churning, boiling mass of spray and there will be screams as everyone races away. Blink and it's over, the water quickly closing in again and settling whilst the escapees fearfully look around and work out who is no longer amongst them. Then the wailing will begin and the bank will be deserted, probably for less than a day before people start to venture back down to the very same spot. It's the African version of Russian roulette, except the local communities often have little choice if they want drinking water or to wash and clean their cooking utensils and clothes.

The reality is that this river is teeming with crocs and hippos. I once said to Don that if his boat went down in the middle of the river, life jackets were useless. You needed to be able to move as fast as you could to get out of the water, not drift around like a floating snack. We should have fins – flippers – hanging from the boat's rails. Even then the chances of making it safely to the riverbank would be pretty non-existent.

On a Sunday afternoon in August the previous year, Don had

gone up the river in the *Pelican* with family and friends. This was something he liked to do at least once a month during the dry season. We would cruise upriver over the invisible boundary into the national park, choose a suitable spot, drop the bow anchor and quietly sit in the middle of the river listening to the hippos grunting and staring at us through large, irritable pink-rimmed piggy eyes, watching for elephant, waterbuck and any other game that happened to come down to the riverside to drink. Sometimes we would get lucky and catch an entire herd of elephant swimming across the river.

When returning to the anchorage, Don had misjudged speed and distance. The stern line from ship to shore had been thrown and the engines put in neutral as the boat glided towards the bank, but its speed was not quite enough to take it there and the current had taken hold, dragging the *Pelican* downstream towards the barrage. Don had thrown the throttle levers forward, applying a burst of forward thrust from the engines in order to recover the situation. In the meantime, however, the stern line had disappeared under the hull and now it became well and truly wrapped around the props and shafts. The engines cut out, but luckily there was now just enough momentum to take the boat to the bank. She was not going to go anywhere in any hurry now until the line had been cut away.

The following Saturday I had returned to the *Pelican* with my brother-in-law Stephen and my wife's cousin-in-law, Michael. Donning a wetsuit and diving gear, I had been gingerly lowered by line into the river off the boat's stern platform. With Stephen and Michael bashing hard on the hull with metal piping, a cacophony intended to deter any watching crocodiles, I had worked in the murk by feel without any visibility whatsoever, cutting away at the tangled line which seemed to be endlessly wrapped around the two props as taut as violin strings – so taut that I was worried that it might have actually bent the propeller shafts. It seemed to take forever, feeling for the line, sawing at it with the diving knife whilst holding on to another section of line with my free hand to help me keep my position, and trying all the time to ensure that I didn't lop off a finger or two in the desperate rush to get the process completed as quickly as possible. One bit of line cut, then feeling for the next bit and so on.

The bashing on the hull, whilst only a few metres away, seemed distant and remote as I lay prone in another world, listened to the catch of the diving regulator feeding me air on demand and waiting for, almost anticipating, a sudden tug on the fins or my legs as a croc swooped in. But ten minutes later the job was done and I was sitting on the top deck, relieved and downing a beer, and wondering in particular what my parents would make of this foolhardiness. I would never tell them. They had had enough tragedy to deal with in their lives without the worry of more.

Opening the chart drawer, I pull out the chart for the area from Fort Johnston to Monkey Bay. The original price of the chart was 6s 0d and it was published in Salisbury by the Federal Government in October 1958 following the completion of the Lake Nyasa hydrographical survey. These charts are like gold dust and totally indispensable. I happen to know Captain Lameck, a wonderful, boisterous old man with twinkling eyes and a ready laugh. He is the most experienced captain on the lake by a considerable sea mile, and although he should have retired years ago he is still the senior captain hard at work. The fact is, there is no one else with his level of experience or who knows the lake as he does. He has a few spare charts and for our journey he has kindly given me those covering the southern and central lake area. The whole of the southern part of the lake, meaning in this case the stretch from where the lake drains into the Shire River in the far south and going northwards to Monkey Bay, around fifty kilometres according to the charts, doesn't get any deeper than forty fathoms, which translates to around 70 metres, but in a number of areas there is less than a couple of metres of depth several kilometres offshore. Along with these shallows there are barely submerged rocks dotting the coastline, teeth rising from the darkness towards the surface, ready to catch out the unwary. Don peers at the map and then jabs a finger down.

'There. You don't want to make the acquaintance of those,' he says sternly.

I look where he's pointing. Crocodile Rocks, just under two kilometres offshore from what is called Mpemba Headland. It's difficult to make out the markings on the chart, but it does appear that these rocks are sitting several metres above the water line and could easily catch out the unwary. And they are more or less exactly on the course you would expect to steer when heading north to Monkey Bay.

'Too right,' I reply. 'From the Bar where we enter the lake we'll steer a course for the eastern tip of Boadzulu Island in the middle of the lake. That should give us plenty of margin.'

Don grunts in agreement. 'Where are you going to try to get to today?' he asks.

'Depends on the weather. If it stays still and calm then I think we should be able to make the northern end of Lake Malombe. If the wind picks up or we're going to struggle to cross Malombe in daylight, then I'll anchor in the river at the southern end.'

Don nods. 'Well, there's no hurry, so best to play it safe.' He pauses, and I can see that something is on his mind. 'She's never done more than potter up and down this stretch of the river, so you may find the odd gremlin needs dealing with.'

And that was it. Like me, he was a little worried. Nothing specific: just what one would think of as normal concerns about a long journey, the unknown and an untested boat. Would the engines behave? Would they get overheated, pick up dirt or water from the diesel tanks? Would the starboard prop shaft, which was not properly clamped onto the engine, cause issues? How stable would the boat be once she was away from the shelter of a confined waterway and out on the lake, exposed to large rollers and strong winds?

'We'll be sure to keep a proper eye on things,' I say with a confidence I don't feel. I'm trying to reassure myself as well as Don.

'Time for a quick coffee and then you chaps must get going,' he says, and abruptly heads up the steps to the top deck. In the event the flasks of coffee are ignored in favour of the champagne that Karen has brought along. She makes a short toast to the *Pelican*, her crew and for a safe journey. We sip away and munch on biscuits, interspersing our small talk with confirmations on the various checks we have all carried out to ensure that everything is in order.

Don hands me his captain's hat, a light cotton one which is a perfect imitation of a tropical captain's hat, white with a black peak and some gold braid, that Karen found in a fancy dress shop a few years earlier. Symbolic and light-hearted in one.

'Good luck,' Don says with a smile before adding, 'You'll probably need it!'

As soon as Don and Karen have transferred from the boat to the bank, I flick the switch for the electric fuel pump and press the two blue starter buttons, one for each engine. Reassuringly, the engines catch immediately and settle into a steady rhythm. I believe in those engines, I know they are totally reliable and virtually indestructible. Their thrumming beat is comforting. In the unlikely event that the manufacturers, Perkins, ever wanted a recommendation, I'm their man.

The remaining shore line is released and hauled on board

and I let the current take the bow round so that we are pointing towards the middle of the river before pushing the throttle levers to slow forward. The props engage and we move slowly out into the river. Stepping from the wheelhouse I wave and shout, 'See you at Monkey Bay in a couple of days!'

Karen shouts back. 'We'll be waiting! Stay safe.'

The ship's log says that it was 09:50 on Sunday, 2$^{nd}$ May 2004. 'Start of the journey to take the *Pelican* to Metangula for cosmetic surgery and charter. Champagne send off with Karen and Don.'

CHAPTER 2

# The Corridor

Around nine o' clock on the morning ofThursday, 7th April 1988, a South African law professor and high profile African National Congress (ANC) supporter called Albie Sachs living in exile in Maputo, the capital of Mozambique, opened the passenger door of his car and placed a small bag of chilled beer on the seat. He was planning to drive over to the beach and go for a run, and the beer was his post-run thirst quencher. Moving round to the driver's side, he paused briefly to wave at a friend who was driving by. As he reached for the door handle his car exploded, and Albie and the car were blown in opposite directions. The car ended up as a ball of twisted metal. What might be termed a complete write off.

Albie, quite miraculously, was not. He survived with the loss of his right arm and the sight in his left eye, a casualty of a targeted hit by the South African security forces and another victim of the civil war that had racked the country since 1977. As casualties go, he was one of the luckier ones. When Nelson Mandela was released from prison in February 1990, he appointed Albie Sachs as a judge in the country's new Constitutional Court. It was a somewhat controversial decision at the time but one which, like so many of Mandela's decisions, turned out to be inspired. Albie became one of the main movers and shakers in shaping and drafting the new South African constitution for the reborn, expectant Rainbow Nation.

The Mozambique civil war in which Albie, as a high profile anti-apartheid activist in exile, and by extension a supporter of the Mozambique ruling Marxist party, FRELIMO (Front for the Liberation of Mozambique), had been caught up and targeted, was in large part a proxy war. Waged over fifteen harrowing years, FRELIMO, supported by the Soviet Union, backed various militant nationalist organisations inside Rhodesia and apartheid South Africa whilst RENAMO (the Mozambique Resistance Movement) was supported by the USA and backed by white-ruled Rhodesia and South Africa. By the time the protagonists realised that neither side could win and called it a day in 1992, the country was in ruins. As is so often the case, the civilian population had been dragged into the fighting and suffered hugely. Those who evaded or survived the horrendous war crimes perpetrated by both sides often faced famine. And by 1992 the country was littered with land mines, as both sides had relied heavily on mines to both defend and destroy infrastructure and terrorise the local population. How many people died war-related deaths has been difficult to ascertain but a number of estimates put the figure at around one million dead and hundreds of thousands maimed and displaced in the fighting, those figures continuing to be swollen post 1992 by those killed and maimed by mines over the following decades.

After such a long and very bloody guerrilla war, life had become cheap. Civilians in the countryside had been left traumatised and impoverished. Both sides had also decimated the wildlife, gunning down elephants to sell the ivory to fund the purchase of arms, and anything else that moved to feed soldiers and guerrillas alike. Some parks saw their wildlife populations drop by ninety-five per cent. Hundreds of thousands of buffalo were slaughtered, many herds believed exterminated 'for sport' from the air by Russian gunship crews. People moved from the ravaged countryside into urban areas looking for work that did not exist. They brushed shoulders with bored, badly paid former insurgents who had been drafted into the new Mozambican army and with de-mobbed ex guerrillas who, in turn, had been left idly kicking their heels, often drifting into petty crime in order to survive. For these former revolutionaries, the chance to make a lot of quick money was too much of a temptation. If it involved violence – even serious violence – well, that was something they were used to. It was, in a very real and warped sense, quite normal.

For Malawians, the road heading south through Têti in Mozambique is the main corridor and gateway to the tourist and business hubs of Zimbabwe and South Africa. When in late 1992 the UN finally declared this road safe for civilians, traffic was extremely light. A few intrepid souls, vehicles moving in convoy, made the trip, hands tight and knuckles white on their steering wheels, convinced that guerrillas would leap out of the thick bush at any moment and gun them down. However, when travellers returned safe and sound, word percolated out and the number of cars and trucks gradually increased. Within a couple of years the borders on both sides of this corridor were busy and the biggest obstacle encountered appeared to be corrupt police looking to impose fines for spurious traffic offences.

Between 1992 and 1997, Karen and I travelled through the corridor probably a dozen times without major incident. There was no doubt that when driving through it your heart rate quickened and your alert status was heightened from green to amber, but five years after opening, most people were primarily resigned to the tedious border crossings. The terrible violence of the war years appeared to be a thing of the past.

CHAPTER 3

# CAUGHT UNAWARES

As the *Pelican* motors sedately upriver, I'm reassured by the steady beat of the engines and the streamlined bow cutting a smooth path through the water. When the missionary David Livingstone embarked on his Zambezi expedition in 1858 to open up the interior and lay the foundations for what he saw as a Christian and commercial highway to help eradicate slavery, he and his small band of explorers had rather a lot to contend with. For transport they had a small, eighty-foot paddle steamer called the *Ma-Robert* (the African name given to Livingstone's wife, (Ma [mother] of her eldest son), in which they ponderously navigated the Zambezi.

In the account of his second expedition to Africa 'To The Zambezi And Its Tributaries,' which David Livingstone co-wrote with his brother Charles, at that time the whole area was in a state of war waged between the Portuguese colonial slavers and rebel tribal slave-hunters under the leadership of 'a [Portuguese] half-caste named Mariano.' According to Livingstone, this 'villain' was aptly termed by one governor a 'notorious robber and murderer' and 'all the Portuguese spoke of him as a rare monster of inhumanity.' At one stage some rebels boarded the *Ma-Robert* and rather curiously seemed to warmly approve when Livingstone assured them that he and his crew and the English nation generally were most definitely anti-slavery. I suppose the deduction was that they were not competition. They were allowed to proceed and later on further upstream they found themselves in the middle of a pitched battle between the Portuguese and the rebels, with lead balls whistling about in all directions. It seems to me that there is something distinctly Monty Pythonesque about two factions arguing over the areas in which they can operate their slave hunts, hacking and shooting each other to pieces on the river banks – the main arterial highways for moving their human cargoes around – whilst the *Ma-Robert* chugs sedately through it all, her mission to end slavery acknowledged and more or less sanctioned by both sides.

Seemingly worse than war, or the ever-present fevers from malaria, dysentery and sleeping sickness, or even Livingstone's dark moods and dogged, inflexible leadership (which led his doctor, John Kirk, to later write "I can come to no other conclusion than that Dr Livingstone is out of his mind and a most unsafe leader"), were the headaches and stresses caused by the *Ma-Robert* herself. The *Pelican's* engines would deal with the river's current with consummate ease, and when we did get stuck on the occasional sandbar a good bit of reverse thrust would solve our problems. Not so the *Ma-Robert*. As she chugged her way upstream she gobbled huge quantities of wood (one day of chopping wood for one and a half days of steam power) and got caught on innumerable sand bars, having to be hauled off with ropes and teams of men. Her boilers were temperamental, the roof leaked like the proverbial sieve and conditions were cramped, noisy and very hot. Cockroaches and rats scampered all over the crew at night and the boat played host to scorpions, centipedes, spiders and snakes, including one particular green snake that took up residence for several weeks concealed behind the deckhouse casing during the day and coming out at night. The Livingstone brothers wrote: 'To be aroused in the dark by five feet of cold green snake gliding over one's face is rather unpleasant, however rapid the movement may be.' Last, but by no means least of all, the hull was made of thin steel which started to rust, so that the boat had to be beached every night to stop her sinking, at which time they would attempt to seal the hull, pretty unsuccessfully, with clay. It's difficult to begin to conceive of the bravery and commitment of these explorers, or the uncertainty and fear that constantly stalked them.

These missions to the interior of Africa were not short-term monthly or even annual excursions. The Zambezi Expedition alone took six years. To do one such journey is really more than man enough. But I'm with the good Dr Kirk. To do three of them smacks to me of a zealousness and determination verging on barking madness. Our anticipated one-week sojourn to deliver a boat and provide a little enjoyment and sightseeing seems extremely prosaic by comparison.

I navigate to the outer parts of the bends in the river to avoid the silted-up inner curves and within less than twenty minutes we have crossed an invisible boundary and entered Liwonde National Park. This is an area of riverine lagoons and marshes, open grassland and deciduous woodlands. A haven for birds and heaven for 'twitchers.' It has a good population of elephant, sable, smaller antelope and waterbuck with the large white circles or 'targets' on their backsides, hippos, buffalo, a handful of black rhino and of course very large numbers of crocodiles. It's also home to countless poachers and many thousands of snares and gin traps (very strong spring-loaded traps).

Everyone is aware that poaching is a major problem, but it was not until some years later, 2012 to be precise, when the then Program Head for an International Animal Welfare Conservation Project, a man with twenty years' field experience in wildlife and environmental law enforcement, carried out a comprehensive investigation into the situation in the park that people became aware of just how big a problem it was. What he discovered was shocking. Covering an area of 548 square kilometres, Liwonde is a small park by African standards, yet it seems that calculated over a three-month timeframe in mid-2012 the number of confirmed poached large mammals alone, which included five elephant, one rhino, two buffalo, twenty-one sable and fifteen zebra, cost the park and nation something like $674,000. Given that only around ten percent of total mortalities of big game animals are detected – game rangers cannot possibly cover the whole park and scavengers and decomposition will quickly remove the carcasses – the total cost is likely to be nearer $6,740,000. That excludes the poaching of smaller animals where the whole carcass is taken away by poachers leaving no sign at all, the loss of fish in the river to around two hundred illegal fishermen, the huge loss of birds to glue traps and poisons and the cutting down of hardwood timber. The real financial cost alone is clearly much, much bigger.

Corruption within management and staff was indicated in the report as one of the reasons given for the rampant poaching. A lack of will on the part of government through the general failure of the civil service to punish corrupt staff was another. For years the future of this park seemed extremely bleak. In the end it was left to an international not-for-profit organisation called 'African Parks' to charge to the rescue and persuade the government in

2015 to hand over all care and control of the park to it. The reality is that it's not really about a lack of financial resources. African governments can easily partner with experienced conservation third parties who do have access to finance. It's simply about a lack of concern and interest about their fate. Many parts of the continent have a single word for animals. In Malawi it's 'nyama' – meat. And the only thing that beats meat is the sale of 'exotic' parts for money, mainly to China to help improve male virility. It seems that the men in that part of the world have some serious fertility and inferiority issues.

We all have to keep a wary eye out for the many pods of hippo lounging in the river and navigate well around them. Although Livingstone came across a small, specialist tribe of hippo hunters, for most of Africa hippo meat is not their favourite nyama and so these grunting and often bad-tempered animals are generally left alone, unless they take to invading villagers' maize crops when grazing on the land at night. A story appeared in one of the national newspapers about a dead hippo floating down the Shire River. Lunch meandering down the river was too much of a temptation for a couple of hungry villagers. They paddled out in their pirogue to cut some large chunks off the bloated carcass. One man stepped off the boat and onto the carcass, and with a cry of alarm promptly disappeared inside. The meat was so rotten he had simply fallen through and into the guts of the animal. Eventually he slashed and pushed his way out and paddled off in disgust. The reporter noted that even after copious washing "the odour bothered him for many days afterwards."

We spot a large herd of elephants grazing in the long grass by the riverbank and I slowly edge the *Pelican* towards them until we are less than ten metres away. These elephants are used to boats and humans and whilst they occasionally get grumpy with the intrusion into their quiet munching, they will generally ignore us or treat us as what we are, a peculiar curiosity of floating heads and arms.

An elephant's trunk is an amazing, versatile muscular implement. It can be used to feel with the gentlest of touches, smell far better than any bloodhound, grasp, strike, lift over three hundred kilos, breathe, snorkel when underwater and trumpet very loudly. I've probably left out something. However, it is the eye of the elephant that I find rather unsettling. Like a large brown marble with a black dot in the middle, it often gives the impression that it is not really looking at you but rather somewhere beyond you, almost as if you don't exist. It probably is the gateway to the soul of this great creature and seems to contain a spark of huge repressed anger on the one hand and communicate a sage and sombre understanding of some intangible, profound truth on the other. And much as they can give the impression that they haven't seen you – much less somehow acknowledge you – you just know that they aren't missing anything. If upset or threatened they won't hesitate to put their massive strength and bulk to use. I've seen a jittery and angry herd communicate in split seconds, circling the young and elderly whilst the younger bulls take up the vanguard, trunks raised, smelling the air and trumpeting so loudly that the ground shakes and you think your eardrums are going to burst before, as one, they advance at a startlingly rapid pace. Today, however, they are at peace and we quietly watch and listen to them grasping great clumps of grass in their trunks and stuffing them carelessly into their mouths. There's something very soothing about these timeless, simple actions and sounds.

Further upriver we pass Mvuu Wildlife Camp, a popular tourist destination, and we wave at the figures moving about on the riverbank. Then in the distance I spot a small green speedboat bearing down on us. It's our mutual friend, Philip, along with a German friend of his called Axel. Philip will be joining us for the entire trip and his semi-rigid boat of the kind known in the boating world as a RHIB (Rigid Hull Inflatable Boat), the *Stingray*, will act as tender and safety boat. Our guardian angel. Passing us and turning, he comes up alongside and he and Axel disembark onto the platform at the stern of the *Pelican* and attach the *Stingray* by way of a short towline.

'You've made good time,' I comment when they step into the wheelhouse.

'An easy run down the lake from the cottage. Everywhere is as flat as a board. Everything all right here?'

'At this point, couldn't be better,' I say, taking in this information with relief. There's a pause, and then Philip says gravely, 'Well actually, it could.'

He peers down at me studiously with one raised eyebrow. My heart sinks. I look at him quizzically. Is he serious or winding me up? I decide that he's going to tell me he's had some engine problems, or perhaps that one of the inflatable pontoons on his boat has a minor puncture. I keep schtumm and watch his face crease up.

'It's too early for a beer but surely the perfect time for coffee,' he suggests with a laugh, and I breathe a sigh of relief. I'm clearly a bit wound up. 'You blighter. Take the helm and I'll go down and arrange that.'

Which I duly do, taking the opportunity whilst in the galley to lift the large horizontally hinged metal hatches that are set into the main cabin floor giving access to the engine compartment. The fans at the head of the two engines are whirring and there's no sign of any leakage of diesel or water. Everything looks, smells and sounds in order and I quickly close the hatches again to cut out the heat and noise.

We spend the rest of the morning cruising up the river in

brilliant sunshine until we reach the southern mouth of Lake Malombe. We've covered around thirty kilometres and it's now gone two o' clock in the afternoon. The sun is already starting its descent towards the horizon as we enter the lake. Deciding that we won't stop and anchor for lunch, we eat some rolls and fruit on the go. I'm anxious to try to get across Lake Malombe before dark, a distance of just over twenty-three kilometres.

This small lake has a bad reputation. It's really a great big pond filled with fishermen and their nets. It's also very shallow, averaging around two metres of depth. Which is what concerns me. At this time of the year the wind tends to blow from the south-east, and the lake is very exposed on its eastern shore. When the wind picks up the friction between the moving water and the shallow lake bed means that it becomes a raging froth of steep sided, closely-knit breakers. A fisherman caught out in a storm on this lake has preciously little chance of survival even if he can swim – and most of them can't. The relentless, unbroken army of breaking waves simply won't allow you to swim. It's like trying to swim or tread water in big seaside surf on a very rough day. It just can't be done.

In the end we motor serenely up the eastern shore of the lake, which remains like a mirror, not a ripple on the surface, the sun sparkling off the water and flashing off the occasional tin roof from the villages on the western shore. On the hillsides smoke rises lazily in vertical wisps. Charcoal burners at work. I'm hoping that we might see a flap-shelled turtle or two. There used to be lots of them in this lake and the main lake, but I suspect they get caught up in the fishing nets and are slaughtered and eaten. A couple of years earlier Philip and I had sailed in the Lake Malawi Yachting Marathon, a ten-day race up the lake in catamarans. On the eighth day the lake had changed from very lively with brisk winds to dead calm. By this stage the little fleet of racers was busy doing a circuit of two islands in the mid eastern part of the lake called the Likhoma Islands. To relieve the boredom we had tracked off course and sailed over to watch a pod of these turtles quietly pottering around on the surface. It's the last time I saw any in the lake.

It's gone five o' clock as we approach the north-eastern end of Lake Malombe and the sun has disappeared behind the hills to the west. Many things in Africa are done at a fairly relaxed pace, but African sunrises and sunsets are not one of them. Within twenty minutes it will be close to dark. Stephen and Philip are on the top deck keeping a look out for nets. There are lots of them around this particular area, close to where the Shire River drains into the lake, and they are almost submerged and very difficult to spot from the wheelhouse. I lever back the throttles until the *Pelican* is moving dead slow.

'Well, Captain Magoo. What do you reckon? Anchor around here or try to find our way into the Shire?' asks Philip.

'Getting dark. I've been checking the chart and the channel leading into the Shire comes quite a long way out into the lake. I think we could traverse east to west and pick up that channel on the depth sounder fairly easily, but I'm worried about the nets. Even using the spotlight we could easily get tangled up in one in the dark.'

'Lake's as still as a graveyard.'

'Easy place to anchor,' I muse aloud.

'Probably easier than risking nets or sandbars in the river,' Philip adds.

It's only a couple of days short of a full moon, and that is not a coincidence. We have timed the trip carefully. The rains commonly start around mid to late November and only generally peter out in early April. We certainly wanted to avoid the huge lightning storms of the rainy season. We also wanted the moon to help light the way in case of dire need, just as one would when tackling a big mountain. I don't like the idea of trying to find the entrance into the river and heading up into it this late. As Philip has pointed out, we don't know what to expect there and anchoring midstream overnight is not a good idea. Who knows what might crash into us? If we take lines ashore that means using Philip's boat and asking someone to step ashore and stumble around the riverbank in the semi dark to find a good anchoring point. Accidents happen in such circumstances. Hippos graze on the land at night and crocs don't care when supper is served.

Philip knows me of old and watches as I cogitate. 'The windmills of your mind' as he once observed, borrowed from the song.

'Let's anchor here,' I eventually say. 'I'll point her up into the wind and we'll set the bow anchor.'

Which is what we do. Then we sit on the top deck watching what is left of a deep red reverse sunset to the east. It's not quiet as one might expect. We can hear the distant clatter and chatter from villages across the water and we catch the occasional whiff of wood fires. Stephen appears with bottles of beer. I believe Malawi has the only Carlsberg brewery outside Denmark and that means that the beer is very drinkable and mostly dependable. Drew has opted to slave away down in the galley heating up some pre-cooked spaghetti bolognaise that Karen put together for us. We eat on our laps and joke that it's probably a good thing that we can't make out what Drew has done to it. The stars come out and the moon provides a steady silver light and reflection on the water. We can see the silhouette of hills near and far. There's an unspoken but palpable relief all round. The boat has behaved impeccably and the weather has been perfect. The nightcap materializes in the form of a bottle of Jameson's whisky.

'Well, so far so good,' says Stephen. 'The perfect end to a pretty near perfect day.' We raise our glasses.

'What's the programme for tomorrow? Can we reach Monkey Bay?' asks Axel.

'It's the best part of sixty kilometres but we should be able to make it with time to spare if the weather holds up,' I say.

'What have we done today?' Drew asks.

'Not much less. Around fifty-five at a very sedate pace.'

'It'll be different on the lake. At the very least there'll be swells and probably a bit of chop.'

'Opportunity to find out how she handles and how stable she really is,' remarks Stephen, the optimist and the pragmatist rolled into one.

I've seen the stability calculations carried out by Don's engineering friend, Basil. His calculations run to fifty-one pages of endless figures. Metacentric stability calculations, centre of gravity calculations, rib points and dimensions, longitudinal moment arm calculations, endless theta numbers and so on. With great understatement in his covering letter to Don he states, 'most of the figures may be somewhat confusing.' Agreed, Basil. To all but you and a few well-qualified engineers.

Despite all the calculations, there's always been an unshakeable niggle in both my mind and Don's about the boat's stability. Metal from stem to stern with a high superstructure and shallow draft. Just like a mini ocean liner. The evidence of your eyes questions the science. It's a bit like believing a compass in bad weather. Your internal 'I think' compass says one thing, the needle another. For all Basil's meticulous maths and obvious knowledge, our eyes just can't quite make the necessary leap of faith. Is she stable? Really stable, or not quite stable enough? Not too soft or hard? Soft stability to me means that the boat will wallow in a leaden sort of way even in small swells. Hard stability and she will move in a jerky, stiff way and when a big swell hits she could just turn turtle. There's only one way we'll know for sure and that will be when we get some reasonable swells and wind out on the lake.

Philip has started one of his famous bush stories. He's a water engineer and these days he heads up projects to provide mainly rural communities with clean, safe, readily accessible drinking water by placing boreholes around those communities. Late one evening a few weeks previously we had been sitting on the veranda of his home at the lake discussing the perennial problem of government and donor funding. We were shrouded in darkness, the only thing visible a necklace of lights strung out along the horizon: fishermen using their paraffin lamps to catch the small fish known as usipa. They are like aqueous moths, blindly swimming up to the light. We did a very basic calculation and estimated that Philip's projects to date had provided safe water for over three quarters of a million rural Malawians. A staggering figure for one man and his small team.

As a youngster Philip's back yard had been a large area in eastern Zambia called the Luangwa Valley where his father, Peter, had been a well-known hunter in the 1950s and 1960s. In those days 'the Valley' was a Garden of Eden, bursting with game. Every trek out of camp was an adventure demanding nerve, concentration and perception. Not just seeing what appeared to be in front of you, or what tracks or scat was on the ground and what birds were up in the sky, or what you could hear and smell; more important was how you interpreted and pieced it all together to make up a picture of what was happening around you and what might lie around the next bend in the track. When on foot, your life really does depend on getting these things right. The instinct for self-preservation meant that young Philip learnt a lot from his father, and very quickly. He also learnt to respect and trust him, which at times made him gullible and ready to do things that his instincts told him were probably not a great idea at all.

'So the rains arrived with a big downpour and a lake has sprung up around this area of high ground, turning it into an island. A young female duiker has become trapped on this island,' says Philip.

'Unable to swim across,' offers Drew.

'Perhaps. She may have been like a badly behaved teenager, still dependent on mum but not following her lead.'

'Why not wait until the water level dropped?' suggests Drew.

'Well that's unlikely once the rains have arrived. If anything the island would eventually be submerged. There was hardly anything to eat on the island. Just some scrubby thorn bushes and a couple of small trees,' replies Philip before adding. 'Poor thing was trembling all over, barely able to stand.'

'So mother duiker left her daughter behind,' says Stephen dubiously.

'Or maybe she didn't quite make it,' suggests Philip.

'Drowned,' says Drew. 'Probably got bogged down in the mud. Did you see a carcass?'

I know this story. Even in the moonlight I can make out the slight grin on Philip's face as he presses on.

'Well it wouldn't have been easy getting across. And if she didn't there wouldn't be a carcass to find. The island was more or less surrounded by crocs.'

Everyone is silent for a moment digesting this information, picturing the mother bravely trying to beat the crocs and splash and leap through the water to safety, and her final struggle as the crocs piled in and tore her apart. Eventually they would get impatient and come for her daughter. There was no escape.

'So I presume you did the decent thing and shot her' Stephen says. Philip gives a deep chuckle.

'Well actually, no.'

Drew is now angry and despondent. 'Oh man. You didn't just leave her for those crocs to rip into her.'

Philip is happy. He's got the reaction he's been looking for before pressing on with his story.

'No. Not at all. My father said to me, "Philip, no need to shoot that duiker. You and Bright" – he was my father's Zambian tracker – "strip down and get over there and bring that duiker back." '

We all laugh at such a preposterous notion.

'So you just shot the duiker yourself,' says Stephen. 'End of story.'

Philip pauses. I'm not sure if it's for effect or because he's not sure if he's about to frame himself as having an IQ the same as his collar size.

'Not quite. My father convinced me that the crocs would scatter when the two of us went crashing through the water. "They'll actually be more scared of you. Are you a man or a mouse?" Or words to that effect.'

'I don't believe you'd do that. I'd be happy to be called a mouse when it comes to a pile of crocs,' says Stephen with conviction.

'Well, we stripped down.'

'Really stripped right down?' asks Drew, trying to be sure he's following this properly.

'Well, down to my jocks. I wasn't prepared to take them off. Not shy of baring all to the bush but the thought of a croc biting into an arm or a leg didn't seem nearly as bad as it chomping off my dangly bits.'

'With you there,' volunteers Stephen holding up his whisky glass and taking a big gulp.

'So Bright and I take a run at it. We're hollering at the top of our voices like banshees and crashing through the water, which comes up to our waists. Bright abandons the rescue and turns back less than halfway across and leaves me ploughing on by myself.' Philip pauses and takes a sip of his whisky before continuing.

'Ever stood on a crocodile? No of course you haven't. I have. Like the bark of a rough tree and it moved lightning fast from under me. Now I'm floundering and really screaming myself silly and bashing the water frantically with my arms. I'm convinced the noise will confuse the crocs, and anyway it's giving me some crazy mad courage.'

'Deranged and barking mad springs to mind,' I interject. Philip is fully animated, his eyes alive and his hands whizzing around, in full flow now and not about to be diverted by anyone's quick quips.

'I make it to the island and I don't stop for breath or anything. Some of you may find it hard to believe, but I was pretty slim and fit in those days.' There's a communal snigger at this remark. Philip is a big man and definitely not what might be termed running fit.

'So the duiker thankfully hasn't moved. It's rooted to the spot, probably in terror of this mad apparition. I grab it low down near the hooves, one hand for the front legs, one for the hind, sling it over my head onto my shoulders and race back through the water expecting every second that a croc would launch itself at me. But here's the thing. Nothing comes for me and we get back to terra firma totally unscathed. For thirty -odd seconds I'm mistaken for some unknown, deranged apex predator and they just watch me stealing their lunch.'

We digest all this in silence for a moment.

'Your dad must have been proud of his brave boy,' says Drew eventually.

'Dad said he'd raised a loon. He didn't expect me to actually do it.'

'But he didn't bother to stop you? Well, that took serious balls,' offers Drew with meaning.

Philip finishes off. 'I can tell you it left me with bad dreams about fighting off crocs in muddy water for months afterwards.'

No kidding.

It's gone seven and the banter is passing to and fro between us, along with the Jameson's, when I feel the first puff of wind. The gentlest of caresses on the side of my face. Then nothing. Half a minute later the caress again, a little stronger. This time I can hear the wind. It's the faintest of sounds like a lover's husky whisper in my ear: 'Don't ignore me. I'm coming to get you.'

Within a couple of minutes the *Pelican* is swaying slightly and the wind has become more insistent. I'm hoping that it's a night-time breeze, a katabatic wind from off the hills to the west. But I know it's not. The direction is all wrong. This is coming more or less from the south, straight up the open lake. A couple more minutes and the *Pelican* is tugging at her anchor. She starts to rock as the wind plucks and pulls at the surface of the lake creating small wavelets. Drew is busy taking all the breakables below decks whilst I'm vainly wishing the wind away, or that at least it doesn't increase in intensity, but within a couple of minutes the force has increased substantially. Philip has his GPS out, his face illuminated by the screen.

'She's dragging her anchor. We're moving,' he announces. Our luck with the weather has clearly run out. I'm amazed that we are moving even given the current force of the wind. The anchor is a ridiculously heavy Danforth, a design having very good holding power in most lake bed compositions. Additionally we've dropped over twenty metres of heavy chain into less than three metres of water. I can't be certain of the features of the lake bed here, though I would lay odds it's soft clay – though it's also just possible that sections may contain some rock, in which case the anchor may have been unable to bite into the lake bed properly. Whatever, we need to jump to action stations.

'Drew. Stephen. I'll start the engines. We need to haul up the anchor and head for the river entrance. Philip, you'd better double check the line to your boat.'

I dive down into the wheelhouse and start the engines, pushing the throttles forward to dead slow ahead. Drew and Stephen are already at the bow busy at the capstan, a large revolving drum, pulling on the drum's outer rail to wind in the anchor chain as fast as they can. It's slow, hard work. I step out of the wheelhouse to get a better handle on our surroundings. The wind is howling out of a cloudless sky and to the east it's inky black, the first few stars now visible. I can just make out the outline of the reeds lining the eastern shore of the lake and so much closer than I expected. Back behind the wheel, Stephen appears to be hauling on the capstan alone. He stands up and turns, giving me the thumbs up to indicate that the anchor is fully raised, before turning back towards the bow, gripping one of the boat's rails to stay on his feet. My hand is on the throttles, about to increase the thrust from the props when he turns again and throws up a hand. A stop signal. He's shouting something, but by now the wind is shrieking around us and I can't make out what he's saying. I can only guess. An obstruction ahead. A rock? A net?

He staggers back towards the wheelhouse and enters through the side door, breathing heavily, soaked from spray.

'Nets. Lots of nets,' he pants. I don't need to say it. We all know. We're in really serious trouble if they get wrapped around the props.

'I can't see them from here,' I say tightly. 'Too dark. Too

much spray and movement. You'll have to spot for me and give directions from the prow.'

That's quite an ask. For him to stand right up at the front, Titanic Winslet style, to check for nets and give directions. I pull the spotlight out of the cubbyhole by the wheel and hand it to him.

'Sorry, you're going to get even wetter.' He doesn't grumble, just checks the light is working and heads off.

Where did these nets materialise from? I can only think that we were already very close to them when we anchored and somehow, just in the last few minutes, the wind has pushed us closer to shore and we have slipped between a couple of them. In which case we've been sublimely lucky that the anchor and props didn't get caught up. Now we have to somehow navigate around and between them.

Someone else has entered the wheelhouse. Drew. And he's absolutely drenched, as if he's been for a swim fully clothed.

'What happened to you?' I ask.

He gives me a quirky half smile and I brace myself for more bad news. Has Philip's boat broken free and he's been trying to rescue the situation?

'I leaned over the bow rails to check if the anchor was out of the water and my wallet fell out of my shirt pocket.' I think to myself that I know where this is going but cannot believe it.

'Please don't tell me you jumped off the bow and into the lake in a storm and in virtual darkness to rescue your wallet.'

'Well that pretty much covers it,' Drew replies nonchalantly. He is compelled to explain himself further. 'Well you know what it's like down at Road Traffic trying to get a replacement when your driving licence goes missing. Police reports, forms, queues.'

'So to save the hassle at Road Traffic you risked life and limb,' I say, partly in anger, partly in disbelief.

'Yup. That just about sums it up. Actually my main concern was not the lake but getting back on board at the stern without getting chopped up by the props.'

'You made it, so I guess your lord must truly love you, Drew, because the reality is that you are a brave but totally certifiable lunatic.'

Stephen has the spotlight on the water and his left arm is up, his hand fluttering up and down impatiently. I increase the revs and turn slightly to port. The relentless army of waves lifts the bow higher and higher until it reaches a tipping point and drops, crashing down with a terrible jarring shudder. It's so brutal and forceful that I'm convinced the hull is hitting the lake bed and is about to split apart.

I try to make out the way ahead, but it's impossible. The reflection of the moving spotlight on the waves and the wet decking leaves me straining to make out Stephen's gesticulations as he waves and points. The spray at the bow lit by Stephen's torch is like a starburst of light which disappears for a second before it lashes against the wheelhouse windows and streams down. For the next hour we fight the storm as the wind shrieks in a rising fury around us and we weave an incoherent track back down the lake, somehow avoiding the never-ending barriers of staggered nets. I'm in a trance-like state, only peripherally aware of the furious, erratic rage of the wind competing with the steady beat of the engines, the bucking, juddering motion of the boat or my hand on the wheel. Everything centres on arms. Stephen is having the roller coaster ride of his life.

At last, when I am beginning to despair that we will ever escape the nets, his right arm goes up, the elbow working like a hinge, his hand moving backwards and forwards insistently. He's pointing ninety degrees to the west, back towards the centre of the lake. I daren't put the *Pelican* broadsides on to the waves so I turn south-west, cutting a line diagonally across them. The motion is awkward with the boat lurching and rocking, but not alarmingly so. We stay on this track for ten minutes and then I turn her smartly to the north-west and we motor back up the lake still tracking away from the treacherous, netted eastern shore. After another twenty minutes we are approaching the northern end of the lake again. The wind has slackened off considerably. It's choppy, but the waves are dying down as quickly as they rose up.

Philip has joined me in the wheelhouse. He's drenched, standing there in a T-shirt, shorts and sandals dripping onto the floor. He never seems to feel the cold. Tells me often that it's something to do with being diabetic rather than a tough man. His glasses are covered in spray so I presume he can barely see through them. He claps me playfully on the shoulders with both hands.

'Well, you'll be pleased to hear that the *Stingray* is still with us,' he announces, almost in disbelief.

'I'm surprised you can see if she's still there or not through those,' I say, nodding at him.

'Wanted to take them off but nowhere safe to put them except the end of my nose. Anyway,' he continues proudly, 'she was never really troubled. Bobbed around like a cork. My main concern was that the tow line didn't snap.'

I pull out the map drawer and hand him a dry handkerchief belonging to Don that I know has been sitting in there for several years.

'Thanks,' he offers.

'Somehow we seem to have sprung ourselves free of the nets. Like it or not we'll now have to find the river entrance and head up into the river tonight in case the wind returns.'

Philip finishes wiping his glasses dry and peers down at the depth finder.

'Okay. You continue to watch Stephen. I'll let you know when the depth starts to increase,' he offers.

We continue to track up the lake and within ten minutes Philip is calling out a sudden increase from two or three metres to six and then nine. We've almost certainly found the channel leading into the river. I continue on the same course until the depth drops off again before turning the *Pelican* north-east to cut across and pick up the channel again. It's a pretty wide channel and we have no difficulty keeping within it until the end of the lake looms and in the spotlight's beam we can finally see the opening into the river. In another five minutes we are moving dead slow upriver until we come to a sheltered spot with tall palms and reeds lining the banks. The storm has dissipated as quickly as it arose and the water looks almost sluggish and black as oil.

We set the bow anchor in mid-channel. We'll just have to take our chances that nothing of real substance comes floating down the river in the dead of night. Stephen squelches into the wheelhouse, quietly dripping, his usual cheery smile back on his face.

'Well done, skipper. Thought we were going to be wiped out there for a minute.'

'Brilliant signals,' I say, clapping him on the back. You just know that he's totally reliable in a tight spot. We would have reason to be thankful for that reliability many times over before this particular boys' adventure was over.

Somehow the relief offered by the sudden calm and relative safety of the river seems like an anticlimax. We make small talk about the last couple of hours and give quick, nervous laughs at our good fortune; but within less than ten minutes we all switch from hyperactive to totally exhausted. Dead on our feet. No one feels like suggesting a nightcap, and within minutes we have all chosen different parts of the boat to roll out our sleeping bags and settle down for the night.

On the top deck I stare up at a totally clear night sky dominated by a large, almost full moon. There's the constellation of Scorpius, the giant scorpion whose sting supposedly killed the arrogant and over enthusiastic hunter, Orion. Both constellations are frozen at opposite ends of the heavens, Orion fleeing the scorpion for all eternity. I know that the main star in Scorpius is a red supergiant called Antares, some three hundred times the size of our sun and a mere 330 light years away. The light I can see at this moment in time emanated from the star in the 1670s when the Merry Monarch, Charles II, was on the throne of England and workmen at the Tower of London were digging up a wooden box containing what was believed to be the skeletons of the Princes in the Tower, murdered by we are not sure who but history records Richard III as being the prime suspect. These overwhelming timelines, the enormous distances and immense vastness of the universe make the *Pelican* and her small crew seem utterly insignificant.

That perspective is not a great comfort. I console myself with the thought that whilst we may be minute in this time and space sense, it does seem to me that we make up what we lack in durability and size with the spark that is life and intelligence, with imagination, emotions and the relatively furious pace it is all conducted. And in terms of our little planet and the globalising Millennium, Africa, more than anywhere else, remains clearly individual with its vast and colourful physicality and deep, raw spirituality. A place where one dares to dream and your pulse never quite settles because you can never be sure what tomorrow will bring. Luck and fate remain ever close companions.

Orion had a gift we nearly had need of tonight. He could walk on water. But the *Pelican* came through this early test with flying colours. That was something to feel relieved about and just a little proud. I can already hear Philip peacefully snoring away somewhere down below in the stern – probably as close as he can get to the *Stingray* without actually being on board her. He's a great bear of a man, sociable and amusing with a warm demeanour and a quiet, disguised intelligence. When you turn up at his house he will be busy with any number of activities. Reading a book whilst listening to music – maybe classic rock or Sibelius or something choral – perhaps building a piece of furniture, servicing the outboard on the Stingray or the motor on his very old Range Rover, using his first qualification as a draughtsman to put together some technical drawings or organising his team for the next community borehole.

My thoughts drift on to another hunter: Philip's father, Peter. He died when Philip was only twenty-four. Like many hunters of the 1950s and 1960s, Peter had had a change of heart later in life and switched from hunting to photography. He was camping in his beloved Luangwa Valley in September 1974 when an enraged lioness with a damaged paw came by and ripped the top off his tent before limping off into the night. The normal practice with wounded predators, which are invariably highly dangerous and opportunistic, is to track and kill them. Peter, however, made a fatal error. In the morning he tracked the wounded lioness but then ignored pleas from the locals to shoot her, advising that her wound would heal and she should be given another chance. The following night the lioness returned to his camp and killed him.

Eventually I drift off into a surprisingly tranquil sleep and I don't, as far as I can know, dream of wounded predators or rushing waves, starbursts of angry water or desperate arms guiding us through the black unknown.

CHAPTER 4

# The Open Sea

We wake before the sun has risen. Nothing, to my knowledge, went bump in the night and the *Pelican* is still on station. I head down to check the engine compartment. Drew is already in the galley, busy boiling up water for tea, and we greet each other with short 'mornings.' Drew helps me to pull open the floor panels and I shine my torch down into the vessel's bowels, peering at the engines, not certain what I'm looking for or expecting. They sit side by side. Twins. Inert and cold yet reassuringly solid, waiting to be injected with life, when they will beat together to a frantic rhythm.

'Looks just fine,' says Drew. 'Looking for anything in particular?'

'Not really. Anything and nothing,' I mutter before adding, 'Mainly water or diesel leaks. I'll just check the oil level on the engines quickly.'

A few minutes later I'm back on the upper deck with a mug of tea in hand. We can now clearly hear the sounds of a nearby village coming to life. People chattering, metal pans clunking and the odd goat bleating. The sun is coming up fast and little faces can just be discerned peering out from behind a wall of tall grass. We are going to be a great curiosity, especially for the children.

The culture of the Western world tends to attach great importance to the individual and individuality, the 'inalienable rights' that include the right for each person to be free to follow and try to realise his or her personal dreams. What in investment parlance might be termed a bottom-up approach. A lot of African culture is based on the opposite premise – top down. The primary concept is the 'life force' that is part of and passes through every individual and everything. The individual, the village, the clan and so on all the way down the ladder, must look after, respect and preserve this life force. The individual is simply a small link in the chain; if he or she is perceived in some way to threaten the life force then that individual can be cut out of the chain and ostracised. It means that individuality is not encouraged; conformity is the order of the day. And this is enforced by village chiefs under the guidance of village elders and by a bewildering array of taboos, rites and superstitions, many of them in relation to sexual relations.

Here are a few. Women are obliged to get married. Don't allow your husband to come 'near' you when your child is sick, the chief is away or there is a funeral in or close by the village – otherwise there will be death or sickness. Similarly when sowing or harvesting your crops or when starting the fermenting process for beer, a couple mustn't engage in sex, otherwise the crop will be poor or the beer bad. If children eat eggs they will become sterile. If a pregnant woman eats zebra meat her child will be born with white stripes.

In theory these taboos give the women a lot of reasons why not. But the existence of a life force creates another, more sinister dimension to things and opens the door for those wishing to cause serious mischief. In most small rural communities on the planet, where everyone knows everyone else, gossip and the green-eyed monster, Jealousy, lurk around most corners.

Here's how it might go in the village. Happy (yes, that really is his English name) Madalitso is doing extremely well for himself. In particular, he has a very beautiful wife, Faith, who runs a successful village store selling foodstuffs and knick knacks – pens, little plastic hand mirrors, some girly things, sweets and cigarettes. Buluzi (meaning lizard) Piri is envious and jealous. He also looks a bit like a lizard with long, prominent fingers and toes, big round eyes and a large Adam's apple. He hangs around Faith's store making silly comments that he's sure she must find hilarious. But after a while he realises that he's not making much progress in developing a connection with her, so he decides that he must be more pro-active in order to teach Happy a lesson for being, well, happy. Hopefully he will also then get his long fingers on Faith.

He pays a visit to the village witch doctor or 'mfiti.' The mfiti tend to stick together and their 'art' (artifice) is generally kept in the family and passed on from father to son or daughter. It is said that they move around at night, invisible and naked, using spells to dig up graves so that they can gorge on the corpses. If they do decide to become visible, you would probably see a white, ghostlike image, tall and thin with a very distended lower lip, big bulbous belly and long fingers and toes. They fly incognito at night, ten together in a small circular wicker basket which looks like a frisbee and is used during the day by the women to remove the chaff from the maize after it has been taken off the cob. Winnowing. It's an age-old process. The women place some maize in the frisbee-like basket and then throw the maize up in the air where the wind takes the chaff away before they re-catch the maize and repeat the process again and again until there is hardly any chaff left. It's an interesting stretch for the imagination. Ten ghoulish, thin, white – but really black – mfitis whizzing through the night in a wicker frisbee at warp speed on missions unknown and unknowable.

What I do know is the story of one old lady whose mental faculties were leaving her. She lost her way in the dark and after walking around for some time she simply crumpled to the ground and started to wail and moan. This led the occupants of a nearby hut to wake up and investigate. Soon a number of neighbours were also helping with the investigations. Nothing approximating to sense could be gleaned from the old dear. An impromptu midnight meeting concluded that she was clearly a witch and had injured herself after falling out of her frisbee. She could very well have been hacked to death on the spot if one of the villagers had not come to her rescue by observing that she didn't appear to be dangerous. Indeed, she was sure she recognised the old dear as the mother of a friend. The reality is that you should never underestimate the immense power of spirituality in Africa. On a number of occasions I have seen perfectly sane and intelligent people waste away and die of an unidentifiable illness simply because they believed someone had arranged for a curse to be placed on their life force.

In our story Buluzi tells the mfiti a pack of lies. That Happy has consulted another mfiti and put a curse on him because he is jealous of Buluzi's marvellous physique and worried that his wife is falling for him. As a result Buluzi now feels sick and has no energy to even tend to his crops. The mfiti must prove that his magic is stronger than that of his rival so for a hefty fee – this requires big magic after all, consisting of one healthy female goat – the mfiti agrees to take the case.

The next morning Happy wakes, puts on his trousers and

opens the door of his hut to greet the day. He's about to step out when he is himself greeted by the sight of a dead, headless snake lying on the threshold. Happy is terrified by this and he dashes back into his hut to wake Faith and tell her. She throws her chitenje (a bolt of cloth used as a skirt or wrapping) around her and carefully steps out of the hut. There is no snake, headless or otherwise, to be seen. Happy peers around in disbelief. 'But it was there,' he says pointing at the ground. 'It was definitely there.' Faith tells him he must have imagined it and he should man up and go weed their maize garden. Headless snakes don't just slither off. Well not that quickly anyway.

The mfiti has cleverly sown the seeds for what is to follow. It won't do for someone to die without the mfiti's powers being acknowledged. He must ensure that belief in his powers remains strong, so strong in fact that many villagers will simply wither away with a strange unknown sickness if he just so much as leaves a message for them. A headless snake on the ground or a dead crow or owl hanging outside the hut are standard messages and the victim recipients will generally head straight for the village medicine man, the sing'anga (many of whom are ex witch doctors), to try to get the curse on their life force removed.

When villagers come across a snake they will invariably kill it. The head is usually crushed beyond recognition, but nevertheless they will also dig a deep hole and bury the head. They know that the snake may be dead but its venom remains toxic and deadly. Our mfiti hasn't buried his snake's head. His art lies in extracting the venom, coating it on acacia thorns and then carefully laying these partially buried on the path that he knows Happy will walk along to get to his garden. And sure enough, Happy obliges. It's just a little prick in the sole of his foot, but some hours later he is found unconscious in his field. By nightfall he is dead and Faith and the whole village are in mourning. The women immediately begin funeral laments to announce Happy's death, going around the village crying out their sorrow with shrill wails. Early the next day a grave is dug. The women's laments, which will have carried on through the night, now reach a piercing, feverish crescendo, many women running haphazardly around and thumping the ground with their fists and even their heads in a sorrow-induced trance.

Eventually Happy is laid to rest. It's not the solemn, controlled mourning and funeral of the Western world, yet when it is all over, it is as if the grim emotions of anger, sorrow and grief associated with death have been vanquished. The village has been brought together in its collective grief and everyone has mourned appropriately, including Buluzi. If he did not, he could find himself accused of being responsible for Happy's death.

But that's not the end of the story. The dead person's relatives now consult the soothsayer to find out who is responsible for Happy's demise. They know that black magic is involved. A crowd gathers as the soothsayer, after an appropriate amount of incantation and ceremony, scatters bones from a special gourd on the ground and reads them in order to detect the evildoer. He won't point the finger at the mfiti. He may choose to say it was Buluzi. But he may also decide it was Faith. She had been unfaithful and Happy had found out, so she had tried to cover up her wrongdoing by poisoning him. In days gone past Faith might have been made to undergo the 'Ordeal Tree' test. Poison from the bark of the mwabvi tree would be extracted by boiling it in water, which then turns an ominous blood red colour. Faith would then be made to drink this potion. If she vomited up the poison then she would be deemed not guilty and would probably survive, but if she failed to vomit she would almost certainly die and must have been guilty.

Sometimes the mfiti, the medicine man and the soothsayer

are one and the same person. It's a curious, incestuous setup.

I look towards the riverbank, smile and wave. There's a giggle, then a hushed bit of chatter and some laughter. The sounds seem to be magnified in the cocoon of grasses and reeds. Eventually a small girl's face appears and she steps forward, smiling shyly. She raises a hand in a brief, uncertain half-wave. I greet this courageous little one with a wave and 'Moni! Madzuka bwanje?' (Hello! How did you wake up?) She mumbles a reply. I wonder briefly what it's like to live a life where your elders still match-make and decide who your husband will be, where your actions and thoughts are influenced and controlled by the mfiti's tricks and the dominant belief in a life force. Where most of the village is your extended family, intimately involved in your upbringing and wellbeing. You'll never, ever be lonely and your business will always be everyone else's as well.

On the top deck we watch the sunrise. The sky on the eastern horizon is changing rapidly from dark blue to a deep firebrick red, then orange red. Just before six o' clock the sun rises majestically from behind a line of hills, a blood-red disc that all too quickly turns to gold. The grey around us fades and our surroundings take on colour.

We've all had what passes for breakfast. A mug of tea and some bread with peanut butter or honey. We can see properly now, so there's no reason to hang around. Soon it will get hot and sticky. My little friend on the riverbank has been joined by her friends so that now there's quite an audience. I start the engines and move dead slow ahead as Stephen and Drew begin the process of hauling up the anchor. Once it's fully up and secured I step outside the wheelhouse, wave enthusiastically and shout 'Zikomo, tikupita' – thanks, we are going. They all start shouting, waving and jumping around. It's certainly a joyful send off. I push the throttles forward until we are making around seven or eight kilometres an hour, dividing my attention between the river ahead and the depth sounder.

Less than an hour later we arrive at the town of Mangochi, sitting on the west bank of the river. Before independence it was called Fort Johnston, named after the country's first Consul General in colonial times and established to try to control the slave trade traffic in the area from moving north towards the lake, destination Zanzibar. Now it's an increasingly busy local trading centre sitting just a few kilometres from the southern tip of the lake.

We pass under the road bridge over the river. Philip and Stephen are keeping me company in the wheelhouse whilst Axel is on the top deck and Drew at the bow checking for any unwelcome obstructions in our path. Philip points ninety degrees to port as we emerge from under the bridge.

'On the roundabout there. That's the clock tower erected as a memorial to Queen Victoria.' He pauses briefly before adding, 'The clock isn't maintained so it doesn't work.'

I know that there's more than just a clock tower there. I've written the occasional article for the national airline magazine, and I've done a couple of stories about the lake and various vessels. I'm torn between saying nothing and sharing and showing off my knowledge. In the end I opt to share *and* show off.

'Either of you heard of the motor vessel *Viphya*?'

Stephen immediately pipes up. As I suspected he would. He has a brain that sucks up information and retains it on things useful, irreverent and useless. But to be fair, most of what he knows is useful and interesting.

'Sank in a big storm up in the northern part of the lake,' he says.

'Correct,' I agree. '1946. 145 people drowned out of just under 200. A big storm that came up very quickly. The ship had only been commissioned a few months earlier.'

Philip is peering at me with a quizzical look. 'And this has what to do with the clock tower?' he asks.

'Well, glad you asked that. There's a simple stone memorial, like a large gravestone, just in front of the tower, which commemorates those who drowned. But here's the interesting thing. The *Viphya* was constructed by the very same company that many years earlier constructed the *Titanic*. Harland and Wolff in Belfast.'

'So did she hit a rock or something in the water?' Philip asks.

'No. She got into trouble when a strong easterly wind kicked up some big waves. Unlike the *Titanic*, the captain of the *Viphya* had the option to run for shore, but for some reason declined to do so.'

'Odd decision,' Stephen offers and then adds. 'Pride comes before a capsize.'

We lapse into silence. I'm thinking that pride won't be high on my priority list if we should find ourselves in similar difficulties.

Another hour, another bend, and suddenly the river before us opens up into a delta of grassy islands and there are a few gentle puffs of wind. The excitement is tangible. We can smell the freshness, sense the lake ahead. The water subtly changes from grey-brown to grey-green.

'And which way now, captain?' asks Drew.

I shrug. 'Lots of possibilities. Not one that says this way.' We both stare through the wheelhouse windows trying to pick out the most likely channel to take us into the lake.

'How about you hop up onto the wheelhouse roof, Drew, and see if you can get a better view?'

Drew doesn't need a second invitation and within seconds he's scrambled up and is shouting down instructions. Five minutes later we reach the 'bar' where the River Shire begins and the lake ends. This mud and sand bar stretches across the delta and if lake levels fall below the level of the bar, then the river simply stops flowing. It did for twenty years between 1915 and 1935, but luckily at that time the country was not reliant on hydroelectricity. If the lake level dropped below the bar now, the country would be mostly in darkness.

There's a collective cattle drive 'yihaa' from everyone as on cue a welcome breeze hits us broadside on and suddenly the *Pelican* really comes to life, swaying and dipping on the growing swells. The depth sounder dives from two to ten and then fifteen metres and with it the water colour changes from green to a light and then a darker blue. I decide we can safely navigate now without the depth gauge, so I leave the wheelhouse and switch to the controls on the top deck where everyone has congregated. We chatter and grin inanely. It's a glorious, seminal moment for the *Pelican* and her crew.

CHAPTER 5

# THE RACONTEUR

Shortly after midnight the rain started to lash down. It quickly turned the soldier's pathetic shelter – a shallow dip in the ground – into a muddy pool, and he'd been forced to decamp onto the exposed hillside, spending the rest of the night huddled under a plastic cape, using his rucksack as a wind and rain break, head resting on bent, weary knees.

The rain had finally petered out just as a weak grey light crept out of the east. It was replaced by a piercing, icy wind that raced up the valley, turning into a roar as it crested the ridgeline and whipped over the bare mountaintop. There didn't seem to be any part of him that was not damp from sweat and rain, and he knew he was quickly becoming dangerously chilled. He'd thought briefly about breaking out his solid fuel stove to try to garner some heat but had quickly discarded that idea as being unworkable. Hypothermia was waiting just around the corner.

Spending the night near the summit of a Welsh mountain in late October had not been an easy choice. However it had been the only real alternative left to him. He'd been canny, keeping to the low ground as long as possible, giving his pursuers the slip by the thinnest of margins. These close calls and small triumphs had sent his adrenalin levels rocketing, giving him added stamina. Eventually, though, as the net had closed, he had run out of options and been forced to abandon the sparse woodlands and head up the valley floor, engaging in an awkward slip-sliding jog across fields which seemed to comprise nothing but mud and sheep shit. He'd worried about putting up flocks of birds that would give away his movements, but his luck had held. In fact there appeared to be a total absence of birdlife, or indeed any life, apart from the flocks of sheep that scurried off at his approach. The landscape became increasingly barren, the primary cover being afforded by dry stone walls, many in varying degrees of dilapidation.

With his energy levels dropping fast, he took a break to rehydrate and check out the land. Scanning behind, his binoculars revealed that they were on to him and moving up towards his position fast. Without the need to worry about cover he now moved much more efficiently and purposefully up the valley floor. Half an hour later he reached the head of the valley, and now there was nowhere to go but up. He immediately struck out, pushing through vast seas of golden-brown bracken and working his way around prickly gorse until finally he broke out into soft moor grass and stumbled, dog tired, towards the bare summit ahead. He knew that even with the benefit of infra-red night vision goggles they would not want to try to pursue him up here in the fading light. Buying time and delaying the inevitable was a matter of pride. But now, swept up in this cold, stark morning, he knew that he was out of options, and he made the only sensible decision left.

Hoisting the sack onto his back, he trudged into the cutting wind towards the ridgeline and started to carefully pick his way down the mountainside. He knew that half a dozen pairs of eyes scanning the ridgeline would have picked him up instantly and his pursuers would be tracking his descent. As he reached the valley floor he sensed their presence, and then suddenly there they were, covering all points – ahead, behind, on both sides. He stopped only when his progress was blocked by someone standing squarely in his path.

"Morning, sir. Bit of a chilly one, eh?"

The sergeant is standing at ease, a very slight grin playing at the corners of his mouth. Andrew looks up towards the ridgeline.

"Too chilly up there for anything but penguins and polar bears."

The sergeant looks up too, peering into the distance, briefly pondering this statement before replying.

"Well, I don't believe you see too many of those around here, sir." His face breaks into a grin.

"You're second to last. Very good effort, if I may say so sir. The only one left is Lieutenant Lochran. Slippery bugger, Lochran. Even slipperier than you."

Andrew grins. Shivers. Even stopping for a brief minute has brought the cold and damp back, eating deep into his body and bones. The sergeant turns.

"Follow me, sir. We've found some accommodations to keep you nice and secure until Lochran is rounded up. Shouldn't be long now."

They set off down one side of the valley floor in single file. After the best part of an hour, roughly halfway down, they stop at a small, stone structure. A sheep pen for when the real winter nights set in. The sergeant extends his arm towards the entrance. He looks as though he is about to bow, but then thinks better of it.

"In you go, sir."

Andrew crouches down and moves into the dark, musty interior. The sergeant calls after him, "Feel free to make yourself at home, sir." He pauses before adding. "We've taken the liberty of making sure that you have some company. Wouldn't want you to get lonely."

"Very thoughtful of you, sergeant. Much appreciated," Andrew quickly replies, trying his best to sound casual and unconcerned. There's a snigger from one of the soldiers and then the wooden door is slammed shut and he hears what he assumes is a large rock being jammed up against it. They move off and he hears the radio squawk. Something about a rabbit in the hole.

Despite the gaps in the stonework, it's a lot warmer inside, and to his surprise the floor feels dry; but he's concerned about the reference to company, assuming there's a live, or more probably decomposing, rat lurking somewhere. Ferreting out his torch and playing the beam around he's surprised to discover one corner occupied by what appears to be a live chicken. Army humour.

It takes another couple of hours to finally flush out Lochran, by which time the two sentries who posted themselves just in sight of the sheep pen, but far enough away to be able to chat privately, are frozen and fed up. When the call comes in on the radio the soldiers head straight to the door of the pen.

"Game's up, sir. Lochran has been bagged. Time to go home." They remove the rock and yank the old door open. The corporal pokes his head inside. The expletive is instantaneous.

"Well fuck me. I don't believe it."

"You'd better believe it, corporal," comes Andrew's laconic reply. "Fancy warming up and having a bite of chicken before we head on down? I've saved you both some."

And that was Andrew. My brother. Practical. Resourceful. Tenacious. Fun. Considerate.

Andrew studied history at Queen Mary College, London University, before heading to the army officer training college at Sandhurst and then joining the First Battalion of the Royal Regiment of Fusiliers. This Regiment is always easy to recognise due to the red and white 'hackle' pinned to the front of the men's berets. He was lucky and had some interesting postings, including Cyprus, New Zealand, running the regimental ski hut in Bavaria, Germany and the Falklands (after the war). On the flip side he had also completed two punishing tours of Northern Ireland, one in Ballykelly in 1985 and the second tour, very much a short-straw posting, to Crossmaglen in 1989. Crossmaglen, a Republican stronghold area, was labelled 'bandit country.' This was part of the period in Northern Ireland's history called 'The Troubles' and in the mid and late nineteen-eighties in particular the military wing of Sinn Fein, the Provisional IRA, were very busy and very well provisioned with Semtex explosive and AK-47 assault rifles, thanks to support in particular from Libya's then President Muammar Gaddafi. The IRA bombed London parks and the Grand Hotel in Brighton, placed a lethal bomb under a Parliamentarian's car, carried out mortar attacks on police stations and army barracks, set time bombs at Remembrance Day commemorations, used snipers to attack British Army and RUC foot patrols, downed British Army helicopters with mortars, organised riots and tried blowing up Army patrols with IEDs (improvised explosive devices). Over the course of three and half decades of terrorist activity the IRA managed to detonate a staggering 19,000 IEDs, which turns out to be around one every 17 hours – perhaps the biggest and most actively sustained terrorist bombing campaign in history.

I remember Andrew relating one near miss. They had received a tip off that an IED had being planted on a particular stretch of road. Andrew and his small team flew in by helicopter, landed in a nearby field and started to search the ditches up and down the road. After thirty-odd minutes they radioed back to base that they could find nothing and were returning. As the helicopter took off and turned for home, Andrew turned to his radio sergeant and told him that he could switch off the jamming device – the electronic transmitter being used to block any external radio signals being sent to set off an IED remotely from a distance. Instantly the telegraph pole under which the sergeant had been sitting a minute earlier, and where Andrew had been standing, erupted in a lethal hail of rock and metal. As Andrew stated somewhat whimsically later, he had a vision of a very desperate and frustrated IRA man hidden away somewhere on higher ground with a nice view angrily pressing the 'ignition button' on his remote transmitter.

Not a lot fazed Andrew. He revelled in working out how to turn difficult situations and problems around. He was easy going and genial with a dry and ready sense of humour, and like my great bush friend Philip he loved telling anecdotes. And like Philip, he had a memory that was stacked full of them. He only needed a gathering of friends, a beer and a café crème cigar, and then the stories would flow naturally. His wife, Caroline, had no doubt heard some of them a number of times, but she rarely seemed to tire of hearing them again, her quick, saucy giggle often leading the way to raucous laughter. Yet watching and listening to Andrew, it seemed to me that he was always aware of and sensitive to the dynamics at work around him and so avoided being labelled a bore, knowing instinctively when to button it and turn from raconteur to listener.

When Andrew and Caroline got serious about each other they decided that whilst they wanted to travel the world together before settling down, they also wanted to do so on their own terms and with their own agenda. It was a very bittersweet moment for Andrew leaving the army 'family,' but he put a brave face on things and pushed on. He completed an MBA at Durham University, packed his bags and headed off to join me in Malawi. As soon as Caroline had landed a job as a maths teacher at Bishop Mackenzie International Secondary School in Malawi, she packed her bags and headed in the same direction. They worked hard and played hard, giving much of their time to the community and voluntary projects.

In the 1990s, Zimbabwe was a country on the move. It seemed that enterprises run by black and white Zimbabweans were springing up every day. It was a happening place with a positive vibe and tourists were flocking in from around the globe.

In early April 1997, Andrew and Caroline drove from their home in Lilongwe, the capital of Malawi, down to Harare to meet up with Caroline's parents, Edmund and Ann, who had flown in from the UK to enjoy the Easter break with them. Together they drove west to the Hwange National Park, the largest reserve in the country with a large and diverse range of mammals and birds. After a few days quiet game viewing they drove one hundred kilometres north to Victoria Falls.

For the vast majority of tourists, Victoria Falls is the main draw in Zimbabwe. And there's no doubt in my mind that Zimbabwe can offer much better views than Zambia when it comes to enjoying the sights offered by the Falls – Mosi oa Tunya, meaning 'The Smoke That Thunders', as the region's makololo inhabitants called it in Livingstone's day. Livingstone was actually quite a wordsmith and in his account of seeing the falls for the first time he wrote that 'on sights as beautiful as this angels in their flight must have gazed.' Inevitably his words have been jiggled around and re-crafted, in this case for the air tours that buzz above the rising mist and the chasm where the water drops into the abyss. The Flight of the Angels competes with white water rafting, bungee jumping, sunset booze cruises, horse safaris, game drives, jungle walks and the raft of curio shops, hotels, lodges and camp sites all catering for tourists and helping them to have a good time and spend lots of their foreign currency.

At the Falls they opted for the Flight of the Angels but that was pretty much the height – forgive the pun – of their exertions. Certainly bungee jumping would never have been on Andrew's agenda due to his unbounded fear of heights.

After a relaxing week they headed back to Harare, where Edmund and Ann boarded a flight home to the UK and Andrew and Caroline headed north to the border with Mozambique. One of the many international border oddities bequeathed to African nations by the short-sighted colonial powers, Mozambique hogs the entire Indian coastline from Tanzania in the north until it reaches South Africa, a distance of just under 2,500 kilometres. As a result, Zambia, Zimbabwe and Malawi, the countries which together were once called 'the Federation,' are all landlocked. Worse again, Mozambique curls around the southern end of Malawi and some four hundred kilometres up the western flank in a hook that neatly cuts off Malawi from Zimbabwe. To get to Malawi from Zimbabwe you have to cross through a part of Mozambique known as the Tête Corridor, a distance by road of around 275 kilometres. The town of Tête sits on the banks of the Zambezi River mid way along this corridor. During the era of Portuguese influence it was initially a centre for trade in gold and ivory before subsequently gravitating to becoming a pivotal control point for the slave trade. It's been described as the end of the earth, a place littered with flimsy shanty huts and desperately poor people scratching around to try to stay alive in the oppressive humidity and scorching temperatures. The annual average temperature is in the mid 30s centigrade, but very often the temperature will climb into the mid 40s. It's not a place to willingly hang around in.

Once they had negotiated the crossing from Zimbabwe into Mozambique, Andrew and Caroline headed for Têtе, crossed the large, decaying suspension bridge over the Zambezi – speed limit 15 km an hour, otherwise the Mozambicans gleefully fine you (they probably will anyway for some made-up vehicle misdemeanour) – and headed north-east towards the primary Malawi border crossing at Mwanza. When they were some twenty kilometres short of Mwanza they cut up a small dirt road heading due north, skirting a line of hills called the Kirk Range – named after the long suffering Dr John Kirk who accompanied Livingstone on his Zambezi expedition – which runs close to the border between Mozambique and Malawi. It's a known shortcut that would bring them out at a small, quiet border crossing called Dedza, only an hour's drive from Lilongwe. In the Royal Fusiliers Andrew had quickly learnt that there was great merit in the army saying 'prior planning prevents piss poor performance'. In this particular case the prior planning involved making a seemingly innocuous and very practical decision to deviate from the primary route. They would save a lot of time and not have to queue up at the busy main border crossing. It was also a pretty drive, offering great views and with very little in the way of traffic or people.

As the car joggled and bounced up the dirt road, at that time of the year in serious need of some grading after the rains, and they drove through pristine indigenous miombo woodland, I can easily imagine that they were in a jubilant mood after a great break, and busy making plans for the future. There had been talk about seeing more of the world before settling down more permanently. Somewhere in the Far East, where Andrew and I had grown up as kids, was high on the agenda. When you're thirty-five without children and not tied into an organisation, the world is your oyster and it holds endless possibilities.

As the twin cab turned a bend in the road near the top of a ridge, an impromptu roadblock confronted them. Two men in military fatigues toting AK47 machine guns; the guerrilla's weapon of choice due to its robustness and reliability. It was early afternoon on Sunday 13th April 1997.

Andrew in Service Dress with General Service Medal and Northern Ireland clasp

Falkland Islands tour, 1990

On night patrol, probably in the Brecon Beacons

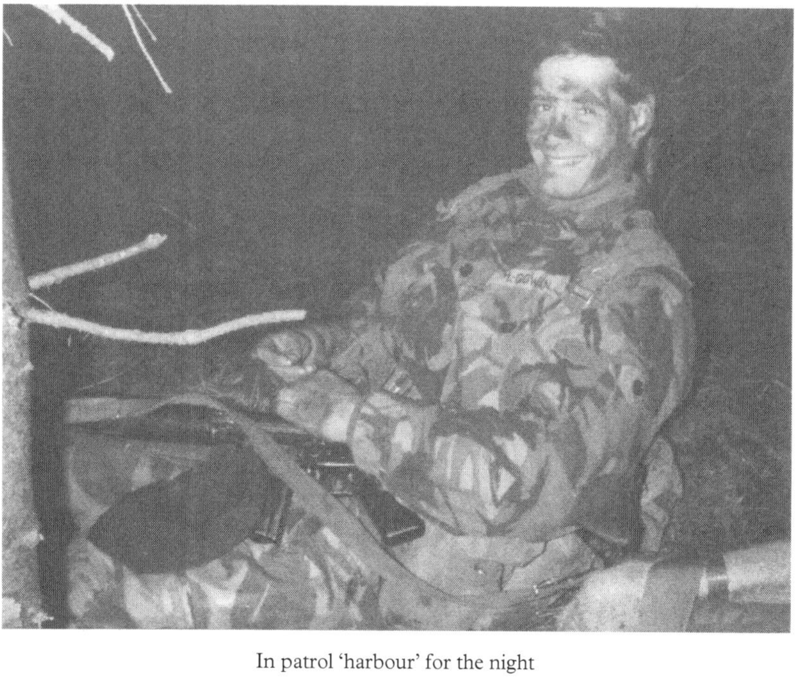

In patrol 'harbour' for the night

On patrol in Northern Ireland with 7.62mm self loading rifle

Andrew and Caroline

On Dedza Mountain, central Malawi

CHAPTER 6

# Steerage Problems

It's nearly eleven o' clock in the morning and we've been steadily tracking north by north-west up the lake a couple of kilometres offshore for nearly three hours. Everyone has had a go at the wheel. We've safely negotiated the Crocodile Rocks on our port side and the large Boadzulu Island some five kilometres offshore to our starboard. We're heading for Nkhudzi Bay, a small bay where Philip's house is located. The plan is to anchor there and go ashore for a serious lunch. It's gone eleven o'clock, over five hours since we had our peanut butter rolls for breakfast, and we're all starving.

Drew is at the wheel and I'm standing next to him, enjoying well pretty much everything. The imposing line of hills to the east stretching north as far as the eye can see contrasting with the flat, unremarkable land to our port which is dotted with small knolls and palm and baobab trees. The baobab is known as the upside down tree because when bare of leaves the branches look like a large root system. The easy motion of the boat riding the swells with a familiar swish and splash. The relief of things being under control and the feeling that we really are going to do this journey and take the *Pelican* right up the lake. And not least, the anticipation of lunch.

Drew breaks in on my thoughts with a fairly casual announcement.

'Hey Ewen. I think you should know that the wheel feels kinda loose.' He could have said something like 'I think the steering is stuffed' but although Drew can let off the odd expletive mostly he's very polite. I digest this information for a few seconds wondering how much significance I should attach to it.

'How do you mean?' I eventually respond.

'Well, just that. It's turning mighty easily now. Earlier it was pretty stiff.'

'It's always been quite stiff. The engineer who built the boat thinks that one of the rudder posts was slightly damaged when the *Pelican* was launched.'

'Well maybe he was wrong and it's finally loosened up?' Drew says, part hopeful and part question. I'm sceptical and my heart rate picks up a couple of notches.

'Okay. Let me take the wheel and check it out.'

As soon as I turn the wheel, I know we have a problem. It more or less spins freely. Whichever way I turn it, the *Pelican* just continues on her merry way straight ahead. I'm pretty sure already that there's a problem with the steering hydraulics. Probably a burst seal somewhere in the system, quite likely in the rear compartment where the hydraulic ram that moves in and out to turn the rudders is located.

I pull the throttles back and think aloud.

'Well we have two options. Continue at a reduced rate and try using the props to steer her. If she goes to starboard then we can increase the revs on that prop and reduce those on the port prop. Or option two is we can dig out the manual tiller and steer using that.'

I try out option one without further delay as the *Pelican* is starting to slew slowly to starboard, the stern being pushed round by the wind and waves. Playing with the throttles hardly makes any difference and we're quickly down to option two. I reduce the engines to dead slow.

By now the rest of the crew has realised that something is up and we're all congregated in the wheelhouse. The atmosphere is bleak. Leaving Philip and Axel on the bridge, the rest of us head through the main cabin to the rear. I haul out the manual tiller – a chunky piece of box metal with a square opening at one end – which is located in one of the hinged bench seats. Outside the back of the main cabin there is a circular six-inch diameter hole in the metal decking with a cap on it. Removing that cap reveals the solid square male fitting and we slot the tiller onto it. The tiller bar faces the stern inclined at an angle of around 45 degrees. Pushing the tiller away from me towards starboard, I find that it moves with little resistance. More importantly, the *Pelican* obliges by turning to port. We breathe a collective sigh of relief. I offer my silent thanks to Don's pal Basil, the engineer, for getting that right and give myself a quiet pat on the back for ensuring the tiller was on board before we left.

Drew offers to work the tiller, but there's a practical problem to be overcome first. He basically cannot see where he's going because he has the main cabin blocking his view and even with the rear cabin doors open and looking forward through the cabin to the wheelhouse windows, all he can see are the five steps at the far end leading up to the wheelhouse. The answer lies in Drew peering around the port side of the main cabin so that he can see Stephen standing up by the bow. Stephen then proceeds with his growing boating speciality. Giving steerage instructions by semaphore and occasionally with a loud bellow. When this is over I'll gladly recommend him for a piloting position.

Twenty minutes later, just before midday, the *Pelican* weaves into Nkhudzi Bay and we drop the anchor. There's an unspoken desperation about the way we pile into the *Stingray*. We're all keen to escape the headache of the *Pelican's* steerage problem and more than ready to devour a hearty lunch.

'No one want to swim?' Philip enquires, and then adds into the surprised silence. 'The exercise can only do you good. There have been no recent sightings of crocs in this bay.'

'Thanks Philip, but I think I speak for all of us when I say that we're happy to pass on the exercise idea today. Perhaps save our strength for whatever trials lie ahead,' I say prophetically.

'But please don't let us stop you,' pipes up Stephen.

'Wimps,' he mutters with a grin, pointing the boat towards shore and thrusting the throttle hard forward. The *Stingray* leaps into life and we fairly fly over the water towards the shore.

There are quotes galore about journeys. John Steinbeck wrote: 'A journey is a person in itself; no two are alike. And all plans, safeguards, policing and coercion are fruitless. We find that after years of struggle that we do not take a trip; a trip takes us.'

Less than forty-eight hours into our journey, it really is starting to feel as though the *Pelican* voyage has its own agenda and we are hapless puppets along for the ride.

Lunch becomes a prolonged affair as we mull over options. Should we leave the *Pelican* anchored in the bay whilst we work on the steering hydraulics? Or do we move her down to the southern end of the bay, where she would be better protected from any storms that whip up? Not having a jetty to dock to means that repairs are going to be painfully slow as we ferry stuff back and forth. Crucially, we don't have access to equipment here that we might need. Eventually the decision is made to press on up to the coast for another fifteen kilometres to Monkey Bay, Malawi's main port. It's sheltered and has docking facilities and workshops. Axel decides that the time has come for him to jump ship and leave us to it. I think he's worried that the *Pelican* may end up floating aimlessly around the lake, an African version of the *Flying Dutchman*.

As we edge out of the bay a fish eagle swoops low overhead and sees us off with its distinctive and piercing call, 'weee-ah hyo-hyo-hyo.' The wind has picked up to a fresh breeze with larger rollers coming up behind us as we cruise up the coastline on a course more or less north-west. Stephen has offered to be our tiller man for this leg of the journey. He sits in a small, collapsible chair, craning his head to peer around the main cabin to get his directions from Drew, who is up at the bow. Frequently he shifts from sitting to standing, from looking astern to looking towards the land and then back again to the bow. A human meerkat on the lookout for trouble or anything of interest.

Less than two hours later we round a headland and steer a semi-circle to port into the harbour. Monkey Bay is ringed by hills and the shelter they provide ensures that the bay remains beautifully calm except on the extremely rare occasion when a strong wind blows directly from the north. The hills also act as a natural auditorium, making the *Pelican's* engines sound loud and throaty.

Docked at the far end of the bay is the MV *Mtendere,* meaning 'Peace' in Chichewa. She is one of two grand old dames of the lake, the other being the MV *Ilala*. Together they have provided a marine bus service for goods and people around the lake for many decades, and it shows. Careworn and bearing all the dents and scars of numerous escapades, they have both had adventures and seen their fair share of mountainous seas and tragedy. They should have been mothballed and scrapped many years ago, but then trade and movement on the lake would have come to a standstill. They are waiting patiently for a new ferry to arrive so that they can slide into a well-earned retirement. In marine speak, be scrapped.

We dock at the main jetty alongside the MV *Mtendere*, a baby David compared to the overbearing hulk of the old ferry. Word quickly gets out and within ten minutes I spot the tall, slim figure of Oscar Selemani in a crisp white shirt, dark trousers and gold-rimmed shades. I know Oscar of old. He saunters down to greet us, cool and inscrutable. He is in fact very smart in both senses. In his late thirties with an MSc in Shipping Management, he works for the Government's Marine Department, part of his remit being the Director of Safety. I imagine he is on a terrible salary and spends a lot of his time bored and frustrated, pushing papers around.

Philip and I step out of the wheelhouse and onto the jetty.

'Good afternoon,' Oscar says in a neutral tone as he holds out his hand, which I shake tentatively. Oscar manages a short, grim sort of smile. His curiosity is plain. We are a temporary answer to his boredom and I wonder what plans he started to concoct when he spied the *Pelican* motoring into his harbour.

'How has your trip been?' he asks politely. He's quietly fishing for information. Anything will do.

'Fine,' I lie smoothly. I daren't look at Philip, but I can sense he is peering at me and wondering if he and I have been involved in the same journey or we are in some sort of parallel reality. Well, to quote again, badly, from Mark Twain, 'as truth is the most valuable thing we have, let us economize on it.' But I'm not good at untruths so feel compelled to elaborate. In any event I doubt that 'fine' will save us from whatever Oscar cooks up for us.

'We have a small problem with the steering hydraulics. Probably a seal has gone. We'll check it out and then arrange for someone to pop down to Blantyre to get a replacement.'

I try to sound nonchalant, though I know that removing and then replacing the steering ram in the tight confines of the rear steering compartment is not likely to be a quick job, and refilling the system with steering fluid is certainly going to be a messy affair.

'So how have you been steering the boat?' he enquires, sounding more disappointed than concerned.

'Manually. We have a manual backup tiller that can be fixed directly to the steering arm at the back of the boat,' I respond proudly. Oscar ponders this briefly and perks up.

'Good. Very good.' I'm assuming that he's pleased we have a backup. But actually he's reflecting on something else he has in mind.

'We need to do a full safety check on the boat including stability tests,' he announces matter-of-factly.

This is worse than I had anticipated. I'd rather hoped that he would just want a quick peek around, a brief inspection, and then some recommendations, followed by an invoice for the Marine Department's time and Oscar's. And that would be that.

'Your man in Zomba has already checked the boat out when it was on the river at Liwonde. We have a valid Certificate of Seaworthiness,' I reply.

'The Zomba Marine Department office is only used to dealing with small wooden fishing vessels on Lake Chirwa. Not a much larger vessel such as this. I'm also sure you agree that the lake is a very different environment to the river.'

I can't argue with that and to do so wouldn't help our cause. I grasp another straw.

'I can show you all the stability calculations done by the engineer when the boat was first launched,' I offer.

'The Marine Department needs to be independently satisfied

about the boat's stability. That's part of our responsibility. You have the ability to steer her manually, so tomorrow morning we'll take her out and do some checks and tests.'

That was essentially what was 'good and very good'. A real, live private mini-ship that he could check from bow to stern and the opportunity to make use of his qualifications by doing a nice long complicated set of stability tests and calculations. Oscar 1, *Pelican* crew 0.

Oscar tells us where we can get some reasonable food and a beer. It's more or less round the corner, where the concessionaires have set up a small guesthouse. We have an hour to kill, so we do some half-hearted cleaning and tidying around the boat. Stephen gets out his fishing rod and casts a lure over the side; I'm sure in hope rather than expectation of landing anything worthwhile. Ten minutes later he gives a whoop and we rush over as he reels in a good-sized sungwa, a member of the perch family, and a very tasty fish. We head off to find the guesthouse and an hour later we are tucking into Stephen's fish with chips washed down by a couple of beers. We're in a sort of no man's land, happy to have safely made it this far – which in truth is not that far – but rather nervous about what tomorrow might hold in store.

'Cheers,' offers Drew. 'Well done to all of us.' He chuckles. 'Especially the amazing helmsmen.' We clink beer bottles and tuck into the food. Our small talk flits randomly around but always veers back to the *Pelican*.

'Anyone care to remember what we were doing this time yesterday?' Stephen asks.

'No, don't remind us,' replies Philip.

'Stephen was rehearsing for a role in *Titanic 2*,' I offer with a grin.

'Yes. *Titanic 2*. Otherwise 'The storm, the ship, her captain and his bit of bother,' Philip flashes back.

'Perhaps we could do with some more Jameson's,' Stephen suggests hopefully. 'Thinking back on it, it was all pretty scary. She bucked around like a wounded buffalo.'

And that last comment is enough to jog Philip's animal memory bank.

'Wounded buffalo,' he muses. 'I think maybe we should have a bit of whisky.' And he magics up a bottle from the travel worn sausage bag by his chair. We charge our glasses and wait expectantly.

'Well, there's a story about a game guide. A character, as many of them are, who had been working in the bush a long time. Larger than life and a couple short of a dozen. Let's call him Bill. Bill has worked out his own signature guiding stunt. Probably the first time he did this he was high on something.' Philip pauses for a little effect and takes a good gulp from his glass.

'It surely can't beat your signature stunt with the crocs,' Stephen pipes up.

Philip nods sagely. 'Let's see shall we.'

He just loves to tell his bush stories. Invariably his audience enjoys listening to them. He peers around to make sure he has all our ears and eyes.

'So Bill specialises in walking safaris. He has a bunch of clients tramping through the bush and behold. A herd of buffalo. Like a commando, Bill's hand shoots up and he turns and whispers to his punters that they must be as quiet as dormice and as still as statues. With maximum drama, nice and slowly, he removes his hat and his rucksack, watching the puzzled looks on the punters' faces before he turns back towards the herd. Suddenly Bill lets out a mighty yell and starts shouting at the top of his lungs, waving his arms in frenzied circles as he races off towards the herd.'

Philip pauses for another sip.

'Which scatters in confusion?' Drew suggests sceptically.

'I think they must,' I say. 'Otherwise it's the final curtain for Bill.'

'Absolutely,' says Philip. 'Totally confused. This isn't something they've ever seen before and they're flight animals. Their first instinct is to run for it. Works like a charm and after the clients have got over the shock and calmed down they think this is just the coolest thing ever. Insane, but cool. They'll be dining on Balmy Buffalo Bill for perhaps the rest of their lives.'

'Different,' I observe.

'Mad bugger,' says Stephen. 'What's he up to now?'

'Oh now. Last I heard he was pushing up the daisies,' Philip responds nonchalantly. We all nod gravely.

'Buffaloes finally get him? Grew tired of the whirling dervish routine?' I ask. Philip has a knowing grin on his face.

'In a manner of speaking. One fine day Bill goes through the routine and sure enough the herd takes off. All of them, that is, except a large old bull that is being sheltered in the centre of the herd. He's been wounded and is in a lot of pain. Certainly in no mood or position to run for it. So he does the only thing he can. He takes Mad Bill out.'

'Amen,' remarks Drew.

And on that note we all head for the *Pelican* and sleep.

CHAPTER 7

# Balancing Act

The Captain's log for Tuesday the 4th May indicates that we woke to a fine day with a fresh breeze blowing and kicking up white horses outside the bay. I brew up coffee in the galley and we breakfast on muesli with long-life milk. Then Stephen and I get to work disconnecting the steering ram. It's not a difficult job even in the cramped confines of the small rear hold. Within half an hour we've removed and taken it apart. It's a relief to see that the problem is exactly as we anticipated – one of the hydraulic seals is damaged.

Philip has a driver for his work as a water engineer and he's arranged for the driver and car to wait at the dockside. By eight o'clock Philip is on his way to Blantyre to get the ram seals replaced. Axel has gone with him. We joke, rather uncharitably, that perhaps Axel has found all the excitement too much and he needs to go home and have a quiet nervous breakdown.

There's no time for the rest of us to relax. Oscar has had last night to think over his plans and he arrives with four dockyard labourers and a second safety officer in tow. He briefly outlines his proposals. The boatyard has lots of old wooden railway sleepers. In not many days gone by the Malawi Railways Lake Service was headquartered at Monkey Bay. So Oscar's plan is simple. He knows the weight of a railway sleeper – we guess it must be around 75 kilograms – and his men will manoeuvre eight of them onto the top deck. He'll then get his little team to shunt them around whilst he takes various measurements.

Plant – as in cranes that can lift things – are in very short supply in Malawi. Most jobs are done manually with lots of labour. Many a time I've needed to move a piece of equipment or put something together and a crane would have been the quick and easy answer. But in the absence of that type of hydraulic lifting power, one falls back on muscle and lots of humour. Typically Malawians are the most humorous, easy going ready to help people on the planet. So with these tricky jobs you explain to them what needs to be done: 'We need to make a bridge so that these ten one-ton logs are positioned like soldiers all in a row across this small ravine.' Except you wouldn't say 'like soldiers' as that would confuse things and a ten-minute explanation of what logs and soldiers have in common would be required. Next you edge away, with the exhortation that they must take care as you don't want anyone to be hurt. Which clearly you don't. They all laugh at the thought and start their own planning. This involves the group having a heated discussion about how to achieve the objective. The conversation will ebb and flow for several minutes and will involve lots of arm-waving until one personality wins the argument.

In general Malawians are not big people. The rural Malawians in particular are slim and whilst I don't know their average height I would guess for men it is around 5' 7". They are used to hard physical work and pound for pound they make most

Hollywood hard men look positively puny. Once they set to and put their muscles to work, there is no pressure apart from peer pressure. The banter flows back and forth and in no time the job is completed. They instinctively know the dynamics involved, the equation relating to energy expended, time taken and diminishing returns. When you judge it safe to return they will all be sitting on a completed bridge chattering about the price of maize or the gossip in a nearby village. Who is marrying whom. Who is playing away. Who is sick, who is pregnant and who is thinking of travelling 'on busyness' to Mozambique or South Africa. What a truly odd bunch white people are. Who in their right minds would want to pick up railway sleepers and stack them on the top deck of a boat?

Oscar's men struggle and sweat. It's not easy lifting and manoeuvring these sleepers up on to the top deck. After that's been done they spend a couple of hours heaving them from side to side and front to back, endlessly stacking and unstacking them as Oscar barks instructions. He has hung a long thin line from the middle of the top deck stern railing, weighted with a large metal bolt tied to the end. The *Pelican* is released from her moorings and allowed to float away from the jetty, held by a single short line strung from the jetty to the bow railings. We all stand as close to the boat's centre line as we can and as Oscar's line drifts one way and then the other he draws lines and marks angles with a black marking pen on the paintwork just above the rear cabin doors. He is in the moment, engrossed in his calculations. I can see the frisky waves outside the bay to the north and imagine the fresh, cooling wind blowing out there. In the harbour the stony hillsides are soaking up the sun's rays and bringing them to life, the heat shimmering and vibrating like a tuning fork, radiating out across the waters of the bay and turning the concreted area around the jetty into a large heat sump.

As the morning drags on we add our sweat to the decking. Many whites, who I'm sure the Malawians tend to view as prone to being impatient and short tempered, would tend to get quite tetchy in such circumstances. We can all congratulate ourselves as we're as good as gold, taking our instructions from Oscar without complaint, helping out as best we can, cheered on by Stephen's constant supply of quips and good humour. He's just one of those guys who seems to have a never-ending cache of happy pills.

By midday, Oscar is finished. So are his men. And so are we. The sleepers are removed and we all take a break for a drink and sandwiches, along with Don and Tam, who arrived earlier in the morning and have been sitting on the dockside patiently watching the show. They have come to see how things are going and to join us for a ride around the bay when Oscar intends to put the *Pelican* through her paces. Don wants to have the opportunity to spend time, just once, on his beloved boat on the lake.

In the early afternoon we start the engines and motor towards the deeper northern end of the bay, well away from a couple of cargo ships sitting at anchor at the south-east end of the bay, which is also a graveyard for smaller boats and barges that have sat moored and neglected for years. Eventually the absolute boredom gets to them and they quietly slip below the waterline to sit rusting on the lake bed, some unseen, others marked by their rusting, damaged superstructures which stick up out of the water like crooked, arthritic fingers warning others of their fate.

The next hour is a riot, one of those vignettes locked into my memory forever. We are like kids on a fairground ride. I stand at the controls on the top deck whilst everyone else is left clinging to the side railings, hair blowing and our loud nervous laughter and chatter competing with the throaty, urgent beat of the engines reverberating around the bay. With the throttles set to full ahead Oscar stands with tiller-man Stephen at the stern giving him directions as we describe crazy circles and figures of eight around the bay, the *Pelican* leaning hard one way and then the other whilst he orders us all from side to side. It's as if Oscar is trying to get the boat to turn turtle, and I suppose in a way he is. Where is that point of no return? Still some way off and hopefully rather further than it feels, I fervently hope.

The situation reminds me of when I was a child and you have that boy thing going on. A competition with the other kids and wanting to prove that you are 'the kid.' You achieve this distinction by being the first to achieve something spectacular. The simple fact that it hasn't been managed before because it's pretty near impossible doesn't enter into our heads. There's a little bit of fear, but not a lot. I think at eight the fear factor is subsumed by the clumsy, brawny boy factor. Also known as sublime ignorance. It's playtime and we're on the school swings, four in a row rocking furiously forwards and backwards to see if someone can do a full circle. There's a grim look of determination accompanying all this effort. You are concentrating on the on-looking peers and on that glorious moment when you go full circle. There's something at the back of your mind that says this could all end in tears but still you press on. If we had all managed to synchronise then I'm sure the first thing that would actually have happened is that we would have taken off because at some point the top crossbeam linking all the swings would have parted company with the rest of the frame and we would all have been flying at warp speed towards those kids quietly playing with their dinky toys in the sandpit.

It's odd having a ship's wheel in front of me that's useless. Instinctively I want to turn it and right the boat, but for now it's just a pretty fixture. I'm sure Oscar at the stern is in seventh heaven, checking his plumb line and wielding his marker pen, adding to his plethora of black marks on the bulkhead.

After the best part of half an hour he has had enough and we cruise slowly back to our berth. Oscar takes some tracing paper and transcribes his markings before heading off to his office. He'll catch up with us, he says rather evasively, in the morning. He's not giving anything away for now. At least not until he's pressed lots of buttons on his calculator.

I do a brew and we all sit on the top deck with mugs of tea and a tin full of biscuits.

'Well, I thought that went pretty well, didn't it?' I ask no one in particular.

'She didn't capsize. That's got to be the definition of a successful stability test,' Tam suggests light-heartedly.

'Yup, all good at that level,' says Stephen. 'I think it all depends on how technical Oscar is going to get.'

Don is surveying the half-sunken boats nearby.

'Well I certainly hope the *Pelican* doesn't end up like that,' he says pointedly.

'Not part of the plan, Don. We may not deliver at the speed of DHL, but deliver we intend to do,' I respond. Don gives a 'harrumph' at this. We all know there's quite a way to go on this unpredictable lake with this unpredictable boat.

'Just keep an eye on the starboard shaft seal,' he eventually adds. 'That's the first thing that needs fixing when you arrive in Metangula.'

Don't I just know it. This shaft seal will be the defining item on our journey, the definition of how something small and apparently insignificant can evolve to become something so huge that it engulfs and consumes you. With the benefit of hindsight we would have stopped right where we were and hauled the *Pelican* out of the water on a trolley so that the offending shaft seal could be removed and properly drilled, as it should have been in the first place.

The steering and propulsion systems for the *Pelican* had been fitted at a small Italian engineering outfit in Blantyre. Both the prop shafts had to be carefully drilled before being inserted through the stern section of the hull and fixed to the back of the engines. This fixing process was simple enough. First you need a key – not the sort you put in a door lock. Imagine a piece of hardened rectangular metal five centimetres long and one centimetre square. On a precision metal router, and starting at the end of the shaft, a slot is cut horizontally along the shaft half a centimetre deep and five centimetres long. A corresponding slot is cut in the circular rotating coupling at the rear of the engine. The key is then placed in the slot on the shaft and the shaft is manoeuvred into the engine coupling. The shaft will now rotate in the direction of the engine – clockwise or anti clockwise – depending on whether the coxswain on the bridge has chosen forward or reverse.

So here's the thing. If you are moving forward, the prop is generating thrust that essentially pushes the shaft against the engine block. But if you are in reverse, the forces are in the opposite direction – the propeller is trying to pull the shaft away from the engine block. In other words, if the shaft is not bolted onto the back of the engine mounting, then when you go into reverse it will try to part company with the engine.

The way to prevent this happening is very simple. Machine drill and thread a couple of holes one hundred and eighty degrees apart through the rotating coupling on the engine block and corresponding threaded holes one centimetre in depth into the prop shaft. Screw a couple of high tensile bolts through the holes in the rotating coupling and down into the holes in the shaft. Now you're good to go.

Unfortunately, some time after the boat was launched it was discovered that a leak had materialised where the starboard prop shaft entered the hull. At first we assumed that this was just due to bad fitment of the starboard seal. Closer inspection revealed a different story. The bolts had been screwed into the holes in the engine coupling, but no holes had been drilled into the shaft. The bolts were sitting there looking purposeful, but this was an illusion. Put the engine in reverse and the shaft could pull away from the engine coupling – not a great distance due to the shaft bearings located at the point where the shaft enters the engine compartment as these also helped to hold the shaft in place, but that reverse pull may be just enough to push the stern water seal slightly up the shaft. Change from reverse to forward and the shaft pushes forwards up against the engine coupling and now a small gap at the seal has materialised where water can enter the compartment.

I imagine an engineer's assistant who wants to please 'the boss' and show how competent and brimming with initiative he is. The port shaft has been fixed in place some time ago. The starboard shaft is lying around in the workshop. He gets some of the workers to help him insert the idle shaft into the hull and manoeuvres it up to the engine coupling. He pats himself on the back for ensuring that he puts the key in place as he does this. He notices the bolts on the port shaft, grabs a couple and screws them into the starboard engine coupling. Et voilà. Job done!

A slightly bigger, well, monumental, example of what happens when a seal fails can be seen by looking at the fate of the Challenger space shuttle.

Eventually Tam, Don and Stephen bid us adieu and head back home. Sadly, Stephen won't be with us for the rest of the journey up to Metangula. He has a farm to run. Axel had departed with Philip. I'm not sure if he has work to get back to. Drew jokes that Axel has decided he's had enough excitement and needs to go home to have a nervous breakdown.

Later, in the early evening, we get a call from Philip. Mission accomplished. He's staying at his cottage in Nkhudzi Bay for the night having returned from Blantyre with a five-litre container of hydraulic fluid and the hydraulic ram fully repaired. Tomorrow we can put everything back together again and test the steering gear. And see whether Oscar is going to give us the green light to continue, or bring our journey to an abrupt halt.

CHAPTER 8

# Deceptive Appearances

I've been hijacked once. I hope never to repeat that experience. It was fifteen years ago and I can remember everything with crystal clarity.

Karen and I set up a project on the farm to grow mushrooms. We purpose built it all – bulk storage, composting pit, sterilising room, growing houses, processing and packaging rooms. Mushrooms are finicky things and need just the right temperature, humidity and $CO_2$ in order to grow. One of the last items we needed were a couple of large air conditioners, so we advertised on a social media site. Bingo. Someone answered very quickly to say that they had a couple that were surplus to requirements. They had been bought for new warehouse offices and found to be too big for the job. Too many BTUs (British Thermal Units) apparently. The seller was very believable and seemed to know what he was talking about. He spoke good English and for no good reason that seemed to add to his credibility. I arranged to meet him in Blantyre the next morning at the Mount Soche hotel, one of the premier hotels in Blantyre.

When I arrived he was already waiting. In his late twenties, he was smartly dressed, tall and I guessed of mixed African/European heritage. David was the name he gave. He hadn't brought the air conditioners – they were still sitting at the factory as his brother had had to dash off on some emergency taking their pickup truck with him. He just needed me to give him a quick lift across town and he would show them to me. We all know that feeling when someone blindsides us and we are left to make a smart – or not so smart – decision in circumstances where we feel uneasy. Unfortunately we don't listen to that little voice that says 'this isn't right.' We listen to the voice which says we need the air cons and we need them now. He looks very presentable. You're being paranoid. Oh how appearances can be deceptive.

We set off across town and make small talk. He says that there are a lot of bad people around and I should really lock the car doors when I'm driving round town. Somehow that comment makes me feel more relaxed. Across town he directs me towards an industrial area and then suddenly away from it across a dirt road towards a large market with stalls and people busy buying and selling. We eventually pull up in a quieter area in front of a house. I think, rather stupidly, that there's no sign of a warehouse. Everything is telling me this is all wrong and yet there's still a part of me trying to convince the intuitive part that all will be revealed and all will be well.

'I have a knife and I'll put it in you if you don't do exactly as I ask.' The tone is conversational. He could have said 'Looks like we might be in for a bit of rain later.' It takes a while to process what he's said and separate out the tone with the meaning. His right hand is low down by my side and I have no intention of checking out whether he's bluffing or not.

'Sorry?' I say rather stupidly. His reply is stronger.

'I have a knife against your side and I'll stick you with it if you don't do as I say. Give me your watch.'

There's no doubt now about what is transpiring. My heartbeat quickens and I have a sinking feeling deep in the pit of my stomach. I undo my diver's watch and hand it to him.

'Your phone.' I get it out from the door side panel and hand that over. He looks at it and I can read disappointment on his face.

'This is an old phone,' he comments, looking at me accusingly. I'm not altogether sure what my response to this should be.

'Well it's my phone. I don't have another.' The truth is that I don't bother with expensive phones. Chances are I will drop it, lose it or it'll get stolen. So as long as it can take and receive calls, as far as I'm concerned it's fit for purpose. But I don't bother to elaborate all this to the knife-toting hijacker. He stuffs the phone in his pocket and continues.

'The money.'

Now I'm confused.

'Money?'

'The cash you've brought for the air cons.'

'I haven't brought any cash for the air cons. I won't buy them until I've seen them and had them checked to make sure they're working properly,' I explain.

'I don't believe you. Of course you've brought the money. No one would let you take them away without payment.'

'I intended to get them checked out by an electrical friend, Mike. He would confirm they are in good working order and then we'd go to the bank to get the cash. I don't like driving around with lots of cash in the car,' I finish pointedly.

He tries not to look disappointed, but this clearly isn't going quite to plan. A rubbishy old phone and now no big payoff. There's a pause whilst he digests this and looks around the car for anything of interest. Outside people are milling around, totally unaware of the little drama playing out a couple of yards away. We are in different universes, those in the fresh air busy with their 'busyness,' and me sitting with this toerag in my car, which has now turned into a metal and glass prison cell. I wonder if I should try to make a dash for it. Not easy, as I would first have to undo my seatbelt, so I pass on that idea for now.

'Your wallet,' he demands. I fleetingly think about saying I don't have one with me. But then he'll know I'm lying. It's compulsory to carry your driving licence with you in Malawi and virtually no one would drive around with absolutely no money on them. I reach under the driver's seat and pull out my bright red and yellow nylon wallet. I don't hand it over but quickly open it so he can see the Malawi Kwacha notes inside. I take them out and hand them to him before nonchalantly dropping the wallet down the side of the driver's door. A few thousand kwachas for him, equivalent to around £10, just about enough to get drunk on. He's got no further interest in the wallet. It's not leather or designer.

'Don't get out or move the car for the next minute,' he says. And suddenly he's out of the vehicle and I just have time to glimpse him darting between a couple of buildings before he disappears. I lock the passenger door and draw in a couple of deep breaths. No point in trying to give chase. No point in telling the police. There's nothing for them to follow up on. After a minute I switch on the ignition, reverse out and head back towards town. I allow myself a wry smile. He didn't get the two $100 notes zipped in the back of the wallet. My emergency fund. But I'll miss my old watch. It was a present from Karen. And I have that gnawing feeling that I've been just a little stupid. Taken for a ride, in both senses.

Roadblocks and hijackings are commonplace in Africa. When I travelled the length of the continent in the early 1980s, the worst offenders for roadblocks were Nigeria and Uganda, closely followed by a host of other countries. They are supposedly on the lookout for guns and contraband, but in reality they are on the lookout for any opportunity to impose a fine or take a bribe. The weary ninety-nine per cent of innocent citizens trying to go about their daily lives and get from A to B are resigned to their fate of constant harassment and threats. Especially those squeezed into rattling old mini buses, which are highly prized and targeted.

The passengers joke that the police roadblocks are where the real highway robbery is taking place. Roadblocks can be fixed in one place for years on end or spring up anywhere on the roadside, usually where there's a nice big tree to provide shade. There's often a confusing mix of officialdom. Police can be mixed in with machine-gun-toting military personnel and often someone in civilian clothes. The civilian may be plainclothes police. He may be something more sinister, a sort of state intelligence guy. He's not going to offer you his name or give you much of a clue as to his purpose or position. You take it he's in charge because everyone at the roadblock defers to him. But generally it's the uniforms that people recognise and give way to.

In Mozambique the traffic police have mastered the technique of indolent authority. There's a big tree in the distance and as you drive towards it you notice with a sinking feeling that something has detached itself from the bottom of the trunk and is moving in slow motion towards the centre of the road. When you're a couple of hundred metres away, with well practised timing, the policeman turns ninety degrees towards you and a white gloved hand languidly moves out sideways and upwards, the palm facing you. You crawl to a halt at the side of the road. You can't see the eyes, which are hidden by a peaked hat and sunglasses. Everyone is careful. You are careful to be polite. The policeman is carefully weighing you up. You go through the motions of smiling and trying to be jovial, pretending that it's perfectly all right that you've been pulled over. Yet again. You have all day and he's doing an important job. Where have you come from? Where are you going? Why are you going there? What are you carrying in the car? Show me your licence. He will take the licence and meander around the car, nonchalantly eyeing it up and checking in particular that the licence disks on the front windscreen are in date. If he's in a bad mood he'll ask you to put on your lights and indicators, check the tyre treads, that you have emergency triangles, and, I always think rather bizarrely, that your windscreen wipers and water jets are working. If all that fails to produce a problem he can pounce on, he can always fall back on the sob story delivered with an ingratiatingly plastic smile. It's a very hot day. He's very thirsty. Can you find your way to giving him a Fanta or Coke? Or some money to buy one?

Sometimes there's a very comical ending. My wife's Aunt Jayn was stopped at a roadblock in Malawi. She sat patiently waiting whilst the policeman unhurriedly checked around the car and then asked her to put on her windscreen wipers and windscreen jets. She complied and the policeman nodded happily.

'Thank you madam. That's in order.' He pauses before continuing. 'Today is your lucky day.' Aunt Jayn smiles in anticipation.

'Oh is it? Why?' she asks lightly.

'Because, madam, today I am only checking windscreen wipers and fluid. And your tax disc has expired.'

The fact is that road blocks are a part of life in Africa. Not a cause for alarm, but certainly a constant cause of irritation. It seems to me that there's an almost unvarying principle, a sort of inverse relationship. The poorer the country, the greater the number of roadblocks.

Sunday afternoon, 17th April 1997. They'd spent a couple of days living rough, filling in the long hours of boredom smoking joints. Ex-guerrillas, with orders but without leadership. Bored and edgy. They knew that the nearby villagers were nervous and unhappy with their presence. Two of them armed and in uniform, but clearly not real soldiers, they could only be up to no good. Sooner or later someone from the village would contact an official, or the local population might mobilise, take matters into their own hands and move them on. Further delay was not an option. They needed a suitable target. And soon.

Rounding the corner as they bumped up the dirt road, the sight of an impromptu roadblock ahead would not have caused immediate alarm to Andrew and Caroline. It was certainly odd out there in the middle of the bush, but at first sight the guerrillas would have had the appearance of officialdom with uniforms and rifles. Stoned out of their minds or not, the hijackers had put some thought into the best place to carry out the crime. Sited a short distance after a blind corner, on the passenger side there was a high bank and on the driver's side the ground sloped away down a hillside covered in tall grass, rocks and bush trees. There was no way to escape, short of running the roadblock. The danger there is that whether official or not, you ran the risk of being chased by a hail of bullets. As soon as the vehicle came to a halt they were ordered out, marched ten metres into the bush and made to lie face down.

Monday, 18th April 1997. Two hundred kilometres away at our house on a farm outside Zomba, Karen and I are enjoying a quiet afternoon with tea and biscuits on the veranda. The rains are over, the grass a lush green. All the vegetation is thick and brimming with insects and reptiles busy in a constant battle to eat or be eaten, to multiply and divide. The frogs and insects will be in noisy competition when the sun goes down. There won't be any lions roaring tonight, but we might hear the yap of a jackal or the whoop of a hyena. There aren't many of either left as the inexorable increase in the human population drives them away into smaller and smaller niches.

The phone rings out in the study. It's my mother in the UK and as always she gets straight to the point.

'I can't get hold of Andrew or Caroline. I've been trying the number since last night. School started today and Caroline hasn't turned up for work.'

'Perhaps they've had a breakdown on the road,' I suggest. 'They may be stuck in Tête or somewhere along the way and unable to get a message out.' This sounds like the most plausible explanation to me. I'm stumped to think of any other, unless they are still in Zimbabwe due to car problems. That's also logical, but not right. If they were still in Harare they would have rung the school or a friend in Lilongwe to pass the message on.

As if reading my mind my mother presses on.

'I have a bad feeling about this. They wouldn't just not turn up without getting a message to someone.'

'Okay, I'll make some calls and ring you back. Don't worry though. There will be a simple explanation, I'm sure,' I respond, trying hard to sound reassuring and unworried though I can hear the sudden strain and rasp in my voice.

Karen and I start to make calls. To the school, to her brother in Lilongwe who is a good friend of Andrew and Caroline. To any others we can think of. We try the Zimbabwe end where they have been staying with friends and discover that they definitely left Harare on Sunday morning for the Mozambique border with the intention of arriving back in Lilongwe mid-afternoon the same day. They must have broken down somewhere quite remote. We can't get a number for the border crossing between Mozambique and Malawi. We're uneasy, concerned but not yet in panic mode. I tell my mother that we'll chase things up first thing in the morning as it's too late to do much more today, but she's already made up her mind and her conviction and distress sends me reeling.

'Something's happened. I know it has. I had a dream.'

The tea is stone cold. I get Karen a soft drink and grab myself a cold beer and we sit in the lounge as darkness envelops the house. We talk it over and make a list of things to do the following day. I feel a knot in my stomach and a growing sense of unease. Though I know it's useless, I can't stop myself from mulling things over again and again to see what simple explanation we might have missed. I brood on the unthinkable. And the fact that Karen is herself not well. She's six months pregnant and has had several miscarriages already, so she is more or less on bed rest. Above all, the doctor says she should not be put under undue stress.

It's generally difficult to keep a balance on life in Africa. When you think everything is pretty much under control, the glass set fair, something invariably happens to throw everything into disarray. It's exciting and exhausting. What I do know is that for Karen and the unborn baby's sake, somehow we have to try to keep things as stress free as possible. From where I sit, this looks as though it's going to be mission impossible unless a simple explanation presents itself in the morning.

CHAPTER 9

# Light and Dark

Oscar peers into the wheelhouse, a small wad of papers in his slim, well manicured hand.

'Morning Oscar,' I say brightly. Feeling compelled to offer an explanation, I continue. 'There seems to be only one way to refill the steering hydraulics and that's through this tiny breather hole on the steering column.'

It's a slow and laborious process. Hold a tiny funnel with one hand, pour a little hydraulic fluid from a small plastic bottle down the spout with the other, put down the bottle and one-handed, slowly turn the wheel to help the system ingest the fluid and expel some air. The seal between the bottom of the funnel and the breather hole is not fluid tight so it oozes out, a strawberry goo that flows around the steering column and drips onto the floor.

Oscar's bottom lip drops into a grimace. He is clearly not at all impressed. 'Looks very messy. Are you sure there's not a proper refill hole somewhere?'

'I'm pretty sure this is the only option. I remember watching Basil, the engineer who put the boat together, and he made just as much mess when he first filled the system.'

'Obviously an oversight,' Oscar says matter of factly. 'I've got a list of safety recommendations and the results from the stability tests,' he continues, holding up his papers. His face gives nothing away. I suppress a sigh, put everything down and step out of my gooey-soled trainers as I exit the wheelhouse. It's the moment of truth.

To be fair to Oscar, he clearly knows his stuff and you can't argue with the need for safety given that the *Pelican* has a crew and in future will be taking on passengers. Unlike Basil's original thesis of stability calculations, Oscar's runs to one page of neatly laid out figures and half a page of script. I pick out the important bits. 'The vessel was found to have a positive GM of an acceptable magnitude of 398.855mm... The Certificate of Seaworthiness as issued at Liwonde remains valid for the stated period.' We are in the clear. Oscar had made various safety recommendations to us the previous day – proper seals on the engine room trap doors, a painted waterline mark, proper seals on the forward compartment in case the boat collided head-on with something, all electrical wiring to be put into steel conduits or replaced with marine cable (it was currently in normal plastic electrical conduits) and the white navigation lights to be placed higher up. And we should also carry a fire axe. I point to this last item on his list.

'This recommendation for a fire axe, Oscar. Is this to ward off pirates or enable us to cut firewood if we get stranded in Mozambique?'

I actually wasn't sure what else we could use an axe for on a steel ship with mainly steel doors. Oscar actually smiles.

'Well, if you think hard enough I'm sure it will have some other uses.' He pauses. 'What about chopping vegetables or meat?'

'Good idea. Or making a mooring post on a barren shore and hammering it in.'

'Or clearing a path through the jungle,' he offers.

'Okay, you win. I get it, Oscar. It's a big non Swiss multi-tool.' I grin widely and feel the relief. The fact is I was worried that he might say we were grounded until these recommendations had been carried out, but thankfully he's not a vindictive person and has taken a pragmatic approach to enable us to continue our journey. He trusts us to carry out his recommendations as soon as reasonably possible after the boat reaches its destination. And I have to admit that it's been a useful exercise that has helped put our minds fully at rest on the stability question. What I haven't told him, because I don't want to run the risk of him withholding the seaworthiness certificate, is that there is the small, irritating matter of the occasional leak on the starboard prop shaft that can only be fixed by pulling the boat out of the water on a trolley and removing and drilling the shaft. In my mind it's just a minor issue that we have lived with for years. The bottom line is that the crew and I don't want to lose any more time. We're impatient to get going.

'When are you aiming to leave?' he asks.

'Tomorrow morning, assuming that we get the hydraulics sorted today.'

'Good luck.' He suddenly smiles broadly again. 'It's good to see another vessel on the lake. We could do with a lot more.' He turns to leave. 'Come and see me later this afternoon. I'm going to sort out the invoices for the mooring fees and safety checks.'

He turns, climbs over the railings and onto the jetty before striding off towards his office. I think that in another situation he would have asked if he could join in our little adventure.

Thursday, mid-morning. The day after completion of the messy repairs to the hydraulic system. There's a steady, fresh breeze, the mwera wind, blowing from the south-east. It's truly invigorating after the stifling heat of the confined harbour at Monkey Bay. A light blue sky with small cotton clouds scudding by overhead perfectly complements the sea, which has changed from green-blue inland to a deep sapphire blue of rolling, sparkling motion gently pushing the *Pelican* along. Land is the best part of fifteen kilometres away and we are steadily tracking north in order to reach the eastern shoreline which curves around in a westerly direction on this section of the lake. We have set off alone and I've spoken to Philip on the radio. He estimates that he'll catch up with us in the *Stingray* within the next half hour. The steering is thankfully behaving fine so shortly after leaving the harbour I have moved up to the wheel on the top deck from where I have the benefit of the breeze and great views of the mountains rising out of the lake in the distance.

Many adjectives could be used to describe the lake today, but one will suffice. Beautiful. Well actually two. Stunningly beautiful. I'm totally immersed in this sublime place and point in time, which is all the more poignant after the trials of the last few days. I have an uncomplicated and clear impression of being an integral part of my surroundings, deeply wrapped up within my own perfect bubble. The sparkling sea and the hazy outline of the rugged mountains on the eastern shore; the smell of the clean, brisk wind and her insistent, pure breath on my face. The steady, clunking beat of the engines and above that the rush and splash of water as the hull sways comfortingly beneath my feet cutting a path towards the distant shore. I feel the glorious, overpowering beauty and vitality of it all and don't want to lose this perfect moment. I want to clasp and hold it tight, yet in the same instant I know with unshakeable clarity that it will not be lost but will remain with me bright and sharp forever, locked into what William Wordsworth termed 'that inward eye.' This radiant, iridescent lake is alive with motion, her colours and moods continually changing. To the north-west there is a vast, boundless disappearing horizon to be explored, a realm known from maps but where the lake's temperament will be less certain. Perhaps quietly sleeping with an impenetrable mirror-like surface hinting at the seemingly bottomless dark depths below. Perhaps playful with small puffs of wind tickling the surface creating innocent, baby wavelets. Or a strong, fresh breeze with some white spray and determined waves rolling together in massed ranks towards that curving horizon. Or a shrieking gale with chaotic, uncontrolled movement. Petulant Poseidon, intent on destruction.

This last is the uncertainty and dichotomy that makes a trip an adventure. You don't want to be out in the middle of the lake when she is in such an ugly mood. Just the thought of it leaves you with a knot in your stomach. Yet it is this knowledge that you are somewhere with such unpredictable, destructive potential that brings many people alive. I guess expectation is everything. How many times does one have the courage and strength to take on an adventure in life before your imagination becomes too vivid or your body too weak? Few or us are as courageous and single minded as the incomparable Bill Tilman, who was still seeking out new adventures and mountains to climb in his eightieth year.

I drop back into reality. Something is missing. Someone. Stephen. With his enthusiasm and banter, Stephen creates his own jovial microclimate, in which everyone around him gets caught up. He has been replaced by a friend of John Fleming's, an introverted, fair-haired youngster called Mark who seems to have little by way of conversation or input. He looks nonplussed by his surroundings and I suspect he is unhappy at being conscripted to join us. A fish out of water. John had asked if Mark could join us for the journey from Monkey Bay so that we could show him the ropes and teach him as much as possible about the boat and how to handle her. Mark would be the person responsible for looking after the *Pelican* once she arrived in Metangula. He had arrived in Monkey Bay on the ferry ship MV *Ilala* a few days earlier and had been a silent presence whilst we did the stability tests and sorted out the hydraulics. On his record to date I wasn't sure that he was up to the job, but perhaps after a while he would come out of his shell and be more proactive. To be fair, who could blame him if he was feeling rather out of his comfort zone? Bobbing around on a vast and often treacherous inland sea in the middle of the Rift Valley is a far cry from the bustling civilisation of Johannesburg. It's often said that real Africa begins north of the Limpopo, the river that delineates the border between South Africa and Zimbabwe.

Drew taps me on the shoulder. 'Here he comes,' he says, pointing more or less directly astern. Sure enough, I can make out a small object in the distance kicking up a short wake. Within minutes the *Stingray* draws alongside and is put on a short tow. Philip clambers up the rear ladder onto the top deck.

'Sorry for the delay. Work issues, but all sorted now,' he declares. 'You've made good time. And what a fabulous day!' He's positively effervescent himself this morning.

'Couldn't be better,' I reply.

'How much longer do you reckon to Makanjira Point?' asks Drew who has magically reappeared from the galley with mugs of tea and a container of biscuits. We're like the Famous Five that Enid Blyton never wrote about, except we're four.

'We're making good time. Probably in excess of twelve kilometres an hour. so I would estimate just over an hour.'

Makanjira was one of a trio of chiefs from the predominantly Muslim Yao tribe which dominated this region. He and his fellow chiefs conspired with the Arab slave traders to capture the more peaceful Nyanja living around the southern lakeshore and transport them eastwards through Mozambique for sale as slaves. After the British explorer and colonial Commissioner, Sir Harry Johnston, had essentially vanquished the slave trade in Nyasaland in 1894, he set up a network of forts in strategic positions to ensure that these slave routes were wiped out for good. Fort Maguire on the coast just north of Makanjira Point, was one of the most isolated of these outposts. I imagine you were pretty much at the bottom of the colonial ladder if you were posted there. Sadly, or perhaps happily, over the ensuing decades it became superfluous to requirements as the slave trade was finally eliminated from the area and it fell into ruin. It certainly had no secondary use as an administration or trading centre. Makanjira Point itself has magnificent sweeping views and would have been perfect for observing all movements on that crucial part of the lake.

As is so often the case when viewing a distant shore from the sea, the land seems to creep nearer agonisingly slowly. You will it to come to you. And very suddenly there it is, almost on top of us. We can make out the rugged, boulder-strewn coastline and the water crashing and cascading against the shore. The area south of the Point is described on our 1954 chart as a 'rocky foul coast' with submerged rocks. But north of the Point there are no dangers marked, and the depth just a short distance from the shoreline is astounding, generally between 70 to 100 fathoms, which roughly translates to 130 –180 metres.

We spend the rest of the day tracking north parallel to the coastline, munching on tuna rolls and cheese for lunch and enjoying the trip. At some indeterminate point we cross the invisible border into Mozambican waters, and by late afternoon we are on the hunt for a suitable place to moor for the night.

This turns out to be much trickier than we had expected. The lushly wooded and boulder strewn hills plunge straight down into the lake. There's no sign of a bay or even the smallest of inlets that we could nudge the boat into. Given the depth of water, mooring offshore is not an option. And even if it were, it would not be an option we would take given our earlier experiences on Lake Malombe. A howling mwera wind arriving without warning, kicking up the water and turning the lake into a raging storm within minutes. Whenever out on the lake you learn to keep a nervous, wary eye on the sky and the state of the lake generally. Unless, of course, you get lulled into a false sense of security by mirror flat water, great camaraderie and Jameson's!

As the sun is dipping perilously close to the horizon on the far side of the lake, we spot the tiniest of bays. More of a bump in the coastline where a small outcrop of rock will provide some shelter from the southerly wind and waves. We edge cautiously towards it and Drew slips into the water with a mask and flippers to explore the terrain below the surface. It's a mission, but twenty minutes later we have negotiated the huge underwater boulders and the *Pelican* is safely moored to an assortment of trees and rocks with a web of lines.

'That'll do nicely,' observes Philip before adding. 'Unless of course the wind backs to northerly or westerly.' It's a bit of a mischievous, throwaway line and I look to see whether he's exhibiting that mischievous grin of his. It suddenly reminds me of when I was a newly qualified lawyer helping put together a complicated set of papers for Richard, one of the litigation lawyers. By helping, I mean doing reams of photocopying and collating. It was all to do with a large claim against an American software company and Richard had painstakingly colour coded the documentation to try to help the judge pick his way through the various intricacies of the claim. It was truly a work of art and

Richard was so excited by the end result that he hauled another lawyer, Chris, up to his office to proudly show him the bulky piles of paper that comprised his pièce de resistance. Chris turned a few pages and looked suitably impressed. He brought his hand up to his chin and massaged it in dutiful contemplation. 'Well,' he pronounced in solemn tones, 'it's certainly colourful and I'm sure the judge will really appreciate it.' He turned to go and then added his throwaway line, 'If he's not colour blind.'

'That has to be a wind up, Philip,' I reply. 'We both know that's unlikely at this time of the year. But in a worst case scenario at least we don't have far to go to shore and it's not exactly a barren coastline.'

'But given our luck to date, not out of the question,' Philip persists.

'I'm confident we'll have a quiet night and the wind will behave – with or without the Jameson's.'

He chuckles and disappears to check the *Stingray's* mooring lines. Drew is already in the galley preparing the evening grub, whilst Mark is at the stern of the top deck sitting on the large metal box that houses emergency lifejackets and other useful paraphernalia, staring into the darkness. He's very withdrawn and I realise with a pang of guilt that I still haven't made any effort to try to get to know and include him. Does he view this little escapade as an adventure or does he think never mind the stability of the boat – what about the captain and his crew! Well, who can blame him? He's certainly a long way from home and the predictable, frenetic world of Johannesburg.

Tonight's Michelin star menu comprises noodles and some pieces of soya flavoured with a hot piri-piri sauce to give it a bit of bite. A full day in the fresh air without any mishaps has left everyone relaxed and famished. We follow up our main and only course with a nightcap after which I slip down below and boil up some water. My appearance above decks clutching mugs of hot chocolate brings the expected flurry of comments from Drew and Philip.

Drew: 'Very domesticated.'

Philip: 'He'll make someone a great wife.'

Drew: 'Is it time for a story?'

Philip: 'Yes, Jackanory. And will you be tucking us up in bed tonight?'

I can only respond in kind.

'Sorry boys but no story tonight. Early start tomorrow. Be good, drink your cocoa and get to bed.'

Later I lie on the top deck staring up at the night sky. Despite being bushed, sleep eludes me. I replay the day in my mind, and then fast rewind to replay the journey to date. Then I imagine the run into Metangula tomorrow. There's barely a whisper of wind tonight. The shore is less than ten metres away, a hillside densely crowded with gnarly bushes and thorn trees, large baobabs and thick, tall grass which stands like the massed ranks of an army protecting the land from the sea. In this profoundly still and black night you might erroneously think that the bush is fast asleep. It's actually very much awake and alive with the sounds of thousands of insects furiously clicking and clacking away, frogs croaking and owls hooting. The wood owl calling 'hu-hu, hu-hu' and waiting for the female's 'hoo' reply, or perhaps the whitefaced owl with his big orange eyes and a loud explosive stuttering 'b-b-b-b-bhooo' call. It's too late in the season now for the red-chested cuckoo, the solitary and shy male endlessly inviting a mate with a call that sounds to me rather like 'I love you' forlornly repeated over and over again. A somewhat cynical and deceptive cry given his polygamous nature. Then there are the stealth predators, in particular the snakes. Endlessly testing the millions of scents in the air with flicking tongues, building a road map to the prey as they silently glide unerringly towards the kill. Perhaps a mouse, nervously darting and quickly feeding, sniffing and peering into the dense dark bush for signs of danger. Never staying in one place for too long as it tries to keep one step ahead. Here the circle of life is short and merciless. And then the bush is drowned out and all I can hear is Philip again, somewhere to the rear of the lower deck, contentedly snoring away. The infinite stars twinkle above, pinpricks of light shining through a black shroud. On the other side lies a universe of light and the stars are wormholes into this parallel universe. And with that thought I drift off into another world that only my subconscious knows and will remember. And rarely shares.

Tuesday, 19th April 1997. Karen and I have tried all the contacts we can think of. We have contacted the Mozambican consulate in Blantyre and their embassy in Lilongwe. They have no news and no interest in making any serious enquiries for panicky British expats. We are a nuisance. We contact the British High Commission in Lilongwe but it's impossible to get through to anyone senior. There are protocols. They arrange visas and passport renewals in the morning and the impression is little else for the rest of the day except, perhaps, high tea at the poolside in the middle of the afternoon. When I think of British Embassies around the globe I cannot shake off that ridiculous, hilarious 'tiffin' scene from 'Carry on up the Khyber' when the English Ambassador – who else but Sid James – mimics the English stiff upper lip whilst the Embassy is besieged and falls apart around him. Anyway, the fact is that you need to know someone who knows someone within the Commission's high walls. British Embassies and High Commissions have proved very adept and had long and remarkable success at keeping out and repelling marauders in all their guises. Today it's less physical and more civilized. We are all treated as potential intruders and they can do the same 'repel job' using a suitable message on a telephone answering machine.

Now, though, the time for phones is over. Physical presence on the ground is required.

Karen and I have a muted dinner and head to bed early. I'm up at 4 am, when it's still dark outside. I gulp down a cup of tea to wake me up and a quick hug later I'm driving north on the road to Lilongwe. A four-hour drive cocooned in our Land Rover. I put the radio on for company and despite my promises to drive very carefully I constantly find myself speeding up and having to make a conscious effort to slow down. My frenzied reflections roll round and round in my head, lending increasing urgency to the situation. In reality there's little I can achieve by arriving early, as the Mozambican Embassy will still only open at 9 am. The road is devoid of cars or life, but the danger of a stray dog or goat, or even a hyena, is very real. And an accident at this moment is unthinkable.

I meet Karen's brother, Bert, and two of his and Andrew and Caroline's friends, Ian and 'Bushman', outside the Embassy. We're in through the doors as they open and quickly complete and lodge the forms and fees along with our passports to obtain Mozambican visas. I manage to talk to someone who purports to be a senior official and he listens to my concerns and says noncommittally that he has heard nothing. He cannot understand what all the rush is about, but he will make some calls and let me know if anyone at the border or Tête has heard anything. In the meantime we must wait. Patiently.

An hour passes. Two. I pace up and down the waiting room, willing someone to appear. Eventually the official reappears. He produces our passports with fresh visas stamped inside and says that he has no news for us. Looking into his eyes as he presents his usual indifference and nonchalance, my heart skips a beat. I know he's lying. He stares with more than usual interest and intensity. He doesn't look sad or concerned. More that he's privy to something.

We drive south in convoy, the Land Rover and Bushman's double cab, and by four in the afternoon we arrive at Mwanza, Malawi's main border with Mozambique. It's not too late to cross the border, but it is too late to make any meaningful enquiries on the Mozambican side before dark. I know we all harbour a wish. That Andrew and Caroline are at the border. That they've been given a lift or a tow after their car broke down. Caroline appearing with a weary smile and hugs all round, just glad to see us. Andrew with his usual big grin and a tension-relieving quip along the lines of 'What took you so long?'

We chat to an immigration official and explain the situation. He nods and disappears. We ask incoming vehicles and passengers if they have seen anything, know anything. Eventually the immigration official reappears, looking concerned. He is holding a slightly crumpled British passport in his hand, and as he hands it to me he asks if we know this person. Opening it, I stare long moments at the picture, confused. Is this a joke? How did he come to be in possession of it? When did he come into possession of it? An unblinking, serious face stares out of the page at me. My brother.

The explanation he gives is simple. It was handed to him early this afternoon. One of the Mozambican immigration officials drove over from the Mozambican side of the border several kilometres away and handed it in. No account given as to where it had materialised from.

'Where's the holder of the passport? The man in the picture?' I ask with growing agitation. He shrugs.

'I know little. Just the passport is given to us.'

'Did the man who handed it to you mention a car crash?'

'He mentioned nothing. No information. Is this the person you are looking for?'

Staring at the photo the situation doesn't seem real. Surely, surely it's a big mistake. There's a pounding in my ears and I start to shake. My fear gives way to an irrational anger.

'This is my brother's passport,' I state accusingly, staring down at the photo. 'What are they doing with it? How can they not know where it's from? Passports don't just come out of thin air!'

By the end I'm almost shouting. Bushman puts a calming hand on my shoulder. I turn and look to him and the others. They say nothing, just look devastated. I'm clutching this passport, the closest link yet to my brother and his wife, and it dawns on me that the Mozambican official must have appeared at the Malawi border with the passport very soon after the Mozambican embassy official in Lilongwe handed us back our visa stamped passports. They clearly know a hell of a lot more on that side than they are prepared to let on.

'You want to keep the passport?' the official asks.

I nod. 'Yes. I'll keep the passport,' I mumble.

He almost looks relieved, as if it's a red hot coal that he doesn't want to handle any more. It's our first lead. An agonising lead. We move away and I stand and stare blankly at the border barrier. My impulse is to cross now and start making enquires. They might be in desperate straits, and twelve more hours might make all the difference. But I know that there really is nothing to be done now. The light is already starting to fail. We need to get properly prepared. We'll have to come back first thing in the morning. For now we'll head to the farm and Karen, get something to eat and make our plans. And try for some sleep.

CHAPTER 10

# Going Down

A warm south-easterly wind is blowing. The breeze is creating small rollers through which the *Pelican* gently dips and rolls as we cut a diagonal line across them. We are approximately four kilometres offshore and our GPS says that we are chugging north at a stately fourteen kilometres an hour, tracking the Mozambican coastline off our starboard bow. At nine o clock in the morning the sun is already high in a bright blue sky dotted with small fluffy clouds.

Up on the top deck I am standing in a T-shirt and shorts, one hand on the wheel sipping coffee from a plastic mug. I reflect that if we have a good run today we should make our destination by late this afternoon. That thought brings a small smile of relief. It would mean that we would have accomplished our mission and survived our little adventure on the lake. But I'm not going to allow myself to get carried away too soon. No one who has lived in Africa for any length of time counts any chickens in advance. Nothing here is ever certain. Africa can be an unpredictable and cruel mistress. She generally likes to leave you guessing right to the very last minute.

I glance astern to check on our safety boat and tender. The *Stingray* is straining on the end of a short towline, Philip dozing in the stern, seemingly oblivious to the tugs on the line and the little rushes of speed as his boat breaks over the crest of each small roller and rushes down towards the back of the next one. The rigid hull and inflatable green pontoons make his boat streamlined and virtually unsinkable. Ideal for its job. Philip's laid-back attitude reminds of that scene from Crocodile Dundee, the one where Mick Dundee, alias Paul Hogan, is out in the bush with his soon to be real-life wife, Linda Kozlowski, and he's arranged to meet his mate Walter on Wednesday. As he's walking away Dundee pauses and turns to Walter. "What's today, Wal?" And Walter says, "Monday" and watches Dundee turn and saunter off before adding to himself, "Doesn't know. Doesn't care. Lucky bastard." Philip isn't that kind of timeless laid back, but he is the kind of laid back that doesn't panic easily or worry unduly. It's part and parcel of having grown up in the bush in the 1950s and 60s learning from a father who was one of the last real white African hunters. A man who later converted to become a game conservationist and a safari photography guide. I'm certainly no Crocodile Dundee but I do have to think about it to remember that it's a Thursday. Five days since we left Liwonde. Though it's not important. We don't have a particular deadline and our day and routine will not change whichever day of the week it is.

Drew is sharing the view with me, and we are relaxed, chatting about the coastline and how different it is to the Malawi side. Drew comes from an American Anglican missionary family with a particular luxury. Rock solid, one hundred per cent faith.

'That was quite a process this morning,' Drew comments.

'Backwards and forwards. Those props were literally inches from the boulders.'

I had had to do a ten-point turn, Drew in the water with a mask and snorkel directing operations to ensure the hull and props didn't crack against the massive granite boulders hidden below the waterline. The rudders were useless in such a confined space so I had had to switch between the props in short, careful bursts, one prop in forward, the other in reverse, trying to gently nudge the boat around towards open water. It had been quite a procedure, and by the time we finally edged out into the lake proper I was very wide-eyed and alert.

'And inches from you too! It seemed much easier getting into that tiny bay last night. Must have been because we reversed in.'

'Can't say I was keen to get into the water this morning. Man it was cold, and then trying to hold on to those slippery boulders whilst watching out for those props. Certainly wakes you up!'

'You'll be pleased to know you were my main concern. Didn't want you minced up. You'd only be good for the crocs then,' I joke.

'Do you think we'll make Metangula today?' he asks. I could be positive, say something like 'Well, we're making good time and the weather is as good as we could hope for so I reckon we'll be there by mid-afternoon.' But I can't help myself. I give him a qualified answer, the product of years working as a lawyer in a previous existence.

'If the weather holds and nothing untoward happens, then we should make it by mid-afternoon.'

The conversation moves on, but I'm not really listening. Something isn't quite right. I've learnt the hard way to trust my intuition, that sixth sense. My heart beats a bit faster, stomach tightens. It was the talk about the props and nothing untoward happening which has set off a warning bell somewhere. Is the boat now rolling more heavily, a bit sluggish?

'Drew, please do me a favour. Pop down below and check on the engines.' I try to keep the rising panic out of my voice. He looks at me quizzically but I don't offer anything more.

'Aye aye captain," he says lightly as he heads forward down the few steps that lead to the wheelhouse, after which he'll turn one hundred and eighty degrees and go down half a dozen more steps into the main cabin, where he'll then have to heave open one of the two large horizontal trapdoors that give access to the engine compartment. I draw a deep, nervous breath and try to convince myself that everything is fine. Imagination just in overdrive.

It was less than ten seconds before I heard Drew's shout. Something unintelligible, but the sense of it was in the high pitch and almost strangled surprise of his yell. It spoke of the unexpected and of frantic panic. He came racing back onto the top deck.

'We're sinking. The engine compartment is filling with water.' He looks stunned. For a few seconds I can't think. My mind is filled with the enormity of this information. Disbelief. And then anger. With myself for failing to carry out this check, the one check we always do every time the engines are started and we move on. Images are flashing away. Water sloshing up from the engine compartment into the lounge. The boat sinking lower in the water until eventually she just gives up the fight and flounders past the point of no return, the bow rising like an accusatory finger pointing up into the vast sky before sliding stern first down into the dark, all enveloping depths. Twenty metres down, the lake is almost pitch black. I know. I've dived it.

I need more information. 'How full? To the top? Halfway?'

'Maybe just under halfway.'

Halfway means we have a slim chance. It means there's time.

Not much, but maybe just enough.

Suddenly, without a word, Drew disappears below decks again. I'm not sure what he's going to do. He can't stop the water which I just know is flowing in around the seal where the starboard propeller shaft exits through the hull. The seal with history.

Now Mark is suddenly by my side. I ask him to go down below and grab all the lifejackets from the locker in the main berth. We have more in the large metal chest at the back of the top deck, along with a couple of large buoyancy rings hanging from the railings. Gingerly I start to turn the wheel, willing the boat to very slowly turn to starboard before grabbing the handheld marine radio and depressing the talk button.

'Philip. Philip. Wake up. Come in. We've got a situation here. An emergency situation. Over.' Peering astern, I see Philip push his wide brimmed safari hat off his face and sit up and move to the main console in the middle of the *Stingray* where the radio is located.

'Say again. What's the problem? Over.'

'We're sinking. The engine compartment is filling with water. I need you to find me a beach. Over' There's a short pause before he comes back on again. When he does he laughs into the radio. Philip laughs easily and quickly, always ready to enjoy a joke or see the funny side of life, even, it seems, in the midst of looming disaster. I can't see anything funny about this.

'You did say beach didn't you? Over.' he queries.

'Yes. Yes. A beach to plonk the boat on. Over.' Relief. He surely understands now.

'You have seen the coastline I take it? We spent the best part of yesterday looking at nothing but rocks. Over.'

'I know. But it's our only option if we are to save the *Pelican*. We don't need anything big. Just something without rocks. Over.'

I'm almost pleading, trying to convince him and myself that it's not a futile errand.

'I think you need a miracle. Over and out.'

Well that makes me feel really good. I watch him move to the stern and start to squeeze the rubber bulb that will push petrol from the fuel tank up into the motor so that he can start the engine. Mark appears from below clutching three or four bright orange lifejackets.

'Hurry Mark. Go and cast off the towline on the *Stingray*.' He drops the lifejackets on the deck and runs towards the back of the boat.

I shout quickly after him 'But wait until Philip gets his motor started.'

If for some reason it won't start we don't want Philip and the *Stingray* floating away as we'll need to evacuate into it. I watch Philip move forward to the console and within seconds I hear the whine of the starter and then the cough of the engine as it splutters briefly and then picks up and Philip pushes the throttle forward to give the engine a short rev. He quickly moves forward, surprisingly quickly for a big man of 120 kilograms, and pulls in and stows the towline Mark has released. I watch the *Stingray* speed off towards the shore, leaving a fizzing white wake behind it. If we go down now, we'll have to swim for shore. That's a big ask. A very big one. The wind and the rollers are blowing right across the lake. We'll never be able to swim against those currents. We'll have to rely on Philip to come and pick us up.

Drew appears at my side clutching a tightly folded black plastic bag but I can't immediately grasp its significance.

'What's that Drew?' He stares at me. It should be obvious.

'My passport and wallet.'

Somehow this feels like a betrayal, an indication of a lack of faith, this getting ready for the almost inevitable worst. It's a bitter thought that he might be right and his actions are sensible and practical. I'm now somewhere closer to despair than hope. But it hurts to think about it. I want to say that perhaps this would be a good time for him to pray to his ever powerful and benevolent god. I don't though. What I should do is ask him to take the wheel whilst I go below decks to rescue the other passports. No point in grabbing the *Pelican's* papers. We won't be needing them.

'We might get lucky,' I hear myself say instead, which of course sounds all wrong. It's also the naive triumph of hope over expectation. I push the throttles forward as far as I dare, trying to coax just a little bit more speed out of the drowning engines. The minutes pass in slow motion. Philip's *Stingray* is now nowhere to be seen, faded and merged into the grey and green coastline of rocks and trees. We're alone. My whole being is concentrated on those engines and the motion of the boat. We're running parallel to the swells now, so the rolling and wallowing is more marked as each roller relentlessly pushes and lifts the side of the hull. The engines are beating rhythmically, like a big sewing machine. One boat with two mechanical hearts. Surely that's enough. I'm waiting for the moment when those pulses catch, the rhythm stalls and the notes waver, becoming rough and fitful. The moment just before the *Pelican* dies.

I think of Don, who has treated me like his son. A man I am very fond of and for whom I have huge respect. How do I explain to him that his boat, his dream, was swallowed by the sea and is sitting on the lake bed in over one hundred metres of water? Irrecoverable. Those piercing blue eyes that flash with a fiery light when angered will look at me calmly and not too reproachfully, wordlessly asserting that a life is more important than nineteen tons of steel. Forgiveness from someone else is one thing. Forgiving yourself is quite another.

The coastline doesn't appear to be getting any closer, the usual trick of the sea against the land where space and time seem to get warped. We have to keep pressing on until, as with the approach to Makanjila the day before, suddenly that distant shore is upon us. It cannot come soon enough. I don't believe in God, though I once prayed to him for a miracle. He came up with a very big nothing. Now I just hope to be surprised by one, though from where I'm standing it seems seriously unlikely that my wish will be granted. We're going down.

CHAPTER 11

# Desperate Moments

Wednesday, 20th April 1997. The four of us leave the house as soon as the grey dawn starts to chase the night from the sky. Two vehicles, two people in each. Karen has arranged marine radios through a contact in Blantyre. The radios will allow us to communicate with each other and also hopefully back to Karen in Malawi. By line of sight these radios work well over great distances, at sea from one horizon to the next, only limited by the curvature of the earth. Using the designated channel, the signal gets boosted through a repeater station somewhere near Blantyre. It's a neighbourhood watch channel used by residents to pass on quick messages and round up the police and a dedicated response unit if anyone is unfortunate enough to be the subject of a night-time robbery. They should work fine, but it won't be private. Word gets out quickly in Africa and we could well have a large silent audience.

Two hours later we have crossed through the border out of Malawi and into Mozambique. There are three armed

Mozambican policemen waiting to join us and we pick them up before heading west on the main road towards Têle. We don't know what we're looking for or what to expect. My fear is Andrew and Caroline's white twin cab, wrecked and burnt out at the side of the road. Occasionally we pull over to make enquiries of local vendors sitting in their little wood and grass stalls or locals trudging along the roadside. No one knows anything.

Some twenty-odd kilometres from the border, we stop where there is a turning to the right heading north. This dirt road leads towards a line of hills called the Kirk Range, eventually coming out some one hundred and fifty-odd kilometres later at the Dedza town border post, the most northerly border crossing from Mozambique into Malawi. It's a natural short cut that would make sense to Andrew and would appeal to him. Off the beaten track, a pretty route, still very unspoilt with good views down onto the plain towards Malawi. But should we head to Têle, the provincial capital over a hundred kilometres away, and contact the police there? Perhaps Andrew and Caroline have been in an accident and are lying in a critical state in hospital. Or perhaps they have been locked up for some reason. Perhaps they have knocked over a pedestrian or cyclist. It didn't seem beyond the realms of possibility that the Mozambican police would actually enjoy quietly locking up a mzungu or two (mzungu translates as white person, originally derived from 'one who moves around' – a reference to travelling European traders) just to let them sweat and see what transpired. It's a sad reality, but whites are still often linked to the colonial era by some African politicians. When the going gets tough for them due to their failings – neglect and corruption mainly – the easiest way forward is to divert attention by shifting the blame onto the colonialists, even though power and responsibility was handed over many decades before. It creates a mind-set and belief in the local populations that is deeply embedded and ever present. A dislike for, and a need to inflict varying degrees of discomfort and trouble, on the present generation for perceived wrongs committed generations earlier.

After a short discussion we decide to turn off the main road and head north. Driving to Tête and making enquiries of the police there would probably cost us a whole day time-wise and if we drew a blank we would then have to retrace our tracks. Somehow, almost intuitively, we know this is the right decision.

The road is lumpy, with ruts and depressions from the recent rains, so our progress is slow, the vehicles bouncing around as we slowly climb towards the ridgeline.

'Ewen calling base. Come in Karen. Over.'

Karen responds within a few seconds. 'Karen here. Reading you loud and clear. Where are you? Over.'

Our link to home, crystal clear, as if she is in the second vehicle just behind us. I'm guessing that it's a lot harder having to sit and do nothing, just waiting for news. Jumping when the radio bursts into life and fearful of what news it might bring.

'We're heading north towards the Kirk Range and the Dedza border post. Over.'

'Is there any news? Over.'

'No, nothing at all at present. How are you doing? Over.'

'Fine. Over.' She tries to lie smoothly, but the fact is that none of us is fine at this moment.

'Okay. I'll call in again in around half an hour unless there's news earlier. Over.'

'Take care. Over and out.'

It's a stilted and unsatisfactory conversation, a reflection of the tension and nerves. We press slowly on for a few more kilometres. Bushman and Bert speak the local language, Chichewa, fluently and we constantly stop and start as they ask the few locals we come across if they know or have seen anything. Nothing at first.

And then something. Bushman looks sombre as he turns away after speaking at some length to a middle-aged woman.

'She says that several days ago, she thinks around the middle of the day, she heard shots from somewhere around here. She's not sure how many. Just a few shots. There were some guys in army clothes who had been hanging around for several days. The locals obviously weren't very happy with them. They were smoking chambva (marijuana) and drinking. Not locals and not friendly. Everyone stayed away from them. They haven't been seen since Sunday.'

My stomach knots as my pulse goes into overdrive along with my imagination. I want to ignore this news. I scrabble in my mind to try to disassociate this information from Andrew and Caroline. It's got nothing to do with them. Some drunken soldiers who have gone AWOL for a few days, let off a few rounds and then headed off. But I cannot escape the facts and the inescapable implications. Same day that Andrew and Caroline would have been on this route. Right sort of timeframe. Shots. The soldiers disappear.

'Has she seen anything else? Anything that might be linked to Andrew and Caroline?' Bushman shakes his head.

'Nothing.'

Perhaps that's good. Nothing is certain until it's shown to be real. We decide to drive on and Bushman talks carefully to the next few locals we come across to see if they can corroborate this woman's story and provide more information. The shots are confirmed by the next couple of villagers, but there's no news about Andrew and Caroline. We make the decision to stop. Bert will stay with the vehicles and call in to Karen on the radio while the rest of us will start to search sections of the nearby bush.

Bushman and Ian head up the road whilst I drop back the way we have come. What do I expect to find in amongst the grass and trees? Best case is my brother and his wife badly injured but alive. Worst case I can't think about. Before I step off the road into the bush I think fleetingly about mines. The advice to everyone travelling through Mozambique is not to leave the roads unless it is to walk on clear, well-worn paths. This was not a big strategic area during the independence and civil wars so I convince myself that there is nothing to worry about, especially in such rocky terrain. During the wars it is estimated that a variety of around two hundred thousand antipersonnel mines were planted, and in 1997 it seemed inevitable that the country would remain cursed with these indiscriminate weapons of death and maiming forever. Yet, as I write this, much to my amazement and thanks to a huge anti-mining effort, the country has been declared free of all known mines.

I move forward, scanning the ground ahead. I'm not thinking clearly any more and I certainly don't have a plan involving search patterns. The sun is high in a blue sky, a dry heat beating down and radiating in waves up from the ground. The scrubby bush trees provide pockets of shade, the grass tall and thick in places, the hillside littered with large granite boulders. It all seems surreal. Above the incessant stridulating noise of the crickets and cicadas I can hear my heart pounding and a rushing sound in my ears as I move haphazardly around. Terrified. Expecting desperate and bloody images to materialise from behind every tree and boulder.

I'm not religious. I have perhaps one per cent of agnosticism, an almost subliminal thought that there may be more 'out there.' Einstein was right about so many things. Perhaps he may also be right about his 'spooky action at a distance' and somehow, somewhere, there are hidden dimensions that will draw in some core parts of my soul if I do step on a mine. Perhaps I will literally get blown into the eternal kingdom. Yet overwhelmingly I'm not convinced about paradise or any of its promises, which seem to me to be rather too splendidly convenient. Faith is so personal, and I'd defend anyone's right to believe in a god, but not in one god or belief to the exclusion of all others. Right now I'm talking aloud in my head to any god or anyone who might be listening in. *Please please let them be found alive.*

I play mind games as I search, grasping at the thinnest of straws. Trying to block out images of men in military fatigues, guns and shots. I want alive, battered and bruised, tied to a tree. Yet overwhelmingly I'm expecting desperate and bloody images to materialise from behind every tree and boulder.

After barely twenty minutes picking my way around in the bush I'm exhausted and my anxiety levels are at screaming pitch. A sense of futility and hopelessness sets in. I stumble back up the hillside to the road and jog along it to the vehicles. Everyone else is there, and it's clear that they have been quietly discussing the situation.

'Anything?' I ask. They shake their heads.

'We think the best thing to do is drive at a crawl up the right hand side of the road. One person on the roof of each vehicle scanning the bush,' says Bert. It makes a lot of sense and I nod. It's unlikely that we'll be able to see anything above the high bank to our left.

'I'll drive the Land Rover,' I offer and we set off in convoy. We have been going less than five minutes when I hear shouts from above. Stopping the vehicle I open the door to hear what Bert is saying. He's pointing into the bush.

'It's them. It's them.'

For one crazy, fanciful split second in time my heart lifts. It's as if he's spotted them in a crowd and is pointing them out. From the driver's seat I cannot see anything but thick grass, so I climb onto the roof of the vehicle and join him. Following where he points, I can make out a form and some red material some twenty odd metres into the bush. It's definitely something, but I'm not as convinced as Bert. We scramble down and cautiously move towards it. And suddenly there is no room left for doubt. Caroline, lying face down as if quietly sleeping. Yet there is an unnatural stiffness in her still form that leaves no doubt in my mind that she is dead. Off to the left, a further ten metres into the bush, I can see a second form, my brother. Also lying face down. I stop right where I am. I'm not afraid of the dead. I've seen quite a number of corpses since coming to Africa. What I don't want is to look any closer. To see any damage, or pain or anguish on their faces. Better to remember them both as they were when alive.

Once again I am stumbling back towards the road, but now with the reality of the scene setting in. We've all seen American cops and robbers movies, and the part where someone gently puts a blanket over the body. I'd often thought, 'What's the point? They're dead. They don't care.' But now in this too much reality, the reason hits me hard and I fully understand. It's not about whether they are dead or alive. It's all about dignity and empathy. Death is in a way the ultimate indignity, and two people I love are lying in the bush, vulnerable and defenceless. I ask for blankets, and Ian and Bushman go over and cover the bodies.

Bert is trying to get Karen on the radio. I'm left standing in the middle of the road, unsure what to do next. Mind blank. I have a desperate urge to rush into action and a white, boiling anger rises in me as I start to walk aimlessly up the road. 'The bastards. The fucking bastards.' I repeat it over and over again like a mantra. I don't know who the bastards are. I just know that if someone put a pistol in my hand and could point me in the right direction I would empty every round into them.

Bert drives up beside me in the Land Rover and I get in. The anger leaves me as quickly as it came on and I'm left numb with a surreal refusal to fully accept. We drive higher up the ridgeline, where the radio signal will be better, and Bert raises Karen on the radio again. Eventually in a cracked and wavering voice I try to lie to her. Tell her I'm doing fine and it's all under control. But she knows and does what she can to console and reassure me.

Less than ten minutes later, a 4x4 draws up beside us. A slim man in his thirties steps out of the vehicle and introduces himself as Tom from the British High Commission in Maputo. His white shirt is open at the neck, but that is the only concession in his attire to the heat and his surroundings. In all other respects he looks as though he has just stepped out of his office. It seems that whilst the BHC in Malawi had proved uninterested and incapable of action, Karen had managed to get someone at the Mozambican BHC to sit up and take notice. They had communicated with their Mozambican counterparts and realised that a real tragedy was unfolding. The third secretary, sometimes known as the embassy spook or intelligence officer, had found out enough to know that he had to get to us as fast as possible. Karen had asked for a helicopter and a search crew. What she, we, had got was Tom, who had chartered a plane from Maputo to Tête and arranged a car and a driver to bring him to our location along with a representative from the Mozambican authorities.

Tom gave us his calm condolences and quickly took control. He would be in immediate touch with the Mozambican authorities and would take care of everything from here. The police would be informed. The necessary arrangements would be made to get Andrew and Caroline back to the UK. He hands me a business card. It feels like some sort of strange and shady transaction, except that my immediate instinct is to trust this man. To believe that he really means well. And as he promised, so it turned out; he did take care of everything, arranging the passage of Andrew and Caroline from Mozambique to South Africa and eventually the UK. Liaising with the Mozambican police, the provincial governor, anyone and everyone as necessary over the coming months. Then he vanished as quickly as he had appeared, and I've often wondered what happened to him. Wherever he is, as Karen said to me some time later, 'I hope he was given a posting to somewhere less stressful with picture-perfect beaches.' He certainly deserved that.

We don't want to desert Andrew and Caroline, but quickly realise that there is little more we can do. We have removed all doubts and options by discovering this terrible reality. There is no reason to remain here. There will be time enough for goodbyes later on.

Bert drives in silence, puffing on his cigarettes. He offers me one – a non-smoker – and I take it and light up. It's more an act of sharing than a need for a cigarette. Yet death, like other negative emotions such as jealousy and revenge, cannot be shared. Like them, it is intensely personal. We have to navigate our own paths through and around the destructive forces unleashed by them. For now, Bert and I sit quietly in the moving vehicle, wrapped in our individual cloaks of despair and disbelief. Lost in our own revolving worlds and thoughts about the scene we have discovered, coupled to snatches of memories of Andrew and Caroline and concerns about the path ahead.

I realise that Karen will now be busy ringing my parents and Caroline's. There just cannot be a more difficult call, telling a parent that they have lost a child. Removing the last vestiges of hope to which they are desperately clinging. I recall that I once had to be the messenger for terrible news, for a friend, also called Andrew, though better known as Andy, who had died at the bottom of a freshwater quarry in an unexplained scuba diving accident. Andy had never mentioned that he had a handicapped older brother called David living in a care home. Driving down the M4 from Bristol to the care home just west of London, a journey it turned out Andy had made religiously every other weekend to visit his brother, I tried to work out how to phrase things, what would be the gentlest way to break such news. I knew that both their parents were dead and they had no living relatives. Facing David, a mentally impaired man in his forties, who looked at me curiously and expectantly, unaware of what I was about to tell him. Would he fully understand? Of course he would, and his wails and whimpers of distress spoke for him as his small, contained world came crashing down. Eventually I had to leave him, still distraught and now totally alone in the world. My only crumb of comfort was the obvious dedication and care of the few members of staff that I had met. I remember thinking at the time that I hoped I never had to break news like that to anyone again.

We arrive home in the late afternoon, and the floodgates containing my grief now open wide. There is no amount of comfort, physical or emotional, that Karen can offer to stem it all. And she is wise enough to realise that this is something that must be allowed to run its course, that all she can do is the simplest and purest thing of all: quietly be there.

In the nights that follow over the next month I have a recurring dream that I cannot escape. A dream to make things right. I know that Andrew and Caroline are heading into trouble. Sometimes I am running like a man with the devil at his back, sweating and heaving for breath as I race up that muddy road. At other times I am driving like a madman, the Land Rover leaping and crashing over the bumpy ground. I arrive at the spot where Andrew and Caroline were hijacked, but each time I am too late. Not by much, but enough to make the difference. On one occasion I find myself reaching for the rifle even as the hijacker pulls the trigger. Each night I dread going to bed; yet perhaps, just maybe eventually there will be one night when I do arrive in time and wake to find that in fact it was, after all, just a really, really bad nightmare. For many weeks and months in my dreams my mind devises alternative realities to try to help me cope with the emotional trauma. The weather is too bad, so Andrew gets part way up the muddy road and then decides to turn back and take the longer route home. They come around the corner, see the roadblock and do a very smart U-turn. Or they are stopped, realise what is likely to happen and Andrew knocks the rifle out of the hands of one of the hijackers and they run for cover in amongst the trees and bush. Or the most persistent one: Andrew realises that the roadblock is too makeshift and the soldiers manning it too slovenly – and anyway why would there be one in such a desolate stretch of the road – so he puts his foot down and smashes through the roadblock, dipping down as bullets rain through from the back of the vehicle. At times my imagination gets lost in these scenarios during the day. What a former girlfriend of mine called 'mind fucking.'

Eventually, with the passage of time, all these alternative scenarios started to fade as reality took a stronger hold. Of course one never forgets. It's a pain you can't remove. It diffuses little by little in time with the relentless forward motion of daily life. Day by day I learn to cope a bit better. But hearing music on the radio that Andrew liked, or the mention of a place we visited together, will bring the past crashing back into the present. Sometimes it leads to a wry smile, even an impromptu laugh, sometimes that unwelcome but familiar feeling of loss and desolation which one simply cannot describe. It is always so much worse when someone close dies unnecessarily, violently and young.

CHAPTER 12

# A Stroke of Luck

From an engineering point of view, it seems like a minor miracle. I make a couple of dashes from the flying deck to check on the situation. The water is slowly and relentlessly climbing up the engines, and on my last visit it has reached the bottom of the fan belts. Yet still those wonderful engines continue their strong, steady beat whilst the fans spray water chaotically all over the compartment. The radio squawks into life, and with it possibly another miracle.

'Come in Magoo. Over.'

'Yes, I'm here Philip. What's your news? Over,' I ask fearfully.

I squeeze my eyes shut and think *beach*. Please, a beach. Even if it's only a few metres wide we'll manage.

'You are one hell of a lucky guy. Just keep on coming. You're heading straight for probably the only beach we've seen in the last hundred kilometres. Over.'

It seems too good to be true.

'You're not kidding are you? Over."

I need confirmation. If this is one of Philip's light-hearted jokes I won't be able to find any humour in it. The response is a short chuckle.

'Have a little faith! Just keep on coming. There really *is* a beach here. Over.'

We're still too far out for me to make out where the land rises out of the lake, but I know Philip is on the level. He of all people would know the importance of time and place and I should never have doubted him. A few minutes later we have, amazingly, entered a small bay that is completely hidden from view out on the lake. A smooth, enticing sandy beach greets us, and behind it thick bush and baobabs dot the hillside. It looks like undisturbed bush without a soul for miles. But this is Africa. There are eyes everywhere you go and as the *Pelican* heads into the bay people materialize on the beach, mainly youngsters and women. The *Pelican* and her crew are a never-before-seen sight. I imagine that this is how it must have been for Livingstone for much of his journey. People emerge from the bush to gape at this white stranger and his curious party marching into their lives and then on into the never-ending beyond. Like us, it would have caused huge excitement, with people running and shouting, passing on the message to the next village and loudly bantering about his skin and clothes, shoes and baggage. Who was he and where was he going? What interesting habits did he have? Did he have a wife? And children? Where were they? What was he searching for? In the excitement the girls' chatter would quicken and become raunchy.

'He looks hot and must be very thirsty,' observes one girl.

'Perhaps he could do with some of your mother's special brew,' replies another. They giggle.

'He looks tired.'

'Yes, he could do with a mat and some nice soft grass to lie down on,' states yet another, nudging her friend and raising her eyebrows.

'Better still someone soft to lie with him.'

'To ease his pains.'

'With a body that moves in a way that will help him to sleep well!' They all shriek with laughter and excitedly chase each other.

I can't hear above the beat of the engines, but I can imagine the noise on the beach as figures run backwards and forwards, some dancing whilst others jump and wave in wild and enthusiastic greeting. Still the *Pelican* keeps coming and I have absolutely no intention of slowing down. I want to solidly beach all nineteen tons of her. It takes a while for the realisation to dawn on the beach party that this small ship is not slowing down. The waving becomes more hesitant, and now I can see their faces, which start to wear looks of uncertainty and puzzlement. Suddenly, as one, the cavorting and waving stops and they scream and race back up the beach into the bush as the *Pelican* encounters the first shore breakers and with a small rush of speed she carves a path into the sandy shore and I throw the throttles into neutral. The logbook says it was 8:20 am.

Almost instantly Drew is at my elbow, greeting me with a big toothy grin of relief. He bats me playfully on the back.

'Man that was the longest twenty minutes of my life!'

'Sure. But the old girl simply refused to let us down.' I'm caught unawares as we both spontaneously burst into laughter.

'No pun intended!'

'Well those engines are absolutely unbelievable,' Drew says in a voice tinged with admiration.

I feel the tension drop away and smile back almost indulgently. 'What do you expect. They're old tractor engines!'

'Well now that we're safely beached, permission to jump ashore.'

'Yes, permission granted. Go make friends with the villagers.'

Drew is the best man to engage with the locals, who are now quickly reappearing out of the bush. His Chichewa is completely fluent and I've noted that he has an animated and jovial manner about him when talking in the vernacular. The *Pelican* has already swung round and is now lying parallel to the beach. I follow Drew off the platform at the rear of the boat and jump down onto the soft sand. An image flits across my mind: a sinking ship and three guys floating in bright orange lifejackets like flotsam on the lake, struggling in vain to keep together and reach the shore against currents that will take them far to the north and west and away from safety. I would have had a radio with me to direct Philip to us but still the thought makes me shiver. Best to keep busy. We need to make a plan. To seal the leak down in the engine compartment and get the *Pelican* under way again as quickly as possible.

Philip brings the *Stingray* in to shore and the locals help him pull her well up onto the beach. He wanders over, a perplexed grin on his face.

'Well Magoo, this is just too much. You are one hell of a lucky fellow.' He claps me on the shoulder. 'I'm in awe. You really must have good connections high up.' I try to shrug nonchalantly.

'The *Pelican's* like a cat. Nine lives.'

'Well it seems that she's using them up pretty quickly.'

We laugh and then fall silent whilst we survey the beached hulk of the boat lying with her starboard side facing us whilst the small breakers crash with surprising energy against the port side. With all the water in the engine compartment, she's not going anywhere for the time being.

'What about a good old English cup of tea?' Or would you prefer something stronger? A hefty tot of the Irish?' asks Philip, raising his eyebrows.

'I need to rescue the batteries, which are underwater. Whilst I do that if you make a fire on the beach we'll have an English cuppa and make a plan,' I suggest.

It's not even mid-morning but I suddenly feel weary, as if I've been battling destructive forces for hours. I call to Mark, who is sitting by himself further down the beach staring out to sea. This, I think, is definitely not what he signed up for.

'Hey, Mark. Want to help me take the batteries out?' I shout. He turns slowly and eventually nods, clearly not enthused. I get the impression that if there were somewhere to run to, he would be off at a sprint.

In the end our plan is not complicated. It feels a lot later but is in fact only just gone nine-thirty in the morning when Philip takes Mark and disappears up the coast in the Stingray to Metangula. Looking at the map, we estimate that they should be able to make it in around two hours if the weather remains calm. Philip will advise John Fleming of our situation and see if he can arrange a couple of guys to come back with him to provide any assistance we might need. In particular, we need a diesel or petrol water pump.

As the *Stingray* drops out of sight I put on my boiler suit. It's going to get soaked down in the engine compartment but it will protect me to some extent from oil and scrapes. With a head torch and armed with a screwdriver, I must make a singular and interesting sight. The villagers crowd round gawping and giggling. What on earth is this mad mzungu up to? Perhaps he is going to perform some strange ritual? In a sense I guess I am. Suddenly I leap towards the nearest of them and let out a loud 'ya-hoo.' They all scream and race off down the beach before turning back, laughing and shouting, part embarrassment and part simple delight.

I climb aboard and drop down into the flooded engine compartment. The starboard prop is well under water, but there's just enough of an air pocket between the existing water level and the ceiling of the compartment to enable me to get to it. I know that I must make an attempt to loosen the prop shaft seal by touch so that I can reposition it to stop the leak. At least then we will be ready, when Philip returns, to start pumping out. Whilst there are small fixed electric pumps positioned in the bottom of the hull – in the engine compartment and the double berth and heads – I don't want to wire the batteries up to the electric pump in the engine compartment and risk running the batteries down. Then we'll have exchanged the problem of a leaky ship for the possibility of one where we can't actually start the engines. We also have a manual pump, but whilst we can give that a go we'll be there a very long time indeed trying to pump out with that. It would be quicker with a bucket.

The awkward jarring motion of the boat adds an extra complication to the task, but I have the advantage of knowing exactly where the seal is and what I have to do. Within ten minutes the mission is accomplished and I'm dripping oily brown water and sweat onto the *Pelican's* rear platform as I struggle out of my boiler suit. When I finally dive into the lake it's cool, cleansing bliss.

Mark has wandered up the beach towards a small peninsula, probably anxious to see what is around the next corner of the coastline. Drew and I put a very early lunch together. We take it up the beach into the shaded treeline. Canned pilchards with distinctly dry, crusty bread rolls and bananas that Drew has purchased from the villagers. Most of the villagers have wandered off but a small group of teenage girls sit nearby watching us intently.

'Ever wondered what it would be like to be famous?' I ask between mouthfuls.

'Not really. Not part of my mission statement.'

'I guess not. But being white in rural Africa gives one a bit of a taster. You must be very used to this sort of attention living on a mission station.'

'No secrets in the villages. Your business is everyone else's. Right down to the most intimate sorts of business.'

I think about that for a moment before replying. 'No, unless I was born into it I don't think I could cope with that. Too used to having space. And anyway, secrets and mysteries are part of what makes people interesting.'

Drew lies back in the sand and puts his hands together behind his head. 'Getting too deep for me, man' he replies. 'After all the excitement I need to get some beauty sleep before Philip gets back and the hard work starts.'

I lie back myself and pull the peak of my cap over my eyes. We're lying in the shade, but somehow it seems necessary. My tiny bit of privacy, like a small child that puts its hands over its eyes to make itself invisible. The group keeping us company grows silent for a while before starting up their conversation again. Africans don't whisper, but at first they do try talking quietly. Perhaps ten minutes pass and I'm dozing off when Drew suddenly snorts loudly.

'Thought you were asleep,' I say.

'The conversation is too interesting. You know that bit you were saying just now about privacy and secrets?'

'Yes. Have you discovered one you want to share?'

'Sure have. The girls have been debating the boat and our arrival. In particular our various merits.'

'Merits?'

'Well, personal situation if you like. So they think that we're probably both single and available. But definitely you, as you're a little strange. Driving the big boat onto the beach and dressing up and shouting around. You might be fun to be with, but it's very likely that you would need some chilangizo in bed.'

'Chilan what?' I ask puzzled.

'Advice. Instruction,' he replies, laughing.

'You just made that up!' I counter, spontaneously defensive.

'No way. They've also been debating the scar on your stomach. They wonder if you got it in a fight with another man or from an angry girlfriend.'

It's actually a scar from pyloric stenosis when as a baby there is a narrowing of the opening from the stomach to the small intestine. I'm told that I was marvellously good at projectile vomiting after being fed.

'Gee, there really are no secrets, real or imagined.'

'Nope. But they sure are having fun imagining yours!'

'And what about you? Come on, spill the beans.'

'They haven't got to me yet.'

'Somehow I just don't believe you.'

'No. Really? Take comfort from the fact that you're the one they find most interesting.' I'm not convinced that this is a compliment.

'Well, I'm going to go and sort out some tea. Then they can move on to discussing my domestic skills.'

It's gone three in the afternoon when we spot the *Stingray*. It turns out that Philip, being the star he is, has found a mechanic, Lazaro, and brought him back, along with his assistant and a small pump. Drew and I had made an attempt in the early afternoon to start emptying the engine compartment using buckets, but although we did make a small impression on the water level, there was still far more left than we had the energy to take out. The pump is quickly lugged over to the *Pelican* and it clears out all the remaining water within half an hour. Without the bulk and weight of all that water in her bowels, the rolling motion of the *Pelican* now becomes much more marked and lively and moving her off the shoreline becomes top priority. Reversing her diagonally away from the beach seems like the best option, not least because of the worry that if the villagers pushed from the rear one of them might slip under the boat and end up with a foot or head sliced up in a propeller. So we fix a line from the *Pelican's* portside sternpost across to the *Stingray*, which is sitting in open water pointing out towards the open lake. I have agreed a fee with the villagers for their help in pushing from the bow.

The moment of truth has arrived. With the batteries back in place and connected to the starter motors, will the engines actually start several hours after being more or less submerged? My nervous push on the starter buttons is immediately greeted by the roar of the engines coming to life without so much as a hiccup. I give a shout and a wave from the wheelhouse as I push the port engine lever into slow reverse. I can see the *Stingray* kicking up a white froth and hear the villagers shouting encouragement to each other.

For a few seconds nothing seems to happen. Another wave, another roll to starboard and back, followed by an almost imperceptible movement of the stern away from the beach. But it is just enough to break the suction gripping the hull to the sand, and suddenly the *Pelican* is free and moving backwards, the stern swinging round towards the open bay. In the wheelhouse I am staring towards the beach and the villagers are doing what they do best: dancing, clapping and whooping.

We've all come across those moments when we believe that we've succeeded in something and can breathe a big sigh of relief, only to have some new problem knock us sideways. As soon as the towline has been released I gently push the levers to slow forward both engines. I feel the push of the props as the gears engage and the beat of the engines increases, but when I turn the wheel nothing happens. We continue on a new crash course with the beach. I push the levers back through neutral and into reverse. The *Pelican* slows and then we back up into the middle of the bay. I try again, but again there's no steerage. Drew and I lower the stern anchor and I cut the engines, don a mask and drop off the stern. It doesn't take any time at all to spot the problem and I surface, haul myself back on board and give Drew the news.

'Both props are fine. As is the starboard rudder. The top of the port rudder post has snapped clean in two.'

He digests this information for a few seconds. 'Don't you mean the starboard rudder post has snapped?' he asks. 'The *Pelican* was lying with the starboard side on the beach.'

'Nope. It's the port rudderpost. Want my best guess on why?' I continue anyway before he can reply. 'As you know, we've always had problems with the steering. Felt it was very stiff at certain points when you turned the wheel. Basil, the engineerio, said it was because it was new and that it would loosen up and settle down after a while. Well, it never has and we then had the issues with the steering when we were heading towards Monkey Bay.'

'You think there's been a problem for a long time?'

'Spot on. It's been a problem since day one. I think that when the launch on the river went wrong and the *Pelican* more or less launched herself, the port rudder post was damaged right there and then. The last few hours of stress as the *Pelican* rolled back and forth on the beach were the final straw.'

'So now we have no steerage. The boat is going to have to be towed the last stretch.'

'No, I don't think so. We just can't use the port engine. If the thrust is coming from the starboard engine and that rudder is working, then we should have steerage. It just means that it's going to be a slow slog up the coast to Metangula.'

We pull up the anchor and I start the starboard engine and slowly motor around the bay testing the steerage. The *Pelican* actually responds well. Problem solved for now. We drop the bow anchor on the port side and move the smaller stern anchor to the bow and lower that as a second safety anchor on the starboard side. Grabbing some provisions, we make a final check of the engine compartment to reassure ourselves that there is no sign of a leak, and Philip then gives us a lift to the beach.

Drew goes to negotiate with the villagers. It looks animated and some of the girls seem to be in virtual hysterics. Sitting in a circle around our beach fire, we grill some of the villagers' freshly harvested maize cobs directly on the fire and complement them with more tinned pilchards, rice and Carlsberg beer, advertised in Malawi as 'probably the best beer in the world.' Right now it's the only beer in the world and has a distinctly heavenly, de-stressing quality about it.

Philip opts to guard the *Pelican* tonight and Mark opts to join him. The *Stingray* slowly motors over and they tie up alongside. Drew and I will be sleeping on the beach. We have thin blankets but it's not cold at this time of the year and there's something timeless, comforting and mesmerising about a natural wood fire on a beautiful beach. Staring into the fire, handfuls of fine sand running through my fingers, we talk about Malawi and family. It's an unspoken agreement that we avoid the subject closest to Drew's heart – religion. We know that we stand far apart on that subject. Our conversation peters out as the fire dies down to glowing embers and the deep reds and oranges of the sky give way to a night backlit by a late silver moon, the clean outline of the *Pelican* at anchor as she gently rocks to the hidden currents entering the bay. Small wavelets quietly rise and dip, kissing the sandy shore. It's all in stark contrast to the rush and drama of the day. I realise that I'm looking forward, a little nervously, to whatever challenges the morning brings. Surely we can't fail now, so close to the finishing line? Whatever else, I am strangely content. A snatch of one of Kahlil Gibran's poems floats across my mind. "This is life, the very life of life. In its brief course lie all the verities and realities of our existence."

Drew brings me out of my dreamy, excessive introversion. 'Ewen, you still awake?'

'Yes.'

'I just remembered that I forgot to tell you something.'

He pauses, I'm not sure if it's for dramatic effect or if I can hear a slight snigger.

'I sort of sold you.'

I digest this and try to work it out. Sold me? I give up.

'How do you mean, sold me?'

'Well, I was chatting to the girls earlier. When I went to buy the maize. They're poor villagers as you know. But I managed to persuade one of them that you do have some value and she should take you on. That the dowry would be worth it.'

'Dowry!' I exclaim. Now I know what the girls were howling with laughter about earlier. And as Drew knew I would be, I'm curious.

'What sort of a dowry?'

'Well she offered a couple of goats. That's all her family has by way of livestock. In the end we settled on one goat and a milking cow to be purchased from the village chief.'

'Ha ha.'

'Well, at least you now know your value. Not many people do.'

'Very kind of you I'm sure, Drew. I think you're forgetting something.'

'What, that you're already married?'

'Quite.'

'I don't think that's a problem for the lucky girl. You've been in Malawi over ten years. You're virtually Malawian. Many Malawians have two wives, one in the city and one out in the village.'

'Except Karen isn't in the city. She's on the farm.'

'Well then, no matter. You can have two in the bush.'

'I think I'll stick with just the one on the farm. We should probably end this conversation before it gets smutty.'

'You should think about it, man. It's a good offer.'

I chuckle. 'Perhaps. But only if you're looking to sell,' I reply. 'However I do appreciate the hard work you've put into this.'

Drew laughs lightly.

'Don't mention it. Good night.'

'Night, Drew.'

Life is tough in the villages. Really tough. Living right on the proverbial breadline, they have to grow everything they need to survive. There's no welfare state to bail them out, no healthcare system to talk of, but plenty of deadly malarial mosquitoes and venomous snakes. Yet the simplicity and insecurity that characterise the vast majority of their everyday lives does contain something that seems to me to be mostly absent from the 'developed' world: engagement. Time to greet each other, friend or stranger, and to smile and laugh together. Wherever you go in rural Africa, with the huge numbers of children crowding around, you will be constantly in the presence of big open-mouthed smiles displaying two neat rows of brilliant white teeth – as opposed to pencil thin grimaces – coupled to uninhibited laughter radiating from adults and children alike. If smiles and laughter are one barometer of happiness, then Malawians have it in spades.

As I drift off to sleep I decide that in fact there's something rather comforting about another familiar sound: the booming racket of Philip's snoring coming to me loud and clear from across the bay.

Just after eight the following morning I sound one long farewell blast on the *Pelican*'s air horn and head out into the lake. It's another blue-sky day and a fresh breeze is driving small rollers up the coastline. Despite running on only one engine we make good, steady progress. The topography changes as the mountains move slightly inland, and the coastline flattens out and gives way to more frequent sandy beaches. Just before one in the afternoon we turn towards the land and head into the small bay of Metangula.

We have hardly had time to drop the anchor when John Fleming appears in a small tender with his 'friends' from the Mozambican Marine, Customs and Immigration departments. They all want to be a part of the welcoming party. To scout out the boat and basically work out what her arrival might mean for them personally. Several crates of beer are hauled aboard and suddenly we are all on the top deck shaking hands, and toasting our safe arrival and the promising future that the *Pelican* offers in terms of tourism. John feels confident that she is just what is needed to demonstrate to the powers that be that he and his sponsors are serious about their project. Now they will start to believe in the benefits that it will bring to the area. Everyone is smiling and clinking beer bottles.

John brings a short, stout man in his late forties over. 'Ewen, I want you to meet Mr Chirinsa. He's the chief of the Marine Department here in Metangula.' Chirinsa nods politely and gives me a tight little smile as I take his hand in greeting.

'Pleased to meet you, Mr Chirinsa. We're very happy to have arrived. This is certainly what might be termed a perfect little bay.'

He nods his chubby, slightly sweaty face in acknowledgement. 'I understand you had some troubles.'

'Nothing that we weren't able to sort out,' I say lightly and add, 'And nothing, I'm sure, that John here won't be able to fix pretty quickly.'

'That's good. We will need to check the safety of the boat and see the Malawian paperwork.'

Chirinsa is wasting no time in staking his claim as the main man in this little scenario.

'I have the relevant certificate of seaworthiness from the Malawi side,' I respond. 'We can go through... '

'You can give that to me later,' John cuts in. 'I'll go through it all with Mr Chirinsa and sort everything out. No need to worry about that now, is there Mr Chirinsa?'

Chirinsa doesn't reply. He simply raises his bottle of beer. John takes this as a cue to propose another toast.

'To the *Pelican* and her crew. Well done for getting here. And welcome to Metangula!'

We raise our beers and the chatter and drinking continues with renewed enthusiasm. Looking back at Chirinsa, I am unsettled. His eyes are quietly locked onto me, and it seems that he is trying to get a handle on me. It took me less than twenty-four hours to realise that the handle was simple and mundane; how much were we likely to be worth to him financially?

A couple of hours later, the official visitors have all left. We do some quick clearing up and then refer to my checklist for putting the *Pelican* to bed when unattended by a proper crew. It is headed up: "Vital checks that must be done *without fail* before leaving the boat." These include checking the prop shaft glands for leaks, checking that all seacocks are fully closed, electrical checks, closing off gas valves, securing windows and doors and checking mooring lines. John puts a couple of carefully hand picked watchmen on board to keep watch over the *Pelican* and the *Stingray* and we are rowed across the bay in a small wooden fishing boat. Some two hours after arrival we get our passports stamped and fill in some Customs forms for both of the boats before meandering up the road to where John and Mark are staying at their project house. It's a couple of hundred metres up the road from the bay and doubles up as a bed and breakfast under the name 'The Bamboo Basket', I assume because some bamboo fencing and partitioning has been put up around the property. The place is run by a taciturn man who shows us silently to our rooms before heading to the kitchen to turn his hand to cooking. As we sit together in the small outside dining area, the conversation is light and interspersed with plenty of laughter as we relive the triumphs and traumas of the last week. It's marvellously therapeutic and by the time Fredrico produces our dinner – a traditional Portuguese dish of peri-peri chicken and chips – the conversation is flowing seamlessly.

It's usually the case when you are animated and in full flow at a party that time passes quickly. I have a vague recollection of lying down on the bed and being surprised when I looked at my watch to discover that it was not even nine in the evening. It felt like midnight. But then we had packed a lot into the day, and those final few hours motoring on one engine towards Metangula had been nerve-racking. I was thoroughly exhausted.

It's Sunday morning and Philip has to get back to Malawi in time for the start of the working week. We have a hearty cooked breakfast and then head off in John's pickup to replenish the *Stingray's* petrol containers before heading down to the bay, where we hire a fisherman's small wooden boat to transfer our gear and us over to *Pelican*. I hand John the keys to the boat and the captain's cap. It's a slightly bittersweet moment. I'm glad to be passing the responsibility for the *Pelican* on but sad to be saying farewell to her. Despite all our problems, we never gave up on her and thankfully she somehow came through for us. It's a new chapter. We hope a really positive one. If all goes to plan, the *Pelican* will get a bit of a refit and be reborn with her quirks and problems sorted out. Passengers can then enjoy exploring the coastline creating hopefully stress free memories.

We head off in the *Stingray* – Philip, Drew and me. It's fifty kilometres to the Malawian side. Immediately we are clear of the bay we can see that the lake is very lively, the top of the rollers breaking into white horses and the wind whipping the foamy tips off into a horizontal spray. It's going to be a rough crossing, but there is no thought about turning back and waiting it out. This sort of weather can last a couple of hours or several days. Philip is the cox, and Drew and I hold the grab bars on either side of the steering console as the semi-rigid jumps and bucks across the waves and cold spray drenches us. The engine roars in defiance, sometimes a deep growl as it powers up and through a roller and the next second, when the *Stingray* leaps through the air to crash on to the back of the next roller, the prop cuts thin air and it makes a fast, high pitched wine. It's pure exhilaration, this howling wind and angry rolling sea. We have, in a manner of speaking, gone over the top without having time to think about it. No time for fear or for 'what ifs.' What if the engine dies on us? What if a rogue wave flips the boat? What if Philip misjudges something? The grey sky is pressing down on the grey lake, obscuring the horizon so that we cannot distinguish where the sky melts into the sea. We are locked in our own tiny universe, concentrating on the unmarked, crazy rolling highway immediately ahead, our path briefly marked by the white wake fizzing behind us.

Three hours later we approach the far side and as we pass a headland into shallower water the chaos immediately gives way to gentle wavelets, and by way of recognition of our successful crossing the sun suddenly breaks through in a brilliant blaze, sparkling off the water leaving us almost blinded as we scrabble around for our sunglasses.

The completed shell of the Pelican

Don on board the Pelican immediately prior to the tow down to the Shire river

Admiring the freshly fitted out interior.

Don standing on the stern of his very big new toy

The Pelican moored on the Shire River

Cruising up the Shire River

Looking across Lake Malawi

Sitting pretty in a small bay, Metangula, 2006

**Hugh Brown Holdings (Pty) Ltd**
Registration No: 2000/024336/07

**Metangula Project Office, Niassa, Mozambique**

13 April 2004

The Chief Maritime Officer
Metangula
Niassa

Dear Sir

**The sailing to Metangula, Mozambique of the boat known as the PELICAN from Liwonde, Malawi**

On May 2 2004, the 18 ton steel boat called the Pelican sets sail from Malawi for the Town of Metangula in Mozambique.

The boat statistics are as follows:

| | |
|---|---|
| Type: | Cabin Cruiser |
| Registered owner: | Blue Breeze Limited (Malawi) |
| Owner's address: | P. O. Box 78, Zomba, Malawi |
| Telephone number: | +265 (0)1 535254 |
| Hull material: | Steel |
| Max. plate thickness: | 6 mm |
| Overall length: | 12.2m |
| Beam: | 3.565m |
| Draft: | 1.092m |
| Waterline length: | 10.3m |
| Displacement: | 18'729kg |
| Number of compartments: | 5 |
| Number of engines: | 2 |
| Engine type: | Perkins 4.236 diesel |
| Power rating: | 81 Brake horse power (60.4KW) |
| Fuel capacity: | 2 X 1200l |
| Electric pumps: | 5 X 500l per hour bilge pumps |
| Manual pumps: | 1 X lever type bilge pump |
| Electrical system voltage: | 12V DC |
| Electric Power source: | 2 X Alternators on engines<br>2 X Engine batteries<br>1 X solar panel |

The boat will be used in Mozambique waters of Lake Niassa by its owners and friends for recreational purposes and will be temporarily moored in Metangula for at least one year. The boat will also be used by the Niassa eco-tourism development project for investment promotional purposes.

Yours sincerely

Metangula Project
Office Site

DATE & SIGNED

**J. H. Fleming**
General Manager, Niassa

13-04-04

18 Angus Road, Bryanston, South Africa, Tel +27 (11) 706 2507 Fax: +27 (11) 463 1751

Directors: Hugh Brown (Chairman), J. Worthing

Pelican Import Permit

The Navy landing craft that gobbled up thousands of welding sticks

The problem

First day - running lines to shore

First attempt at pumping out - day 5

Stephen the day after head-butting the awning superstructure

Looking a lot happier than I felt

Heeling to starboard

Captain William of the tugboat MV Thyolo

The ever dependable Geller (right) and the MV Thyolo engineer

The inexhaustible Bastia

Stephen pondering how to raise the Pelican

Evening of day 6, immediately before pumping out the stern section.

Ready for the tow home. The girls from the morning parade would take turns lolling in the Pelican's floating rings. Our rescue mission provided them with great excitement and merriment.

Anchored off Nkhota Nkhota on the Malawi side of the lake.

Success! Smiles all round from the tugboat engineer,
Captain William, Stephen and Geller.

CHAPTER 13

# FAREWELLS

'After the darkness comes the light.' How long will the darkness last? Over the period immediately following the murders of Andrew and Caroline I live in a blur at one remove. Things are happening around me, but I am barely aware of them. Karen, heavily pregnant, is making arrangements to get Andrew and Caroline home to the UK along with me and Bert. She wants to come with us, to be at our side, but I worry about the flying and the situation we will meet with when we arrive in the UK. Mostly I worry about the potential effect on her in her condition. This is the furthest she has carried into any pregnancy. She liaises with the BHC in Mozambique. Within forty-eight hours the bodies are flown down to Johannesburg and post mortems carried out. Flights are booked with Virgin Atlantic, which is prepared to take the caskets. I'm told that the other airlines are not so accommodating. She fields a stream of questions from parents and friends and friends of friends, a rock to my swirling, treacherous ocean of shifting, destructive emotions. Cards and letters of condolence stream in, but I read very few. They are genuinely well meaning, but each one is a stab to the heart. The sincere, placatory language – resting peacefully together, live on in our wonderful memories of them – is at odds with my feelings. The truth is that I am absolutely certain Andrew and Caroline would not be at peace or happy for a second, let alone an eternity. They would be spitting mad to be cut down in such a manner in the prime of their lives.

I am obsessed with justice. Or is it revenge? The two seem to be intertwined and inseparable in my mind. The BHC tells us that the Mozambican authorities in Tête are making enquiries, but they are not releasing any information at this stage. At this stage? What stage would that be? Do they have any ideas or are they busy covering up? We can only guess at things from what little we know and have seen. Not a lot to go on. And my mind tends to invariably make illogical jumps and think the worst. That either they are not doing anything at all, or they are putting together their own version of events, covering this uncomfortable event up so that they can obfuscate and obstruct and eventually magic the whole thing away. My fears and frustrations are eating me up.

Then in the morning, the day before I am due to fly to London, Karen comes to the rescue with some good news in relation to the investigation into the murders.

To understand it, one has to go back in time. The Saudi authorities are well known for their strict attitude towards a lot of Western liberalism, which for the most part they view as irreligious and potentially anarchic. High on their very long forbidden list are alcohol and physical intimacy, in public or out of wedlock.

On the evening of the 19th May 1979, on the sixth floor of a flat in Jeddah, a farewell party was underway. The hosts, a surgeon named Dr Richard Arnot and his wife, Penny, were providing alcohol in the form of homemade wine, gin and black-market whisky. This was a very 'wet' apartment in a 'dry' country. The partygoers were there to say farewell to Tim Hayter, a New Zealand diver. Perhaps by way of a proper farewell, at some stage during the evening Penny had sex with Tim. However, it was the discovery made in the early hours of the following morning that led to worldwide headlines and resulted in a body being held in a UK mortuary for thirty years, the longest known period that someone has remained in a mortuary unburied or uncremated.

The story put out by the Saudi investigators, and endorsed in hindsight with almost indecent haste by the British Foreign Office, was that a young British nurse named Helen Smith, and a Dutch tugboat captain called Johannes Otten, had at some stage fallen off the apartment balcony into the street 70 feet below, probably whilst having sex. Johannes, his underpants around his thighs, was found skewered upon the spiked railings that surrounded the apartment block. Helen was found on the ground nearby with her knickers partly off.

The Saudi authorities locked up the Arnots and a number of the guests for several months in one of their dirty, overcrowded prisons. Richard Arnot was charged with drinking and 'social offences' and he was eventually sentenced in March 1980 to a year in prison and to be flogged, while his wife was sentenced to a public lashing for unlawful intercourse. Diplomatic manoeuvring secured their releases and the sentences were never carried out. Their fates, however, were essentially a sideshow.

Helen Smith's father, Ron, was a gritty retired policeman from West Yorkshire in the north of England. The preparations for his daughter's funeral were underway when an article appeared in *Private Eye* indicating that there had been a cover up. Ron Smith immediately flew out to Jeddah to check on the story for himself, and this was the beginning of a campaign for justice that lasted over thirty years. Six post mortems were eventually performed on his daughter, with differing conclusions. What was clear from some of the PM reports was that there were serious grounds to believe that the official explanation of a fall from the balcony was too simplistic and failed to explain away a number of inconsistencies and possibilities.

For instance, Ron Smith noted, when he saw his daughter's body in the mortuary, she appeared to have no broken bones and subsequent medical statements indicated that Helen's body had no injuries consistent with the fall she had supposedly taken. In rigor mortis, her arm was positioned at an angle above her head that would actually have been impossible if she had been alive when she fell. There were injuries to her face that included at least one blow to her head which could not be accounted for by a fall but which would have rendered her unconscious. There were signs that she had been roughly handled and quite possibly sexually assaulted. These signs included bruising to her inner thighs and genital injuries. The balcony also appeared to be too high for someone to accidentally topple over it. Friends of his daughter, who wanted to remain anonymous, told him they believed that his daughter had been murdered. Add to all this the fact that there were a number of people at the Arnots' party who were never traced, and allegations that some of the guests included Saudi nationals, and it is not a stretch to understand why vested Saudi interests aided by 'incompetent' investigators might have reasons to conceal the truth.

Helen's body was flown back to the UK in June 1980 and in December 1980 the first autopsy was performed, after which the then Home Office pathologist, Dr Michael Green, stated: "If I was to say Helen Smith's death was an accident, I would be a liar."

All in all there was evidence that in fact Helen Smith had been raped, received a potentially fatal blow to the head and had then been carried down to the street to make it appear as if she had fallen from the balcony. Clearly the hapless tugboat captain had fallen. But was he helped? Was he collateral damage? Had he threatened to blow the whistle and paid the ultimate price?

Ron Smith poured his waking moments and his money into trying to prove that his daughter was murdered. His allegations of a cover-up by the Saudi and British security services led to a diplomatic crisis between the two countries. When he finally agreed to his daughter being cremated in November 2009, he was a frail old man of 83. He died eighteen months later in April 2011, still resolute, angry and haunted by his belief that his daughter had been murdered.

The relevance of Helen Smith's death and her father's dogged campaign for truth and justice is that it led to a change in the rules in relation to the deaths of Britons abroad. The West Yorkshire coroner at the time, Philip Gill, had declined to hold an inquest on the grounds that the case was outside his jurisdiction. The High Court subsequently concurred with him, but in July 1982 the Court of Appeal overturned this and ruled that Britons who die abroad in violent or unnatural circumstances should have a British inquest once their bodies are returned to the UK. The 'inquest of the century' held in December 1982 failed to reach a conclusion in relation to Helen Smith's death and the jury returned an unsatisfactory majority open verdict, which prevails to this day.

The Court of Appeal's landmark ruling led to other high profile cases being examined and re-examined. Six years later, in September 1988, Kenyan officials came up with the most improbable story. They theorised that Julie Ward, a young 28-year-old photographer and publishing assistant who had gone missing in the Masai Mara Game Reserve, had had the double misfortune of having been eaten by lions and her remains struck by lightning. Or perhaps struck by lightning and then eaten by hyenas. One cannot fail to be staggered by the wild imagination and desperately inept attempts of the Kenyan officials to cover up the truth in order to protect their tourist industry and those responsible.

A week after Julie's disappearance her father, John Ward, found the burnt and dismembered remains of her body. And so another father began another long, patient and persistent fight for truth and justice for his daughter, which included around 100 visits to Kenya and a financial outlay of around £2 million. Two separate murder trials in Kenya of two game wardens and the head warden in 1992 and 1998 respectively delivered acquittals.

Eventually John Ward got one step further forward that Ron Smith. In May 2004, after a British pathologist showed beyond doubt that her body had been dismembered with a machete, doused in petrol and set alight, the inquest held in Britain recorded a verdict of unlawful killing.

What has always struck me about both of these cases is the extraordinary lengths that government officials, both abroad and in the UK, will go to in order to protect reputations and preserve diplomatic ties. Ron Smith found that Saudi and British officials were not prepared to offer any substantive assistance in order to get at the truth in case this harmed diplomatic relations. And an investigation in 2008 by *The Sunday Telegraph* revealed that the British authorities had deliberately obstructed John Ward in his pursuit of justice over his daughter's brutal murder. The Foreign and Commonwealth Office (FCO) and the BHC in Kenya were also heavily criticised in an unpublished independent police report on the case by Jon Stoddard, at the time the Chief Constable of Lincolnshire police, which highlighted mistakes and cover-ups over Julie's murder. That report was originally suppressed, ostensibly on the grounds of national security, but in reality simply because it shamed Britain's reputation for honesty and fair play. Diplomacy, it seems, is only interested in justice if it happens to coincide with good diplomatic relations.

Like many Britons, I was well aware of the cases of Helen Smith and Julie Ward, which had been very high profile over many years. I was unaware of the Court of Appeal ruling relating to inquests until now. Following receipt of the post mortem report carried out in Johannesburg, it seemed that the Surrey police were prepared to investigate the murders and the Mozambican Authorities had agreed to this. Interviews for Bert and me had been arranged at Mount Browne, the Surrey police headquarters, which was located literally around the corner from where I had attended Guildford College of Law.

This was a positive development for all. The families would have the benefit of knowing that a proper investigation would be conducted, making it harder for the Mozambicans to organise an investigative whitewash. The British authorities would be seen to be aiding and assisting Mozambique, which had very recently been admitted to the Commonwealth family, in a case involving the brutal murders of British nationals. The Mozambicans would be seen to be concerned and helpful, and assuming that the killers were caught, it would show the Mozambican authorities up in a good light, keen to co-operate and enforce law and order. They would also have the benefit of forging some useful ties with the British police and learning something about their investigation techniques.

I have a number of recollections of the events that flowed in the aftermath of Andrew and Caroline's deaths. The emotional goodbye to Karen at the airport in Malawi, another emotional meeting with friends who met us as we rushed through Jan Smuts (now O. R. Tambo) airport in Johannesburg. Sitting through the night in the darkened fuselage of the plane as it flew up the African Continent, unable to think of anything beyond the caskets lying cold and secluded in the fuselage somewhere below my feet. I remember my image of them lying 'together alone' in a profound silence that completely transcended the rush of the plane's engines. From somewhere the images from the film *The Piano* came to me, specifically of when Ada deliberately tangles her foot in the rope as the piano is thrown overboard and is pulled in with it, down into the deep. Michael Nyman's strong yet tender music and Thomas Hood's haunting words 'There is a silence where hath been no sound, there is a silence where no sound may be, in the cold grave – under the deep, deep sea.' Writing this, it seems almost contrived and excessively sentimental. Yet whatever was surreal about what had happened since we had discovered Andrew and Caroline, their deaths and loss became inescapably, utterly real for me that night. Sitting in a plane filled with passengers, I felt utterly bereft and alone. There were emotional days to come, but this was one of my own darkest hours.

The joint funeral was held at St Joan of Arc Catholic church in Farnham, a big old stone church with high ceilings and plenty of stained-glass windows, so packed that people were left standing outside. The confusion when the caskets arrived as to which casket contained who. Reading the eulogy I had painstakingly pieced together and my determination to hold myself together. I delivered the same eulogy a couple of weeks later at the Memorial Service held at Caroline's school in Malawi and the children – god or someone bless and thank them – clapped when I eventually finished.

Only twenty-four hours after the funeral service in Farnham, Bert and I went over to Mount Browne. We sat in a small office making small talk to a couple of policemen. The door opened and in strode a sturdy, muscular man in his mid fifties. Without preamble he shook hands and introduced himself.

'Good morning. My name is Detective Superintendent Brian Woodfield of the Surrey Police. I am very sorry indeed for your loss. I will be leading the investigation into Andrew and Caroline's deaths.'

There was genuine empathy and concern in his demeanour, but his words spoke of efficiency and professionalism. There was no doubting that he was in control. He was not unfriendly – subsequently he and his wife Elizabeth became very good friends. But he made it clear: he had a job to do and he was going to do it properly and to the best of his ability. No question about it.

He took off his jacket and rolled up the sleeves of his crisp white shirt. It was time to take statements. And instinctively I began to feel confident that this person would get results and we would not get sucked into an enduring battle for justice like the ones that had been forced on and had consumed the lives of Ron Smith and John Ward. In this belief, I turned out to be both right and wrong.

The funeral was not the final farewell. That took place later at Heathrow, when I said goodbye to my parents before boarding the flight back to Africa. We were all heartbroken, but there is something doubly tragic about a parent losing a child. I think about the young men and women killed in two world wars and this personal moment of tragedy gave me just the smallest of glimpses into the sheer horror and scale of the heart-rending losses suffered. I think about the ripples on a pond, how so many people had been directly or indirectly affected and touched by Andrew and Caroline's deaths. It seemed too much of a stretch to imagine that on a global scale. What they lived through explains a lot about the strength and resilience of my parents' dwindling generation. I tried to hold that thought and buoy myself up in the knowledge that there was some light at the end of this tunnel for all of us. Karen and I would shortly have a child. Their grandchild.

CHAPTER 14

# Bureaucratic layers

One should not assume that never-ending layers of bureaucracy are pointless. Yes, it probably means that the true objective behind the bureaucracy has been lost somewhere along the way so that at first sight it seems rather than being a means to an end it has become an end in itself. In Africa the British were said to be – and to be fair, for the most part were – extremely good administrators. I think of administration as being something slightly less murky and complex than bureaucracy. The Mozambicans learnt their administration from the Portuguese, and if there is one thing the Portuguese love, it is paperwork. Even by African standards the Mozambicans have endlessly fine-tuned it and brought it to an altogether new level. To create work and jobs, find reasons for extracting payments and setting up hierarchies of power and patronage. Their administration has become a truly monstrous bureaucracy.

Within a couple of days of the arrival of the *Pelican* in May 2004, the bored head of the marine department had given

John Fleming a list of *'Documentos Para Registo Provisório da Embarcação Pelican'* (documents required for the provisional registration of the *Pelican*). This list contained twelve items that he had dreamt up and included:

1. Confirmation of the vessel's radio call sign;

2. A copy of the vessel's construction plan (well, we had large chart sized blueprints of every square inch of the *Pelican* provided by the original design company and enlarged and detailed by Don's engenerio friend, Basil);

3. All the manuals and leaflets showing the characteristics and specifications of the engine and equipment;

4. A request for '*cópia do certificado de garantia de construçâo do motor e casco passado pela sociedade de classificaçâo de navios*' (a copy of the engine and hull construction warranty certificate issued by the Ship Classification Society).

Ha! I imagine he must have really enjoyed thinking that last one up! Such a warranty certificate would be great, but rating societies are generally located in places where ships are constructed or insured – London, Gdansk, Piraeus, etc. And they are primarily for large cargo and passenger ships, oilrigs and submarines. To my knowledge there is no satellite office of a Classification Society within a thousand miles of Lake Malawi.

It had taken John Fleming several months and heaps of diplomacy to get Chirinsa to settle down and modify his list. The thought of now re-awakening Chirinsa's ingrained bureaucratic tendencies brought me out in a cold sweat. We will go through the motions of feigning friendship and respect though in truth we both know it's all an act. I think that by now I should be inured to these charades but it seems not.

'Good morning Mr Chirinsa. Good to see you again. It's been a while. This is my brother in law, Stephen.'

Chirinsa offers a quiet 'Good morning' of his own and nods as we shake hands. He introduces his deputy, a slim, younger man in a tight white shirt with a limp, wet handshake. He has a doleful demeanour, frequently nodding in agreement with whatever his boss says. He has rather bulging eyes that immediately remind me of the actor Christopher Lloyd as Doc Brown in 'Back to the Future,' but minus the frantic hairdo. We subsequently nickname him Agent Glum.

It's the 13$^{th}$ May 2006, a Sunday morning at the Marine Department Offices in Metangula and almost exactly two years since the *Pelican* first arrived. Chirinsa's office is a sparsely furnished, large room in a long, low building on the hillside looking down on the lake glimmering below. It's cool but with a neglected look and a musty smell. It was probably built with great things in mind, but the reality is that nothing great is happening around Metangula or the Mozambican side of the lake. My impression, perhaps rather uncharitably, is that Mr Chirinsa's biggest decision of the day probably centres around arranging lunch, and his biggest challenge is how to fill in the time until then.

He plonks himself down behind his large wooden desk and indicates that we can sit in a couple of the rather decrepit chairs reserved for visitors. Chirinsa's office seems to be almost paperless, which is certainly not representative of virtually every other official's office I have entered in Africa. The norm is heap upon heap of dusty files and papers littered all over the floor and on top of all available furniture and filling cabinet surfaces. Chirinsa gives another slight nod, an indication that the meeting can proceed, and we are first up, having asked to see him. Still very economical with words, I note. His eyes stare inscrutably out of his round, smooth face whilst his elbows rest on the desktop, hands clasped neatly together. It's a deliberate attempt to convey relaxed authority. Agent Glum sits on the edge of a chair, a respectful distance to the right of his boss.

Stephen and I had arrived on the Malawi passenger ferry, the *Ilala*, the day before. The ferry has now left heading north but will be back again on Tuesday for her return trip south. Assuming the *Pelican* was still afloat, the captain of the *Ilala*, Lamek, had agreed to take her on tow and haul her back to the Malawi side. Stephen and I had come to check out the situation and smooth the way.

It's a very civilized game of cat and mouse. We are the mice. The way it works is that both sides must remain diplomatic and excessively polite, even when grinding your teeth and wanting nothing more than to do something violent. A good old-fashioned punch to the face probably. I'm not prepared to give up on the *Pelican*, to surrender her. We need to get the go ahead to tow her away, and Chirinsa knows this. So the real question is how much his consent will cost.

'Thank you for agreeing to see us on a Sunday. We really do appreciate your assistance,' I offer ingratiatingly, and for this comment I am rewarded with nods from Chirinsa and Agent Glum.

I press on. 'Captain Lamek told us that he had heard the *Pelican* had sunk. Thankfully that is incorrect. She is moored in a bay around the headland near to the naval base, but there is a sunken cabin cruiser in the smaller bay next door. They have obviously been mixed up.'

Another nod, accompanied this time by a small, knowing smile.

'We have established that the *Pelican* is undamaged,' I conclude.

I pause, and Chirinsa decides it's time for him to speak.

'The boat is sitting here for two years now and continues

to fall under my jurisdiction and responsibility. What are your plans?' he asks, not unreasonably. Stephen steps in smoothly.

'The *Ilala* returns to Metangula on Tuesday. Captain Lamek has very kindly agreed to put her on tow and take her over to Nkhotakota on the far side of the lake. This will release you from your obligations and I am sure you will be glad not to have the ongoing responsibility for her.'

Chirinsa nods slowly, acknowledging the logic of Stephen's argument. Crunch time and we wait for his response.

'If the *Pelican* is seaworthy then I have no problem with the removal back to Malawi. I can arrange a letter confirming this.'

I'm stunned and stare rather idiotically at Chirinsa. He's enjoying the moment, I'm sure, though his face gives nothing away. It's almost too good to be true, and probably is.

Chirinsa reaches for the dark green file in front of him, which he opens to reveal a wad of papers. This is his way of saying 'See, we have paperwork. We have had a job to do in relation to the *Pelican*. Now you must pay.' He removes a flimsy A5 sheet of paper from the file and slides it across the desk towards us. I know what this is. He gave me one on the day the *Pelican* arrived in Metangula, just as he was leaving the boat after our little celebratory arrival party. Then the 'Aviso De Pagamento' (Payment Notice) was bright pink. Not one to miss a trick, on that occasion Chirinsa had charged us for bringing not only the *Pelican*, but also the *Stingray*, into his realm. The 'embarcação dneumatica' (dinghy) cost $60 but interestingly the 'embarcação chada' (live on board) *Pelican* was only $30.

'However,' he continues, 'there are, you understand, certain charges due to the Marine Department that have to be paid first.'

I'll bet. I take the flimsy paper invoice and prepare for the worst. My main concern is whether we have brought enough dollars with us to pay these fees which, I have a suspicion, are calculated not particularly on the basis of any schedule but on what Chirinsa thinks he can wrestle out of us. It's for meticais 8,250,000, which seems like a truly huge amount. Ever helpful, Chirinsa has indicated the hard currency equivalent for us, a neat $350. It refers to various items – mooring fees, costs for a permit for the *Pelican* to leave, inspection and maintenance fees. The last is something of a joke, as we have already checked with the guards we employ to look after the boat and they have confirmed that Chirinsa has never shown his face, let alone stepped on board to inspect her or embark on any sort of maintenance. It's actually for less than I expected, but the show must go on.

I show the invoice to Stephen and try to look suitably worried and shocked.

'Thank you Mr Chirinsa. This is a lot of money.' Chirinsa unlocks his hands and splays them outwards to signify that it is what it is.

'Do you or do you not want the boat?'

I sigh and nod. 'I'll arrange to get the payment. Perhaps if it's convenient I can come by on Tuesday morning to pay and collect a receipt?'

Chirinsa nods and stands. Stephen and I follow suit.

'That is fine.' He pauses and looks at us intently before continuing. 'You should understand that I have no issues with the *Pelican*. I am pleased that you have come to remove the boat. It is not good to have such a big boat sitting on the water unused for such a long period of time.'

Stephen nods. 'Absolutely Mr Chirinsa. It was not part of our plan for the boat to be left like this. John Fleming was keen to get the boat repaired and working, but he was unable to obtain access to the dry dock at the navy yard.'

Chirinsa nods politely. I sense that there is more, something that he knows but is too diplomatic to mention or wishes to remain hidden. I wonder if I have got Chirinsa all wrong. That my suspicions and prejudices about his motives are ill founded. Perhaps he's just a decent guy at heart stuck in a backwater of the Republic. Not exactly the heart of darkness, but nevertheless very quiet and neglected. It would be enough to make the most virtuous rot, mentally and morally. I shake off the thought. Only time will tell.

Getting the *Pelican* repaired and renovated to the standard that John had wanted, or indeed any standard at all, had proved to be impossible and the whole charter had turned into a disaster. Early on the Mozambican Navy had professed interest and the Commander of the Navy Base had come to inspect the boat, offering any assistance needed. John had taken him at his word and negotiated a deal that in return for his Project – the Niassa Project, rehabilitating one of the navy's landing craft for them – as a quid pro quo the *Pelican* could go up on a trolley in the navy dockyard. The Project used some 500 kilograms of welding rods, countless cutting disks and hundreds of litres of diesel running their generator. They had cut out the rusted areas of this hulk and welded in new plates. Days had turned into weeks, which had turned into months.

Yet it had all started so promisingly. Within a few days of the initial delivery of the *Pelican* John had emailed to say that he had 'four guys on board with scrapers and sand paper and... Mark has moved on board.' New solar panels and high-cycle batteries were in the pipeline, along with a completely new electrical system, new tarpaulins and soft furnishings, hardwood decking and panelling, a paint job and a floating pontoon that would provide a very nice bespoke mooring. The *Pelican* was to become a five-star entity. John wrote in early December 2004 to say 'work is now in full swing' and he was 'confident that the renovation of the *Pelican* will run on as planned.' C-Day (Completion Day) was set for the end of February 2005.

Some Irish embassy staff had stepped aboard when they called in to Metangula on a lake tour and they were impressed and ready, indeed itching, to book voyages. But all this was in vain if the boat could not be taken out of the water so that the broken rudder and the problem with the starboard propeller shaft could be fixed.

In late May 2005 John wrote to say that work had stopped. Despite his best efforts he had been unable to complete the repairs to the landing craft, which meant that he had been unable to get the *Pelican* out of the water. Worse still, 'the Swiss,' who were the major investors in the Project, had pulled the plug. Their European bankers, sitting in nice plush ivory towers in London and Geneva, had had a crisis of confidence about ploughing millions of euros into a project in such a far out of the way place in a far out of the way African country. Who could blame them? Spinning a story to bankers of an undiscovered paradise that promised big returns once developed was a bridge too far, even for John's exceptional persuasive talents and enthusiasm.

Perhaps this is a good time for a very quick diversion into African debts and bureaucracies. In the 1980s, a period that in the context of the African Continent has become known as 'the lost decade,' most African countries were close to paralysed by increasing debts. It seemed that the only growth areas were mismanagement and corruption. Overall, standards of living were no higher, and in many cases lower, than at independence. The revenue bar had never been particularly high, but it had sunk in real terms to levels which left everyone, whether in the civil service or private enterprise, ducking and diving to make ends meet. Those with suitable qualifications fled abroad, leaving behind a flourishing black market where staple foods, goods and currencies thrived in an informal sector over which governments had little or no control. With tax revenues plummeting and no banks crazy enough to lend, in the early 1980s these failing regimes turned to the lenders of last resort, the World Bank (WB) and the International Monetary Fund (IMF).

Recognising that the main cause of Africa's ills rested with its leaders and their massively bloated bureaucracies that rewarded their supporters and legions of relatives with contracts and jobs, the WB and IMF decided that a quick, firm hand was all that was needed. Shake the tree nice and hard and all the rotten apples would drop to the ground. Instead of recognising the state as the principal engine of growth and development, their plan was to switch the emphasis to private enterprise and the free markets. Those regimes seeking assistance were required to remove subsidies and allow commodity prices and currencies to find the proper market level – which in effect meant devaluing their artificially strong currencies and raising agricultural commodity prices. Leaders feared this would lead to serious unrest and blood in the streets. But worse was to come. They were also required to cut back their bureaucracies and sell off state-owned enterprises. And lastly, horror of horrors, reduce deficits and make meaningful progress towards balancing their budgets.

Given the dire situation that governments found themselves in, they had little choice but to sign on the dotted line. When it came to the crunch, a signature would cost nothing. As the WB and IMF were to find out. By the end of the 1980s it was clear that the structural adjustment programmes inflicted by these two institutions were not working. In fact, they appeared to be having the opposite effect. If you could obtain lots of aid, accumulate massive debts and then get it written off or re-scheduled time and time again, then why bother with any meaningful reform? Just pretend to be implementing the requirements. And if the WB and IMF wanted public companies to be sold into the private sector, that was no problem. By the cartload they were sold to relatives and chums at knockdown prices. Patronage became even more worthwhile and entrenched, whilst investment reduced alarmingly. African countries became hooked and reliant on aid in its various forms and used to flouting or weaving a way around the conditionalities attached to it. In effect, they became dependent rather than independent.

Eventually the penny dropped and the WB and IMF realised that economic assistance was virtually guaranteed to be ineffective in helping to drag the majority of the continent's impoverished population out of poverty unless it was linked to other conditions, most notably political changes aimed at creating real Western-type democracies protected by the rule of law.

I'm sceptical that even this combined economic and political approach has had much impact. A handful of dictators in places like Benin, Chad and Mali found themselves out on their ears, but dictatorships have survived and continue to do so. Some twenty-five years later there are still a handful of 'real' dictators, and a new breed of twenty-first century 'democratic' dictators. They are politicians who win by various nefarious means at the ballot box, and once in power subvert and bribe the opposition until they have a stranglehold on the political process and can divert and utilise state funds and resources for their own political and private purposes. By paying just enough lip service to the democratic process, they keep the aid money flowing. Debts continue to accumulate with no end in sight to either the re-scheduling process or the plethora of loans, grants and budget support packages, or the increasing misery of the poor.

In a speech at Yale University in April 2018, the British MP Rory Stewart, who had worked as a minister at DFID (the UK Government's Department for International Development), stated that over a period of around half a century little Malawi had received and gobbled up around £4.5 billion – yes, four thousand five hundred million pounds – in aid, yet was probably poorer now than when the aid had started. Indeed donor success in sustainable job creation appears to be virtually non-existent. At the time of writing, the country is being propped up with over $1 billion in annual aid, which is more or less the same as the amount raised through domestic tax revenues. So whilst I'm admittedly no expert, I do struggle to see what has been achieved with all that aid apart from creating a culture of dependency and corruption. Corruption appears to be as deeply embedded as the Mariana Trench, because as a system of governance and wealth creation for the powerful it quite simply cannot be bettered.

With a ballooning African population, the WB and IMF are trapped in an endless cycle whilst many of the developed nations set their own example with enormously impressive budget deficits that are growing exponentially (the US government debt has gone from a manageable $6 trillion in 2001 to a whopping, staggering $24 trillion by 2020 and is currently on a breathlessly steep upwards trajectory, particularly in the wake of Covid 19). There is such a massive wealth gap that Oxfam's wealth report for the year 2018 found that 26 people on the planet together own as much as the whole of the poorest 50% of the planet's population, around 3.6 billion people.

A number of years ago, around 2005 I think, a friend of mine took a job at the World Bank and moved to Washington. He had spent five years working in Africa before this move. He was put on the International Desk and was beavering away at his statistics when the phone rang. He was asked if he could lead a small delegation to Southern Africa on a fact-finding mission. He respectfully pointed out that he was not on the Africa desk and perhaps it would be more appropriate if someone from that desk led the mission. It was respectfully pointed out to him that he appeared to be pretty much the only person within the Bank who had actually lived and worked in that part of the world. He relayed this news to me with a sort of awed shock when we met in Malawi during his short fact finding mission. And in a nutshell it tells me, very simply and eloquently, a lot about the level of knowledge and experience, of the real importance placed on the Continent. Perhaps by now the situation within the World Bank has changed.

At first sight it seemed that the Niassa Project was a dead duck. John indicated that he was heading back to South Africa to study for a Masters degree in Business Administration. Mark had panicked and could not be seen except by the dust raised from his hasty departure for Nacala, where he was hoping to find work on the coast. John's boss in Johannesburg was prepared to make an offer for the *Pelican* payable over twelve months. We don't know his boss but believe he is something of a wheeler-dealer and are sceptical that all the payments will be made.

Less than a week later it was all back on again. It seemed that the project was going ahead in a scaled-back format and John had been offered money by his boss which could be used to finally finish the landing craft and get the *Pelican* out of the water for repairs. Rather than taking her back across the lake to Malawi, a fresh new slimmed-down tourist operation would be set up on the Mozambican side totally independent of the original large, lavish project. All headed up by John, who now felt invigorated by the change in direction and the possibilities of running something over which he had personal control and some real ownership. He has put together a very comprehensive list of works and items needed over the coming months in order to get the *Pelican* ready to operate as a five star vessel.

Over the next six months we got emails from John, who was

busy flitting all over the place within Mozambique and South Africa. I got the impression that the Niassa Project and the *Pelican* were now rather small cogs in a growing list of ideas and projects that he had on the go. Some works were carried out whilst the boat sat on the water, but still access to the naval base ramp eluded him. Finally, in January 2006, he advised me that the Niassa Project really was closing down. The *Pelican* was sitting in a little bay next door to the naval base, loved but neglected. John had been concerned that her fuel tanks, after so little use over the last couple of years, were internally rusted and needed flushing out, so these were disconnected. If on arrival the *Pelican* had been the equivalent of someone moving with the use of a Zimmer frame, she was now indisputably bedridden and totally incapable of independent movement.

Stephen and I tramp across the peninsula and ten minutes later we reach the top of the hillside that looks down on to the small bay where the *Pelican* is moored. It's a quiet spot ringed by ancient trees with thick canopies, the shoreline littered with huge granite boulders that look as if some heavenly hand has carelessly thrown them down. And whereas the trees are hundreds of years old, the boulders have been rounded and smoothed through millions of years of rain and the persistent slap and lick of the waves. It's a little Eden, the boat sitting quietly moored on the calm, twinkling water. We strip down to shorts and splash into the lake for a short, blissful escape from the humidity, swimming sideways holding our T shirts and trainers in the air.

On board the *Pelican* we go through the boat from stem to stern to check that everything is in order. The guards have done a good job looking after things. Everything is clean and tidy and the engine compartment has an insignificant amount of oily water swilling around. In short, she's ready to put on a towline.

We swim back to shore and head back up the hillside to the dirt road that leads down to the main harbour.

The sun is now fully overhead, the air cloying, with little in the way of wind coming off the lake. My throat is parched, my whole body assaulted as I am fried by the sun above and waves of heat rising from the baking earth under my feet.

Some one hundred metres from the harbour is a crossroads. To the right leads inland and then steeply up into the mountains and eventually to the provincial capital, Lichinga. Ahead leads north along a road that snakes along the side of the lake, whilst left takes you down to the harbour. A ramshackle structure with a small rickety wooden veranda sits at the crossroads facing down the road towards the bay. It's a bar, and Stephen and I are gasping.

We sit in the shade of the veranda and order a couple of cervezas. It's not as busy as a normal weekday, but there is still plenty of activity. Everyone knows someone and there's a constant jabber of shouted conversations and greetings accompanied by smiles and easy laughter. Barely anyone goes unnoticed or unacknowledged. I reflect that there are large areas of England where saying 'hello' or 'good day' is viewed as pretty bad form, almost akin to a threat. Loaded bicycles are being pushed or cycled in all directions whilst many people mill around. The women are mostly homeward bound with containers filled with water effortlessly balanced on top of their heads, gliding along with perfect postures and swaying hips.

People start conversations from afar when they first spy their friends, a shouted conversation punctuated with laughs and noisy 'aahs' and 'ayes.' The volume barely decreases as they come level and perhaps have a couple of minutes further commentary face to face before continuing on their way, shouting over their shoulders as they move on.

The beers, when they arrive, are ice cold and go down far too quickly.

'So what's our plan?' asks Stephen.

'Find a fisherman down in the main bay who has a boat with an outboard. Agree a price for him to come round to the bay tomorrow morning and tow the *Pelican* back around the headland so that she's ready to be taken on tow when the *Ilala* arrives on Tuesday.'

Stephen thinks about this for long seconds.

'Seems too simple. Aren't we missing something?' he queries.

'Not that I can think of. Chirinsa made it clear that he has no argument with us. Pay the money and he'll be glad to see the back of us and the boat.'

'And customs?'

'We saw the chief of Customs when we arrived yesterday and he seemed to have little interest in us. In fact customs have never expressed any real interest in the *Pelican*.'

'I'm just nervous about the way Chirinsa said that *he* personally doesn't have any issues with us or with the *Pelican* leaving. He almost seemed to imply that he couldn't speak for others...'

We ponder this in silence, people watching. We order another beer and make small talk about the activity around us. Eventually, reluctantly, we leave our shady oasis and walk up the baking road to the Bamboo Basket Guesthouse. Arrangements are made through John's agent, Thomas, for a boat to head round to take the *Pelican* on tow the following day. Stephen and I read and chat. Fredrico makes us fried usipa (whitebait) and chips for supper which we spice up with plenty of sabola (a hot chilli sauce) and another beer. We decide – not that it was ever a serious thought – that we won't try to paint the town red but rather aim for an early night.

The fan in my room is covered in dust and hangs lopsidedly. It looks ready to part company with the ceiling and not surprisingly it doesn't work. I have brought a mosquito net with me and I stand wobbling around on the soft-springed bed and tie the net to the fan, hoping that it doesn't all come crashing down on top of me in the night. Pushing the window as wide open as it will go I clamber into bed and try reading. Underneath the net the air is stale and clammy, and very soon I'm sweating and restless. The single naked bulb provides a stark, inadequate light for reading, so I give that idea up and switch it off. Outside there is still plenty of activity – the clicks and whirring buzz of cicadas, birds finishing their evening conversations with a flourish, a melodious chorus of chirrups and cheeps intermingling with the chatter of people passing along the road on the other side of the garden wall. Much closer by, I'm assailed by the irritating whine of mosquitoes, haphazard formations of tiny drones crisscrossing backwards and forwards outside the net on the hunt for blood. Lying there, hot and sweaty, I'm ticking all the meal boxes, visual and chemical.

My mind follows a very vague and abstract thread. I think of the very real discomfort of the troops in the trenches of the First World War and some of what they put up with in the mud and cold of those trenches. Of Winston Churchill banishing himself to 'Plugstreet' on the Western Front in January 1916 after losing his job as First Lord of the Admiralty following the disaster at Gallipoli – his strategically interesting idea to put an end to troops 'chewing barbed wire in Flanders' and break the bloodbath that was the result of the stalemate on the Western Front. Churchill was known to have been generous to a fault in sharing his cigars and brandy with the men and whilst cigars are not my thing, it occurs to me that a good swig of peach and apricot brandy might be just the ticket to help me relax and get to sleep.

At some indeterminate moment the whirring thoughts and

mosquitoes cease, and my last thought before I tumble down a dark tunnel and drop off to sleep is that I should pay more heed to Stephen's concerns. We really must get the *Pelican* out of Metangula and back to Malawi as soon as possible, before we get caught up in a bureaucratic web.

CHAPTER 15

# JAMIE

The radiographer smears gel liberally over Karen's tummy. Thursday, 22nd May 1997, barely two weeks since the Thanksgiving Service for Andrew and Caroline in Lilongwe. We have flown back to the UK. Karen has sensed that things are not right with the pregnancy and we need to be somewhere where she and the unborn child can be given all the necessary care and help. Her doctor from when she lived in the UK previously has been a star and arranged for her to have an ultrasound scan and see a consultant at Exeter Hospital.

Holding her hand as the probe is moved over her tummy, bringing black and white images swirling around on the screen, I'm just another excited, nervous expectant father. The room is bright and warm, rather like the friendly, chatty radiographer, who clearly loves her work. She stares at the screen and moves the probe around at different angles. After a while her conversation dries up as her concentration on the screen increases and the smallest of frowns creases her brow. Eventually she looks round at us.

'Just bear with me. I'm going to get my colleague to pop in.'

She is back very quickly with a female colleague who stares at the image locked onto the screen and then moves the probe around herself. Eventually she looks up and nods to her colleague. I feel Karen's hand squeeze mine ferociously. She is now as certain about what is coming as I am blithely ignorant. I'm thinking maybe twins. She speaks softly.

'I'm so very sorry. There's no heartbeat. Your baby has died."

It's as though an invisible hand has smacked me in the face. A feeling of unreality envelops me. Even as Karen's resolve finally crumbles and she breaks down into sobs of deep grief, I am struggling in this secure and comfortable environment to take it in. The radiographer is gently wiping the gel off Karen's tummy with a white paper towel. My throat is dry, skin suddenly hot and prickly.

'Are you absolutely certain?' My voice is scratchy and strained.

'I am truly sorry. Yes, I'm certain.' I stare vacantly at her, at the ultrasound screen locked on to an image of our son, Jamie, frozen in time.

'We'll leave you and Karen alone for a while,' she says as she and her colleague quietly leave, closing the door behind them.

We cling desperately to each other, a crumpled island of beings, two living, and one gone even before he has had the chance to take his first, tiny breath. There are no words to capture these emotions, nothing that can bring any solace to help break away from the clutches of this blackness.

Time passes. A nurse is in the room, gently explaining the next steps. I absorb snatches. A liquid concoction. Induction. Stillbirth. Several hours.

Karen is taken to a small ward with no other patients and made as comfortable as possible. She's regaining control, thinking and preparing for what is to come. The flush of raw emotion has left her face and she looks pale and weary. Totally drained.

'I think you should ring Charles and arrange for him to pop down,' she says. 'He's probably only an hour away. You can both go to a local pub for a beer.'

I'm stunned at this suggestion. It strikes me as preposterous to head down to the pub with an old university friend whilst Karen copes with an impending stillbirth.

'Absolutely no way. I'm staying right here with you,' I reply instinctively in my 'I'm not for swaying' voice.

'This is going to take hours. I really need you here for the birth. In the meantime you need time out to talk to someone other than me. And in all honesty I need some time alone.'

Her voice is soft yet firm. We have entered the preternatural calm that often precedes a storm. A time to gather thoughts and strength in order to prepare for what is coming. Yet I'm still not convinced and in my dazed state I utter an awful analogy.

'I'd feel terrible. Like a captain abandoning his ship. Worse.'

'Ewen, I'm not a ship and I assume you are coming back. It's all fine. Give Charles a ring. Please.'

As so often, I realise that she is several steps ahead of me. She has thought it through, and like so many women faced with such dire situations, she instinctively knows what to do for the best. She is also, as always, thinking primarily not about herself, but of others. Right now, me.

I still have misgivings, but I make the call. An hour later Karen has popped pills and is pacing up and down the hospital corridor as she has been instructed by the doctor. A nurse comes by to tell me Charles is in the reception area.

'Are you really sure about this?' I ask yet again. Karen gives me the brightest smile she can muster.

'Of course. Just remember that this is not the time to come back plastered.'

Charles and I sip at our beers in the pub. He's a great friend, a good listener with an innate sense of how to tactfully diffuse things with some well-timed humour. We talk about everything and nothing.

A couple of hours and a couple of pints later the call comes in and I head back to the hospital. Out of nowhere a thought pops up and dread grips me. I've been immersed in my grief for my brother and his wife and now my lost son. What if something happens to Karen? She is about to go through the trauma of a stillbirth. I pick up my pace until I am running – running into the hospital, ignoring shouts to slow down, running down corridors. I want to run forever, but I slow to a walk for the last few yards before I arrive. Karen is lying on the bed, clearly in a lot of discomfort. She takes in my breathless, dishevelled state and smiles.

'No need to sprint. As you can see, I'm not going anywhere. And nothing's likely to happen in a hurry.'

In the end it took over six long hours of labour before Jamie came into the world. Crumpled, silent and tiny, his hand as small as my thumb. A perfect baby that Karen and I hold until eventually the nurse gently lifts him away and we hug and comfort each other, an island of two again.

It's surreal, heading down to the Registry of Births, Marriages and Deaths to register the birth and death of our baby, a baby that never lived outside his mother's womb. I return clutching the certificates, the only record of his arrival and passing.

On a bright, crisp morning a week later, Karen and I are in the chapel at the crematorium. Jamie lies in the tiniest of white coffins. Karen is desolate and her tears stream whilst I'm assailed by a kaleidoscope of emotions and images of what might have been. We both need this closure, but my tears won't come. I'm looking into an abyss that is ready to suck me in. If I go down there I'm might never find a way back out. So I tell myself that I must stay strong. Stoical and deadpan. For my sake and Karen's. She is confused, unsure why I am so stiff and almost emotionless, and I stumble around trying to deliver a muddled explanation.

Later that afternoon an appointment with the consultant obstetrician gives us no answers. He can't explain why this has happened other than to say that these things do happen. There's a suggestion that Karen might have to accept that she won't ever be able to have her own children, and if she continues to try it may well be detrimental to her health. Perhaps we should therefore rather look at the alternative of adoption. It seems inconceivable, surreal, that our lives have been turned so upside down over the last month. I think about those well-known verses from Ecclesiastes that we often hear at funerals: a time to be born and a time to die, a time to weep, laugh, mourn, dance. Jamie's span of life was as brief as a passing shadow. A vignette as sad and tragic as could be, but I knew that I couldn't push it into some dark recess of my mind. Far better to choose to remember his peaceful, sleeping form. We are all, I suspect, a little barking mad. I think of those magical lines from Lewis Carroll's 'Alice in Wonderland':

Mad Hatter: 'Have I gone mad?'

Alice: 'I'm afraid so. You're entirely bonkers. But I'll tell you a secret. All the best people are.'

Many years later, Jamie lives on. I still talk to him, my silent alter ego; how he'd have loved this or that, agreed that 'that' was not a great idea, talk through a pickle of my own making. His tree and his ashes are at the bottom of our garden, a constant and reassuring reminder and presence. The child is indeed father of the man. This child tells me that I should continue to chase dreams for as long as I possibly can.

CHAPTER 16

# THE TRIAL

Wednesday, 15th October 1997. The same day Andy Green was busy going supersonic and breaking the world land speed record in the Black Rock Desert. Karen and I drive over to Tête from Malawi to attend the trial of the men responsible for the murders. It's the culmination of months of waiting. Mum, Dad and Edmund will be flying in from the UK via Maputo.

At this time of the year it's the build up to the rains and the daytime temperature is in the mid thirties Celsius and the humidity clings like a damp, sweaty cloak. Driving down the hill towards the hulking old iron bridge over the swirling Zambezi is like arriving on the set of some film collaboration on Armageddon by Tim Burton and Ridley Scott. The eye is gripped by the vast panorama of a crammed shantytown of mud, sticks, torn plastic and rubbish that pans out before you. Dust devils, mini swirling tornadoes of fine red dirt, rise suddenly from nowhere, weaving crazy, unpredictable paths before dying down as quickly as they have materialised. If you don't manage to close the windows in time the dust clamps itself to your throat and hurls a fine grit into your eyes. I had thought many times in the past when travelling through Tête that if there is a hell on earth, this might well be it.

The following morning we are all sitting in the courtroom, nervously waiting. Juiz Presidente Antonio Romao Charles sits in an ornately carved mahogany chair. He is flanked by two assistant judges and two elected judges. These five make up the Judicial Tribunal for the Province of Tête. On the light grey wall behind them hangs a large, simple black and white line drawing of the scales of justice, a motif that is repeated in a carving on the wooden panelling fronting the long desk behind which the tribunal members are sitting.

The courtroom on the first floor of the building has a distinctly new feel about it, all the pews and fittings freshly made from hardwoods, mainly dark red mahogany. It's in stark contrast to the building in which the court is housed, a dirty white rectangular double storey which, from the outside at least, looks more like a warehouse than a courthouse.

In his mid-forties, Judge Charles is elegantly dressed in a double-breasted grey suit. His fellow tribunal members, two men and two women, appear older, perhaps in their mid to late fifties. They talk among themselves until Judge Charles says something in Portuguese and the chatter in the courtroom quickly gives way to an apprehensive hush. The air seems to suddenly hang inert and heavy, all eyes trained on a side door that has been opened. Three murderers are about to walk into the room. What should I expect? How do I imagine them?

I remember waiting in the Crown Court in Bristol as a young lawyer. I cannot remember the case I was involved in, but I have never forgotten the bail application that preceded it. A steel-haired ex-marine with a reputation as a no nonsense "flog 'em and hang 'em" judge. The prison cells are located directly below the court and the stairs led directly up to the dock in the middle of the court. The accused appeared almost by magic, handcuffed and flanked by two prison guards. If someone could be said to exude an air of malevolence, then this young man did. Tall, wiry and of mixed descent – perhaps Italian and Middle Eastern – he had olive-bronze skin, deep-set dark brown eyes and long black hair slicked back. His aquiline face was dominated by a very large, hooked Roman nose. Let's call him Nero.

Nero was snappily dressed in a light brown suit and open-necked white shirt and exuded an air of sneering contempt and frustration, pulling angrily at the guards holding his upper arms. He had been remanded accused of a very nasty attack on his girlfriend which involved slashing her face with a flick knife. To this single count of grievous bodily harm had been added a second charge of GBH in relation to a prison guard who had been unwise enough to approach him in his cell.

The barrister representing Nero looked distinctly uneasy, and despite the cold courtroom I watched him wiping sweat from his brow. It was astonishing to me that he was even attempting a bail application, but one has to bear in mind that he was bound by his instructions, however barmy, which had no doubt been put to him in appropriately threatening vocabulary. Given this judge's reputation there was always the distinct possibility that on flipping open the file his honour would explode and ask why the hapless barrister was wasting his time with such a hopeless application.

Very sensibly the barrister got under way quickly and prefaced his application with a plea for the judge to hear him out. His unspoken appeal was 'Yes, the application's bonkers, but so is my client. And as you can see he's a rather nasty toe rag so please help me out here.' He was rewarded with a curt nod and he smartly got underway, balancing the need for his client to be assured he had given it his best shot whilst not wanting to over-extend the judge's short fuse. When he had finished, the prosecution gave the anticipated response in rebuttal, citing the nature and seriousness of the offence, the likelihood of the accused re-offending and interfering with witnesses. The judge appeared to give the matter some weighty thought, leafing through the bulky court bible, the Rules of the Supreme Court otherwise known as the White Book. Finding what he was looking for, he peered down at the accused over his half-rim glasses and then read out all the reasons why bail might be refused under the Bail Act. His conclusion was swift and succinct.

'Application for bail denied. Take the prisoner back down,' he barked.

At which point the area around the dock exploded and the court reverberated to the sound of a roaring bellow. I couldn't be immediately sure but thought Nero was saying 'I'll kill you, you bastard.' The two guards seemed to have been cast aside and Nero had somehow leapt over the front of the dock and was scrabbling over the pews to get to the judge's bench. The judge, I noticed, hadn't moved a muscle, though both barristers and the court clerk were beating a hasty retreat towards the nearest exit. It's not easy to balance and leap around when your hands are in handcuffs, and by the time Nero reached the front of the court the angry and seriously unamused prison wardens were there ready to rugby tackle him. He was dragged off screeching obscenities, the muscles of his neck bulging like a knot of snakes. One seriously hacked-off guy. The judge remained unruffled and in stern, measured tones gave Nero an on-the-spot six-week custodial sentence for contempt of court before calling for the next case. Business was to resume as usual.

I'm not sure what I expected, but I do know that the three prisoners now stepping into the courtroom in Tête were as far removed from Nero, or in this case from former RENAMO guerrillas, as it was possible to imagine. In their mid and late twenties, of medium height and slim builds, they walked unhurriedly, chaperoned by one casually dressed court administrator. Not a handcuff in sight, they managed to present themselves as both relaxed and respectful and they looked for all the world as if they had been groomed and prepared for an important job interview and had not just arrived from the hell that is Tête prison. Clean shaven, with blank, impassive expressions, they did not look ill, mistreated, starving. Or worried. For a brief, ridiculous moment in time I wanted to stand and say 'There's been a mistake – we're in the wrong courtroom.'

Looking at them, it seemed hard to believe that they were capable of the crime. They looked as though they had just stepped out of an office. Or perhaps more likely, given their casual attire, a primary school classroom. The first defendant, Paulino Nguaza, wore a short-sleeved shirt depicting fish swimming in horizontal blue columns, dark blue designer jeans and an intricately stitched brown leather belt. The second defendant, Ernesto Francisco Ferro, also known as Paulino Conde and Paulino Paulo, wore a spotless white T-shirt and Levi jeans and the last, Joaquim Quembo, of paler complexion and wider, bushman-like features, wore a rugby shirt with blue and green squares complemented by cream trousers. I could see freshly ironed creases in all the clothing. On the second and final day of the trial the first two wore crisp, white long-sleeved shirts and the third swopped his rugby jersey for a long-sleeved shirt with dark blue and grey vertical lines and dark trousers. Immaculately presented, throughout the two days of the trial all three remained totally composed and unemotional, sitting together almost motionless on a low bench immediately in front of the tribunal members, their hands clasped together and their attention apparently focused unwaveringly on the tribunal.

The proceedings were conducted in Portuguese. The State Prosecutor outlined the case for the prosecution and then two accused were taken out of the room and the remaining accused was questioned about the crime at length by Romao Charles, followed by the other members of the judicial panel and lastly by the prosecutor and the defence lawyer. Then that defendant was taken out and the whole procedure repeated with the second accused and then the third.

There were a couple of short comfort breaks during which a new-found friend, Severiano Molande, who worked as the Programme Co-ordinator for HelpAge International in Tête Province, would give everyone a quick précis on what was going on and what had been said. Severiano had become our primary link with the Mozambican side and a constant source of support. He had entered the picture initially as the translator for Brian Woodfield and the Surrey Police team and continued in the role now for us. Over this period and the years following we discovered a brave and jovial man with a heart of gold. He and his family took a big risk in being seen to be identified with and helping the police and us. Yet he never faltered in his support and clearly never had any expectations. A compassionate man, he simply did what he believed was right.

The morning wore on. The tempo inside the courtroom never wavered. Nor the emotional temperature. It was all ridiculously civilized. Sitting there, listening to people talking in inexpressive, deadpan tones in a language of which I had no knowledge – apart from being able to say rudimentary things like 'please,' 'thank you' and 'no problem' – you look for other indicators. Voices raised in agitation or anger, arguing or pleading. Body, hand, arm and head movements to help emphasise a point. But sitting behind the defendants we were unable to see their faces and even if we had, I know that they were devoid of emotion. Deadpan. It was as if all spirit and passion had been physically sucked out of them and everyone else involved in the proceedings.

Romao Charles adjourned the court early in the afternoon and we drove back to our lodgings, a house near the river shaded by large canopied trees. We had done little but sit all morning and yet despite this and the dispassionate court proceedings everyone was drained. We all headed off to our bedrooms for a late siesta, to privately mull over the proceedings and our impressions of the killers.

At dinnertime everyone tried hard to lighten the mood. Would Liverpool and Michael Owen be able to stop Ferguson's Manchester United from winning yet another league title? Would we be cloning humans after the cloning of Dolly the sheep? Was Tony Blair a political breath of fresh air or just a beaming fake? The demise of Woolworths. And then another demise, one that had the UK and the world at large reeling. The death of Diana, Princess of Wales. Was she effectively killed by the voracious, tenacious paparazzi or was there, as some quarters of the press were now suggesting, a more sinister explanation? Almost inevitably, it seems, we were back to the topic we were trying hardest to escape.

The following morning the prosecution and defence lawyers make very short closing speeches. From the written translation taken from the audiotape obtained later, the prosecutor accuses all three defendants of 'the crime of robbery concluding with the crime of murder.' In additional there are the further crimes of illegal possession of firearms and the impersonation of military personnel. He says that these crimes were premeditated and no one was an accomplice – all three were perpetrators under the law. That an example has to be made of the accused in order to deter others from committing such crimes

The defence lawyer is also remarkably brief. He refers to the fact that all three defendants have cooperated and confessed to their crimes. That they regret what happened and are sad about this. They have all been caught up in the sixteen years of recent civil conflict in the country, are unemployed and have to look after their families. I'm sure he knows only too well that there's not a lot to be said apart from the obvious, so there's no point in antagonising the court by being over verbose. Yet to my mind there's more going on here. I have this nagging thought that this is all being stage-managed, as if the attorneys, the accused and the judicial panel have had a dress rehearsal. I wonder how far the dress rehearsal went. Did it end when the prisoners entered the prison and the iron doors were slammed shut? Or did it reach further forward?

Edmund and I are invited to make statements on behalf of the families. Edmund wants to bring Andrew and Caroline into the courtroom, and he passes around photographs of them. He explains that Caroline was his only child. She and Andrew worked hard and had built good relationships within the local community. "With Andrew she was working for the future of Africa. Their reward was to be murdered in a cowardly and brutal way." He thanks the court, Mozambican authorities and the British police and concludes by saying that he hopes justice will be done by applying the maximum sentence.

I reiterate Edmund's thanks to the authorities and court before continuing.

"These murders were very clearly carried out in a premeditated, callous and violent manner without any mercy shown to a completely defenceless couple. Andrew and Caroline had given a lot in life and in helping their community and still had a lot more to give and contribute... For myself, my wife, the parents, family and friends of Andrew and Caroline, we have all been given our life sentences as a result of this totally meaningless, cruel act."

I also hoped that justice would include the maximum sentence. "Perhaps their deaths will not be totally meaningless if a proper example is set and the message is clearly given by this court that criminals like these and those who support crime can and will be found and dealt with sternly."

I know even as I utter them that these words would be far more appropriate in a Western context and are unlikely to have any real impact or meaning in a Tête courtroom.

It's past 2 pm. Romao Charles adjourns the court for the day. This gives the judicial panel the rest of the afternoon to discuss the case. The court will reconvene the following morning at 9 am for the judge's summation and delivery of the agreed verdicts and sentencing.

To my mind the verdict is a formality, given that the bandits have pleaded guilty, and it's unthinkable that they should be given anything but the maximum sentence. Predominantly I am apprehensive about the summation of the crime and whether that will present us with any surprises. Frustratingly we will have to rely on Severiano to give us an outline translation of what Romao Charles says. We won't know the finer details until I get a translation of the court audiotape around a week later.

Surrey Police team with Severiano Molande (second from the right) and translator

Judge Romao Charles in his chambers

Paulino Nguaza, Ernesto Ferro (aka Paulino Conde and Paulino Paulo)
and Joaquim Quembo the leader.

Judge Romao Charles addresses the accused

CHAPTER 17

# THE DRUNKARD

'You are going to die with this fine.'

Antonio Vilanculos, Metangula's very newly appointed Customs Chief, has his face in mine. His hand rests roughly on my shoulder as he peers through bloodshot eyes, his sweaty profile swaying in front of me, his breath rancid and hot. It's as if he's trying to read my mind but can't quite focus through his alcoholic fug.

He straightens up and completes a creditable pirouette before shuffling back towards his desk. The outer edges of the heels of his shoes are so worn that he is forced to adopt a swaying, dislocated inside-outside step. A dirty triangle of his white shirt covers his grubby trouser seat. I'm sure he's been sitting on a step – probably his office steps – whilst boozing the afternoon away. He's not the finest example of a government official at this moment in time.

Six of us are squeezed into his tiny oven of an office, sucking on the stale fetid air. Outside, the late afternoon sun is still brutally hot. Stephen and I are sitting whilst Vilanculos wanders between the chair behind his desk and us. His audience, the retiring former head of customs and two deputies, line the walls.

Forget European football hooligans. They couldn't hold a candle to many Africans, who can consume vast quantities of diverse alcoholic beverages and still remain standing. I first found out about how strong their constitutions are very soon after arriving in Africa. I had helped arrange a leaving party for the manager of the local club. We had stocked up heavily on the staples – beer, 5-litre boxes of white and red plonk, gin and whisky. I realised that I was in the company of alcoholic Olympians when I saw that the wine was being poured into pint glasses and then consumed as if it were light beer. Their strong constitutions allow them to cope with and survive physical deprivations that I know would leave me following far in their wake. Take, for example, malaria. It is often graded on a simple scale of one to five. One means that it's not that bad, five means you are knocking on death's door. Many Malawians have had malaria so many times that they know instinctively when they have got it and drag themselves off to the nearest chipatala (local clinic) to get the drugs for treating it. Those who do get tested often get a three or four rating. They have probably been working or carrying out daily chores for days but have eventually decided that the headache, sweats, chills and aching limbs have become too much. Within twelve hours of taking the remedy they will be up and about again.

I've had malaria three times to date, all rated as a lowly one on the sickness scale. Each time I've thought I was going to die. Bedridden and incapable of carrying out the simplest of tasks, it usually takes me at least three days to start to feel ready to venture anywhere, and around a month to start to feel vaguely normal again. And I'm certainly not alone among the white population in being so delicate compared to the indigenous population.

I wonder how many beers Vilanculos has consumed. Ten? Twenty? Given his state, my money is on the latter amount. I know it's pointless trying to reason with him, but I also know I have to try. We've spent most of the day towing the *Pelican* round to the main bay and getting her ready to take on tow with the *Ilala*, which is due to arrive the following afternoon. Stephen and I have a lot of time and effort already invested in the rescue of the boat.

'Mr Vilanculos, the document I've just shown you has been stamped by the Ministry of Customs and Finance in Lichinga, the Provincial capital. It clearly indicates that the boat was coming here and why. We made enquiries at the time and the Ministry said that they don't have a procedure to issue temporary import permits for boats, so this is the reason why they have stamped this document.'

Vilanculos stares at me with vacant hostility. It's as if he's staring at a pesky bug and is undecided on precisely how to squash it.

Stephen steps in to try to reinforce our viewpoint. 'My understanding is that the Customs department here indicated that they were happy with this document when the *Pelican* first arrived in Metangula back in May 2004. They have never indicated since then that there were any problems with it.'

Vilanculos flicks his hand dismissively in our direction and picks up a piece of paper from his desk. 'I'm not interested in your papers. You must see the paper I have prepared for you. You are fined. Five hundred and forty million meticais.'

He flourishes his handiwork triumphantly in the air. How can the assembled company not be impressed by his unwavering pugnacity? And the astronomical size of the fine. I'm busy trying to do the mental arithmetic, grappling with all the zeros.

I think I've worked out that the fine is somewhere in the vicinity of twenty-three thousand dollars. The size of the fine makes the idea of negotiating our way to an agreement a nonstarter. In his drunken zealousness and desperate need to impress his colleagues he has led both sides down a blind alley. Agreeing to pay him something more realistic for nuisance value, say five hundred dollars – which would certainly have gone into his grubby back pocket – would be a huge comedown for him. In any event, I don't do bribes. I'm too tired to do the outraged shock bit which he is no doubt hoping for. I can manage tired resignation.

'Perhaps we can arrange to meet tomorrow morning to discuss this further?' I offer.

Vilanculos seems not to have heard me properly. He peers down at me, and then Stephen, trying to ingest my words.

'Tomorrow?' I repeat. 'It's been a long day for us. And I think for you? Can we meet again in the morning?'

He looks genuinely deflated. Where is the pleading and grovelling he has been expecting and hoping for? He lowers his hand and replaces his bit of paper on the desk.

'Tomorrow. Yes, tomorrow,' he says, pausing, and then as if he has made an important decision. 'Tomorrow in the middle of the morning.'

I nod. That should give him enough time to sober up. Stephen and I stand up. We shake hands with the ex-chief and the deputies and I hold my hand out to Vilanculos. This dispassionate, excessive politeness is more than he can bear. He stands and waves both arms, wagging his fingers at us and shouts.

'Don't try towing your boat away. I forbid it. It must stay here. This is my jurisdiction. We have guns. Ka-la-shni-kovs.' He utters the last word slowly, trying to enunciate each syllable. 'To ensure that people don't break the law.'

I nod dumbly, wondering if he is about to try to lock us up. The new ex-chief of Customs, Lazamo, who appears to be equally drunk, chimes in in support of Vilanculos, his new bosom friend.

'If you try to tow the boat our men will shoot you,' he concludes.

I look around to see how this speech is going down with his deputies. They are both staring in alarm at their current and ex-bosses.

Stephen steps in, his voice super calm and measured. 'We note what you say, Mr Vilanculos and Mr Lazamo. We are not going to take the boat away without first sorting things out with you.'

Outside fine dust motes hang in the air. The ochre-red road leading down to the bay is bathed in a warm golden light thrown by a blood-red sun on the far side of the lake. As we head up the hill towards the guesthouse we turn and pause to watch its slow, silent descent among the faraway hills. Tomorrow is another day, the first day of the rest of our lives. The optimist in me hopes that the morning will bring with it a fresh start and a return to sanity. Livingstone spent a week encamped at the village of one Chief Kabinga just east of the Bangweulu wetlands and lake in northern Zambia. He described the chief as a niggard who tried to sell him sheep at exorbitant prices, but observed that 'we must take [the Chief] as we find him, there is no use in growling.'

We head down to the bay. I want to check on the *Pelican* and put her to bed for the night. Standing on the shoreline a string of kayakers appear, paddling slowly into the bay followed by a gaily-painted wooden vessel chugging along and bringing up the rear like a mother duck with her ducklings. The kayakers paddle over to where we are standing and Stephen and I hold the kayaks and help the paddlers extricate themselves. We fall into conversation with them, and it quickly becomes apparent that they are from different corners of the globe – South Africa,

Europe and America. And they are disabled, many with prosthetic limbs. Tired they may be, but they are also an exuberant bunch, kayaking together around the periphery of this huge lake. The lady in charge of this happy group rows over from the support vessel to check on her charges and arrange for the kayaks to be towed back to the support vessel. We chat with her about the lake, her band of kayakers and the expedition generally. Her name is Marzi, and she strikes me as an interesting personality – well organised, with the relaxed demeanour of someone with the experience and confidence that comes from knowing how to run a good operation, yet also a free, easy-going spirit, very comfortable within herself and this environment. (Several days later, back on the farm in Malawi, I hear terrible news. A couple of days after our meeting with Marzi, further north on the lake, she had vanished. Search parties were organised, but she was never found. It was believed that she had slipped whilst coming down the ladder from the top deck of the support vessel, hit her head and was knocked out. In a heartbeat she had fallen into the lake and been pulled down into its deep, dark depths. It seemed shockingly tragic and unfair to me that such a vibrant, happy individual should be robbed of life in such an arbitrary, freakish accident.)

The following morning, we pack up and head off early down to the bay. I'm troubled about the prospect of the boat being left unsupervised in the bay over the long term. It's sheltered to a point, but would not provide any proper protection from a strong northerly or southerly wind. I don a mask and dive down to check that both bow and stern anchors have a good grip on the part-sand, part-rock lake bed.

Mid-morning we head up to the Customs office to see what awaits. We find the two deputies, Claudio Calisto and Anselmo Florinto, hanging around outside. I greet them and ask if Vilanculos is around. They look uneasy and say no, he has not appeared yet. Perhaps we should come back around five pm. Which we do. There's still no sign of Vilanculos and when I suggest that perhaps they should ring him or go and check at his house, they come clean. He's gone to Lichinga and has told them he will not be back today. And of course, they won't discuss anything as they lack the authority to make decisions. We eventually persuade them to ring Vilanculos and the message coming down the phone is that there was to be no negotiating. The boat stays.

I pull out my notebook and ask the deputies for their names for future reference. This smacks of potential responsibility for their actions or their chief's and they again look very uneasy.

Calisto solves the problem. 'Names cannot be written down. Names are confidential. Customs officers are classified as military personnel.'

Eventually Florinto writes a letter confirming that customs are refusing to release the boat. He tries to insert words to the effect that the reason is because the engines are not working. We get him to re-write his letter omitting this. The *Pelican*, we point out, doesn't need engines for a tow behind the Ilala and this was in any event the Marine Department's domain and we have a Clearance Certificate from Chirinsa. Reluctantly Florinto and Calisto sign their letter. They are distinctly uncomfortable. This all goes well beyond their usual levels of responsibility. I anticipate that all too suddenly they feel like chickens with their necks on the block.

A short time later we hear the booming horn that signals the approach of the *Ilala*. Colourful wooden fishing vessels with small buzzing outboards head towards her like bees around their queen. There's the usual flurry of activity, shouted greetings and instructions as passengers and cargo are ferried back and forth from ship to shore. Our two trusty watchmen are in place on board the *Pelican* and we arrange a transfer for ourselves. Within an hour of arrival, the *Ilala* is heading out of the bay. Stephen and I stand high up on the stern and watch the *Pelican* gently rocking as small wavelets thrown up by the wake of the *Ilala* lap at her newly cleaned hull. She is very easy on the eye with her neat, flowing lines, but to me, in the current circumstances, she already appears forlorn and abandoned.

'You can't do more than your best, so don't sweat it,' says Stephen reading my mind. 'I'm sure she'll be fine.'

I'm grateful for his attempt to make me feel better about the situation. 'I suspect you're right. No point in moping around, though I'd love to see Vilanculos strung up from the top deck,' I say with feeling.

'Some beer and food?'

'Yup. Let's go and make a plan for the next phase of the *Pelican* Liberation Operation.' The meaning of this new title that I've dreamt up for the next stage of our battle is not lost on Stephen. He grins happily.

'Hmm. The PLO. Probably appropriate. They'll also never give up their struggle. You realise that you'll be able to write a book when this is all over!'

CHAPTER 18

# ACCOUNT OF AN ATROCITY

9:00 am, Friday 17th October. The court is back in session. As always, immaculate and virtually immobile, the prisoners are sitting together in their usual place on the bench seat in front of us. Romao Charles is the embodiment of composure. He commences his summing-up, his face deadpan and his voice dispassionate yet firm. So, after later translation, what did the court audiotape reveal about what he had to say about what had happened leading up to and on that fateful Sunday afternoon?

The three hijackers had, it seems, all been friends for a long time and had fought as guerrillas with RENAMO during that conflict. At the end of the war and following the signing of the Rome General Peace Accords on 4th October 1992, some RENAMO fighters were demobilised and others were integrated into the newly established national army, the Forças Armadas de Moçambique – FADM. Only Francisco Ferro, alias Paulino Conde, was taken on by the FADM. The other two were demobbed.

Ferro became a furriel (corporal) in the 4th Infantry Brigade of the FADM based in Têtе and was seconded to their Military Police division. After several years he was approached and recruited by Quembo, who subsequently became the de facto leader of the small band of three. The plan was simple. To earn a lot of money in a short time by hi-jacking foreign registered vehicles at gunpoint with a view to stealing money and valuables. 'Ferro,' said Judge Charles, 'left the military life in order to embrace a criminal life.' Before leaving the army he stole some 'camuflados' (camouflage uniforms) to facilitate his criminal activities. Quembo had by now recruited another ex RENAMO colleague, Nguaza, and in early 1997 the three embarked on a number of criminal activities and were spotted in the cities of Beira on the coast, Têtе and the surrounding District of Angonia.

On Friday, 11th April the three hijackers arrived near a village called Zongo close to the small town of Dedza on the Mozambique/Malawi border. Prior arrangements had been made for two AK47 firearms to be stashed away for safe keeping with a contact in Zongo. These firearms were to be brought to an agreed location outside the village. Having met the contact at the drop off, the band headed south down the road on foot and away from the border to find a suitable location for a hijack. The choice was good: a route that a Malawi vehicle would take to the border but with very little traffic because it only led to a minor, rural border post. There were very few villages around and only the occasional local using the road. And there was plenty of surrounding bush in which to hide their presence from passers-by.

The remoteness of the location was born out by virtue of the fact that on the Saturday, 12th April, not a single vehicle with foreign plates passed by. The band moved down the hillside to a nearby stream, where they cooked a meal and slept the night.

Late the following morning Nguaza, dressed in civilian clothes, hid himself further down the track at a bend in the road where he could assess approaching traffic and signal his comrades. Around midday a double-cab with a middle-aged white male at the wheel came bouncing up the road. It didn't appear to be loaded with baggage and would probably provide slim pickings, so Nguaza ignored it. Around half an hour later a white Toyota double cab appeared, loaded with baggage and occupied by a young white couple, it was the perfect soft target, and Nguaza gave the agreed signal to his comrades.

Quembo and Ferro had donned army uniforms and were toting AK47 rifles. Stopping the vehicle, Quembo demanded money. Now pumped up and ready for action, he tells the court that he felt the response to his demand was too slow. I think back to when I was hijacked in Blantyre and how it took me time to process what was going on. If someone pretends to be one thing and turns out to be something entirely unexpected, you are left numbed and dazed. You need time to get your wits together. And so I am sure was the case with Andrew and Caroline. You approach and stop at what looks like a military police roadblock only to find when you've ground to a halt that in fact it's manned by gun-toting hijackers. No normal response would have been enough, or quick enough. Even someone experienced in the world of violence and who is half expecting trouble would be hard pushed to save himself.

I offer an illustration. Tom, a friend of Karen and myself, was stationed in the 1980s with the South African Defence Forces on the border with the South West, now Namibia, during the period that South Africa applied their concept of apartheid to South West Africa and was busy with counter insurgency operations against communist-backed freedom fighters. In those days there was conscription when at least one year's National Service was compulsory for whites. Tom was engaged in many cross-border counter insurgency operations, which often involved attacking SWAPO (the South West African People's Organisation) guerrilla camps. He had an impressive scar to show for his active service – a deep pink bullet furrow running from the hairline on his forehead all the way along the top of his skull. If he'd been standing just a few millimetres taller in his armoured vehicle, it would have been curtains for him.

When on leave in Johannesburg his training and recent operational alertness meant that he remained vigilant. Those on orange alert do things that would give police forces in the Western world apoplexy. Not the simple precautions such as not wearing a seat belt in town because they want to be able to move fast. Not the fact that they constantly check their mirrors and the movement of the traffic and vehicle occupants around them. Nor that they never allow themselves to be boxed in, choosing the inside or outside lanes and keeping a car's length between them and the vehicle in front when in heavy or gridlocked traffic. They never sit bumper to bumper. But they do sit with a fully loaded handgun, safety off, wedged between their thighs.

There is one situation in particular that even those on orange alert cannot control: getting held up at traffic lights. If you get caught at the front of the traffic at a red light with rows of traffic crossing in front of you, there's nowhere to go. And that's when you are particularly vulnerable. One afternoon in Johannesburg that was Tom's scenario. Looking in his side mirrors, he saw the passenger doors of the vehicle behind him spring open and two people move very rapidly towards his vehicle, one on either side. He barely had time to shout a warning to his friend in the front passenger seat before the hijackers were upon them. Grabbing the handgun between his thighs he let off a double tap – two bullets in quick succession – through the side of his door, killing that assailant. He turned the gun to the passenger seat, but he was already too late. His friend had been shot in the head and killed. That assailant realised that things were not working to plan and fled across the waiting traffic. Tom leapt out and fired several rounds at him, but he escaped. Blood subsequently found at the scene confirmed that he had managed to wing the second hijacker. The remaining hijackers waiting in the vehicle behind jumped out of their stolen vehicle and fled.

Tom, military trained and recently back from a war zone, sitting in the midst of the Johannesburg traffic, gun at the ready and on high alert, had some warning, and even then he only just managed to save himself. He did not have enough time to save his friend.

Andrew and Caroline were forced out of the vehicle, marched sixteen metres into the bush, made to lie on their stomachs and summarily executed.

Why had Ferro and Quembo shot them? In court the killers had been vague and unconvincing in their reply to this question, remarking only that Andrew and Caroline had been slow to respond to their demand for money. The appalling reality, unspoken in court but acknowledged later by the prosecutor and police, was that if they had been left alive they could have identified the gang members, so they had to die in order to ensure the gang's anonymity. This totally bleak and ruthless logic is difficult to get your head around, especially from a Western point of view. In Johannesburg cars are hijacked at the entrance gates to homes or, as with Tom, in the middle of busy traffic in broad daylight. The word 'compassion' does not exist. For professional hijackers life is cheap – dirt cheap – and ruthless expediency and self-preservation is the name of the game. Dead men don't talk, so dead men can't make emergency phone calls. Dead men can't chase you or retaliate. Dead men can't identify you.

In Andrew and Caroline's scenario, a long way out in the

bush, there was no impelling urgency. Tying the victims to a tree and gagging them would have served the same purpose. They only needed to scarper before the locals saw what was happening and raised the alarm. There had clearly been no real resistance or threat. There was a suggestion that the gang were high from smoking cannabis and that it was fuggy thinking, a sudden panicked reaction fuelled by the marijuana. Or perhaps it was also their background as guerrilla fighters, an entrenched mind-set that didn't allow them to consider alternatives. As a local English newspaper subsequently reported, Caroline was shot twice in the back by Ferro and Andrew once by Quembo. Straightforward bandit executions, with anything but straightforward ramifications.

The hijackers were now in a tearing hurry. The locals would have heard the shots and very shortly people might come to investigate. Nquaza, the lookout and designated getaway driver, turned the car around and drove off at breakneck speed. Reaching the main highway, he turned right and headed towards Têté. There are straight sections on this road but for the most part it comprises some sustained bends and lots of undulations. At one point the road drops and curves steeply down off the escarpment towards the plain below. Hurtling down this escarpment – several witnesses later attested the driver was going at breakneck speeds – the vehicle swerved to avoid a bus and flew off the road into the bush, rolling down a steep bank. The hijackers were lucky. None was seriously injured. As the locals converged to investigate they abandoned the vehicle, along with the knapsacks containing their clothes and both firearms, and fled the scene.

For the villagers, an abandoned vehicle loaded with baggage was a gift from heaven and not to be passed over. It was quickly ransacked. Bags, radio, seats, wheels, battery, canopy. Anything that could be lifted or prised off and carried away was. Within hours the double cab resembled nothing more than the skeleton of a vehicle. All that was left for the authorities to recover from a local villager were Andrew's passport and Caroline's international driving licence. The hijackers decided to split up. Two headed for Beira on the coast, the third, Nguaza, made for Harare in Zimbabwe.

Within an hour of commencing their hijacking, the bandits were on the run with less in the way of possessions than they had started out with before the executions. And two young people lay dead.

CHAPTER 19

# THE MAN WITH A BIG JOB

Frustrations. None of us likes to give up our time and put vast amounts of effort into something unless we anticipate some positive results. The next move seems obvious. Go and visit Vilanculos' boss, the Provincial Chief of Customs, who is based in Lichinga, the provincial capital. It takes me three and a half months of constant phone calls and faxes to finally chase down and make contact with Crisologo Cintura, the Customs chief. I pin him down to a date for a meeting. John Fleming seems to be a body in constant motion, whizzing around Africa and Europe, but eventually I get him to coordinate his movements so that he can fly up to be in attendance as well.

Early morning on Tuesday, 5th September 2006. I drive two hours on good tar to the north-eastern border with Mozambique, and a further three hours on hot, dusty roads to Lichinga to meet up with John Fleming. After a brief lunch and discussion with him, at three o'clock in the afternoon we are on Cintura's doorstep. John has done his homework. He's been told that Cintura is a young, educated guy from Maputo who has been fast tracked. He has very recently been sent up to Niassa Province and his first job in the fast lane is to sort out the provincial Customs department. Niassa Province is, it seems, something of a mess and revenue from Customs is appalling. That doesn't surprise me one bit. Cintura will be a Frelimo man trying to make headway in RENAMO territory. RENAMO don't like the idea of sending their revenue down to the faceless Frelimo bureaucracy in Maputo to be pocketed down there by 'the enemy.' So they have probably been rather slack on the collection side. Or more likely diverted taxes into their own pockets.

Cintura's office is a cramped space in a small, dilapidated little building. There are neat piles of files stacked around the dark-wood-panelled walls. I wonder if they have just been neatly piled up to give visitors the impression of efficiency and order, or whether Cintura has actually been wading through them. He is certainly young for the position, probably early thirties. Medium height and build, his eye contact is direct. He greets us with a cocky confidence that stops just short of arrogance. Apparently the requirement for uniforms does not apply to young fast-tracked Customs chiefs. He wears a crisp, casual white shirt, jeans and well-polished pointed black shoes accessorised by a large gold watch. He's a very different breed from the likes of Vilanculos. I wonder, very uncharitably, how long it will take for the rot to set in with him.

Yet again I explain everything. Why and when the *Pelican* first came to Metangula. What has happened over the last two-plus years. I pull a piece of A4 paper out of my folder and hand it across to him.

'Mr Cintura, here is the relevant document dated 13th April 2004.'

Involuntarily my thought processes stumble. I simply cannot

help myself. The 13th April. Quite simply the worst date in the calendar. The date Andrew and Caroline were killed. Also the date Apollo 13 announces, "Okay Houston, we've had a problem here." There's something about 13th April that's cursed. John and Cintura look at me curiously as I draw in a deep breath before continuing.

'You can see that this document has a picture of the *Pelican* giving her vital statistics – details about the boat and the reasons why the boat came to Metangula.'

Cintura takes his time to read through it. He stares at it for a while before looking up.

'I have not seen this document before. But I am new to Lichinga. This was long before I arrived here.'

'Well, if you look on the right-hand side there,' I say, pointing, 'you will see the Lichinga Customs stamp. There should be another original of this document in your files somewhere.'

I pause to look up at him. His face is impassive, but I detect a flicker of something in his eyes. Anger? Uncertainty? I don't want to antagonise him, so I choose my next words with care, giving him my best award-winning smile.

'You can hardly be expected to know the history behind this matter after such a short time. You have a lot of very important matters to deal with.'

Pump him up a bit. Feed that ego. Cintura actually runs a finger over the Customs stamp as if to verify somehow that it is an original. He opens a file on his desk marked 'Confidential' and shuffles through the thin wad of papers inside. Really it's a play for thinking time. Eventually he looks up.

'It's not in here,' he says simply.

John now cuts in.

'I had about six originals made, all with original stamps and signatures. And I definitely arranged for one copy to be placed in your predecessor's file here, one in Metangula, I kept two and I passed two to Mr McGowan.'

'I have my other original back at home, so you must take this one,' I say, sounding, I suspect, rather magnanimous. If Cintura doesn't have the original of this document in his file then I'm very curious to know what it does actually contain. Presumably Vilanculos' report. I'd dearly like to have sight of that.

'What would you suggest we should now do? Can you write a letter releasing the *Pelican* to me?'

Behind his round, metal-rimmed glasses, Cintura blinks slowly. His brow creases into frown lines. Then he drops his bombshell.

'Well the matter is no longer in my hands. It has all been passed to the judge in Nacala where the Customs Court is located for this Province.'

I'm stunned. Now we have to deal with a faceless judge located hundreds of kilometres away on the coast.

'May I ask what papers have been passed to the judge? Perhaps you could let me have a copy?'

Cintura hesitates briefly, I guess mulling over whether he can safely let me have a quick look in his confidential file.

'That will not be possible at this time.'

I'll bet. Vilanculos' report will be a vengeful pack of lies woven around a largely imaginary storyline. There's no point pressing Cintura now. Better to try another route and create some bonds. If at first you don't succeed one way...

'I understand your difficulties, Mr Cintura. It's getting late and I am sure you have other matters needing your attention,' I say forcing a smile and lightly waving generally at all the files stacked around his office. He smiles back.

'I have a big job to sort out here.'

John and I nod in unison.

'We would be very happy if you could join us for dinner this evening. We can talk about much more interesting things,' says John.

There's no hesitation in Cintura's acceptance of this offer. His interest is piqued and I'm sure he wants to find out more about the *Pelican* and John's involvement in the Niassa Project.

In the evening we are joined by Drew, who has travelled up to Lichinga to visit friends at a nearby mission station and is happy to come and see what he can do to help. Over standard fare of piri-piri chicken and chips in our hotel dining room we make small talk about Malawi's food problems and the effect of the recent drought on food production, and the sorry state of football in both countries with neither able to qualify for the Africa Cup of Nations. Drew talks about life as a missionary and the orphanage they are building.

Cintura appears relaxed and is happy to join in the conversation. Eventually his curiosity overcomes him and he wants the whole story of the *Pelican* from construction to arrival in Metangula. And we provide it over the course of an hour and several beers. Eventually the offer we have been hoping for is forthcoming.

'I must contact the judge and explain things to him,' he says.

'You said the judge had been sent a report by your predecessor. So hopefully you will be able to correct any errors in that report?' I suggest.

Cintura's look turns more serious as he drops another bombshell. 'The only papers the judge has are a report written by Vilanculos.'

Our expressions clearly told Cintura what we thought of this news.

'I don't think that report will be very accurate. In fact I doubt it will contain anything accurate,' I say glumly.

'I fear you are right. Vilanculos says at the end of his report that the only way he could prevent you from taking the *Pelican* away was for his men to get out their machine guns!'

Drew splutters over his coke and this turns into a coughing fit. We all wait until he has recovered before I press on.

'This is, as I am sure you realise, utter rubbish. There were many witnesses, including Lamek on the *Ilala*, who could verify that this is nonsense. Vilanculos was extremely drunk and was not even around on the day that the *Pelican* was supposed to be towed away by the Ilala.'

'I know you are right in this. The truth is that Vilanculos has been causing problems. He has been removed from his post at Metangula.'

I cannot help myself. 'To cause problems elsewhere?'

In general, crooked or incompetent officials don't get fired. They just get moved on sideways to more and more distant and lonely outposts.

'No, he was sent to Maputo and shortly afterwards fired.'

'Well, I'll drink to that,' Drew declares with feeling and raises his Coke to the demise of Vilanculos.

I imagine a dishevelled Vilanculos in some seedy bar in one of the shanty areas of Maputo slumped over a bottle of beer. I'm not revelling in this news, but equally I cannot find any compassion in me for the man. I'm just relieved that he is now out of the equation.

John poses a question. 'Have you been able to find someone good to replace him? Malawi Lake Services are very fed up with Customs in Metangula constantly thinking up ways to take money off the *Ilala*'s passengers. They are seriously thinking of cutting Metangula out of their lake schedule.'

Cintura grimaces. 'I am aware that problems exist. I can reassure you that I will be sorting them out.'

Cintura wants us to know that he is busy trying to get a good handle on what is happening on his patch, that's he's no slouch. I fervently hope that he is no louche either – forgive the pun – or we really are sunk. He takes a large swig of his beer before continuing.

'It would be helpful to your situation if before you leave you put together a signed statement outlining the facts. I will then send it to the judge in Nacala.'

Early the following morning Drew and I pick up Lazzamo, the Metangula Customs chief recently appointed by Cintura to replace Vilanculos, and we drive down to Metangula. It's a predominantly quiet dirt road with unremarkable scrubby bush trees on either side. Just over an hour later we reach the edge of the escarpment leading down to Metangula and the lake. I stop the vehicle on the ridgeline and we all get out to take in this absolutely stunning sight. The slopes below the ridgeline are densely packed with the canopies of large indigenous trees stretching down to the shores of the lake, a huge shimmering body of water spreading out into the distance, right and left as far as the eye could see.

In his epic, tormented final expedition, which began in March 1866 and lasted over seven long years culminating in his death, Livingstone travelled from the Indian Ocean along the course of the Ruvuma River, which forms the northern border between Tanzania and Mozambique. His objective was to finally solve the riddle of the source of the Nile. Trekking inland for over five hundred kilometres along a route that was predominantly used by the slavers, he encountered the grisly horrors of that trade. To prevent those slaves, mainly women, who were unable to keep up with the slave caravan, from becoming the property of someone else, the slavers would tie them to trees and shoot and stab them to death. It was a truly wretched path through the heart of darkness. Reaching the source of the Ruvuma, which was well short of Lake Nyasa, Livingstone struck off south-west, leaving the grim route of stunted trees and burnt grasslands behind him to enter mountainous terrain and finally a land of gently undulating hills. He never saw the precise view where we have now stopped as he arrived on the shores of the lake further south on the 8th August 1866, but he certainly appreciated coming 'back to [his] old home' and looking down on the lake's glinting, pellucid waters. He wrote about how pleasant it was "to bathe in the delicious waters again, hear the roar of the sea and dash in the rollers... I feel quite exhilarated." A far cry from a journal entry from his previous expedition when he had first discovered the lake. Then, in September 1861, he had written: "while sailing pleasantly over the blue water with a gentle breeze, suddenly and without any warning was heard the sound of a coming storm, roaring on with crowds of angry waves in its wake... our seaman, John Neil, who, having been a fisherman on the coast of Ireland, understood boating on a stormy coast... had never seen such waves before." After experiencing this terrifying storm he wrote: "did we not believe the gales to be peculiar to one season of the year, [we] would call Nyassa the 'Lake of Storms.'"

Storms are most prevalent in the months of July to October, but Livingstone is incorrect in saying that storms are peculiar to one season of the year. The reality in my experience is that storms can erupt on the lake at virtually any time of the year.

We head off, driving down the snaking mountainside, negotiating tight switchbacks. I'm dreading what I am going to find when we arrive. Less than an hour later Andrew and I have donned masks and we are in the cool water inspecting the underside of the *Pelican's* hull.

The previous month, August, a fierce storm had blown up on the lake and my worst fears had been realised. A vicious south-easterly 'mwera' wind had swept across the mountains and down into the main bay at Metangula. Wrenching both the *Pelican's* anchors off the lake bed, it had driven the boat out into the lake. It was to be the first and last time that the maritime chief, Chirinsa, actually did something proactive and useful.

The rescue, he later tells me, required no fewer than thirty-three people (including six of his 'administrators') in various small fishing boats. It had taken three days to catch up with the *Pelican* and tow her back. Sensibly they had towed her around the headland back to her original little bay near to the naval base. If the mwera wind picked up again, the worst that could happen was that the *Pelican* would be grounded in her little bay.

The hull is in a very sorry state, badly dented and scraped. Both rudders have snapped off and are missing. I imagine her reeling and spinning around like a drunkard as she crashes and staggers along the rocky shoreline before finding the entrance to the bay and the open sea. It was an absolute miracle that she had not been holed and sunk.

We head over to the Maritime offices, where I spend half an hour discussing the situation with Chirinsa. It's all very déjà vu, but I go through the expected motions. He wants twenty-nine million meticais for the rescue. Eventually we settle on fifteen million ($650).

Mid-afternoon we drive back to Lichinga, and the following morning I head over to Cintura's offices to brief him on our trip. The rest of the morning is spent with John and me putting together the sworn statement. We explain that before the *Pelican* came to Metangula, enquiries had been made of the Mozambicans as to what documentation they wanted for the boat. We state that they had no standard documents for the temporary import of a boat and that the result had been the permit stamped by Customs at Lichinga. We explained the purpose of the boat in aiding the Niassa Project, the inability to get access to the ramp at the naval base to carry out necessary repair works despite all John's efforts in aiding the naval base in repairing their own craft, and the necessity to now get the boat back to Monkey Bay in Malawi, given the damage caused after she dragged her anchors.

By three in the afternoon the following day, Friday, the report had been finalised, translated into Portuguese, sworn by John and myself and delivered to Cintura's office. John hopped on his plane back to Johannesburg and I drove, recklessly fast, for the border with Malawi, arriving about a minute before it closed for the night.

The final part of the journey home, much more sedately in the dark, gave me time to reflect on the situation which seemed to be going from bad to worse. It was like being stuck in a bog. The harder one tried to work one's way out the deeper, more stuck fast one became. The *Pelican* was now extensively damaged. Her release was subject to the whims of a Customs judge in Nacala who now had two versions of a story. Our main hope seemed to lie with Cintura being able to convince the judge that our version was correct and persuading him that he could either quietly ignore and return the papers or make an order for the release of the boat.

'A snake you can see does not bite' goes one African proverb. Cintura came across as efficient and wanting to be popular. He seemed benevolent and congenial, but of course appearances can be very deceptive. Was he really on our side or actually a snake in the grass? I had no idea what hand Cintura has and how he is going to play it. Whatever the legalities and rules might be, or even what constitutes right and wrong, I feared that in all likelihood he would proceed purely on the basis of what would promote his own personal agenda and ambitions. After all, why had the go-ahead, fast tracked Cintura apparently gone at a snail's pace and ignored my earlier requests to have a meeting for so long? He gave the impression that his predecessor had sent Vilanculos's report to Nacala, yet Cintura had been in his new post for several months, so why had we not heard anything from the judge or the court in all that time? What had happened to the original import permit? Had Cintura's predecessor destroyed it at the request of Vilanculos to help corroborate his outlandish report? Or had Cintura? Webs within webs, patronage and favours, all leading to lies and half-truths. The reality is that one never really knew what was going on behind the scenes and never would. As an outsider, not one of the cognoscenti, you decipher things with a mixture of known facts and a large dose of conjecture, peering through a dark, opaque glass hoping for a little light to be shed on the winding path ahead.

CHAPTER 20

# JUDGMENT AND THE JUDGE

After Judge Charles has completed his summation of the facts, he calls for a comfort break. It gives Severiano time to give us a potted summary of what the judge has said. Twenty minutes later Judge Charles calls the court to order and presses on with an outline of the law applicable to the crimes of robbery and murder.

The perpetrators are those 'who carried out the crime or are indirectly involved with it.' In the present case the two accused who shot Andrew and Caroline are perpetrators, but so is the lookout driver, as his intention also is to benefit from these crimes. In addition there are 'aggravating' factors: that the crimes were clearly planned and premeditated and that they used firearms to attack people who were defenceless.

"From the beginning the intention of this armed group was to kill. So, all things said, analysed and considered... the maximum penalty is required of 24 years in jail."

The judge also ordered the three to pay the maximum 'Tax

of Justice' – compensation – to the relatives of the victims. Five hundred million meticais, around $21,000. By Mozambican standards a truly huge amount of money. Clearly there was absolutely no chance of that compensation being paid, in whole or part.

Romao Charles also demanded "the capture of the two men who supplied the guns... for [trial] and our interpretation [is that] all are perpetrators: there is no accomplice."

Around the time of the trial a friend of mine who had lived in Tête for many years had made discreet enquiries of his contacts there. The word was that one of these two men – the 'Moatize Two' – was a senior serving army officer and it was believed that it was this officer who had persuaded the corporal, Francisco Ferro, to carry out the hijacking. The Moatize Two would help Ferro by secreting two AK47s and ammunition in a 'safe' house in the village of Zongo near the border. In return the Moatize Two would be entitled to a share of the spoils. Whoever the Moatize Two were, the Mozambican police made no comment and as far as I am aware no attempt, either before or after the trial, to apprehend them. I was subsequently told by my mole that the senior army officer had been smartly transferred from Tête down to Maputo around the time that the British police arrived to help with the investigations. It would, of course, be very bad publicity for the army and the army commandant if a senior serving army officer was implicated as being part of a gang hoping to profit from murders and hijackings.

Looking at the three in court as they stood ready to file out after sentencing, it was difficult to believe that they were taking everything so phlegmatically. Still no evident emotion. Not even sweat on their brows. Edmund had requested permission to take some photographs. All three stood, in the main staring obliquely away from the lens, expressionless. It left me feeling distinctly uneasy. Why were they so 'relaxed' about what they had done and accepting of their fate? Had they seen so many horrors during the war that 24 years in jail was regarded as virtually meaningless? Or did they know something we did not? Had they also been promised a get out of jail free card once the dust had settled?

Afterwards Romao Charles asked to see us all in his chambers, a room brimming with neat piles of paperwork. I counted seven piles, each about a foot high, on his desk alone. He was happy for me to take a couple of photographs of him standing beside his overloaded desk. I cannot recall what I said, but I remember how all of a sudden he relaxed and his stern, magisterial face creased into a beaming smile. We chatted and I discovered a sensitive man who accepted without fluster or complaint his almost herculean task of finding a way to implement justice in an unsettled province in the wake of a long, bloody civil war.

'What do you do in Malawi?' he asked me at one stage.

'I work as a legal and financial consultant. And I help on my father-in-law's farm, though my training is as a solicitor, not a farmer. My father-in-law would say I dip and dabble on the farm.'

'Did you train as a lawyer in Malawi?'

'No. In Malawi I'm what they term an import. I originally qualified and worked in England.'

'So what do you think of our court proceedings?'

'Very civilized indeed. I was amazed at the calm manner in which the proceedings were conducted.'

'I'm sure it would be the same back in England?' Romao enquires.

I think about that briefly. 'I doubt it. The accused all came into court without any handcuffs. Given the crimes involved, in the UK they would have been handcuffed. And with three in the court together there would have been a team of prison guards inside and outside the court.'

Romao chuckles and says simply, 'There is nowhere for them to run to.'

'Well, the system in England is much more adversarial. Your advocates here are astonishingly courteous and respectful of each other and of you and the court.'

Romao's eyebrows rise in unison and then he smiles again. 'We can't afford to be too adversarial here. There are very few lawyers and even fewer judges left after the war. We have to be able to greet each other when we meet. We cannot afford to hold grudges any more.'

'Let's just say in England the advocates tend to be a bit more forceful and robust. But they don't bear any ill will afterwards. They also want to be able to share a drink with their colleagues.'

'And are you all happy with the way justice has been carried out here?' he asks.

I look at the strained and tired faces, no doubt reflecting my own, of Edmund, my parents and Karen. The consensus is yes. After all, they had pleaded guilty and have been given the maximum sentence available under the law. I'm holding it together, but beneath the outward calm my emotions are churning, raw and confused.

'Yes,' I say hesitantly. I am thinking that it's Mozambican justice according to the law. Not the justice I would like to see meted out at this point in time.

'But I would like to request that the prisoners are transferred from Tête prison to Maputo. Tête is an area where they have friends and perhaps some influence.'

'I fully understand,' Romao replies. 'You must put this request to the Provincial Governor.'

Later that afternoon we meet briefly with the Governor at his villa residence, an opulent mansion with large open rooms and high ceilings, marble floors and light pink walls. The pink colour even stretches to his business card. A large, educated man, Governador Virgílio Ferrão is welcoming and quickly makes us feel at ease. A consummate diplomat. We drink English tea from delicate china cups. He offers his condolences, hopes that the result of the trial will be of some comfort. He mentions the challenges faced in administering his province, but is optimistic that over time things will turn around for the better. If there is anything he can do for us, we should ask.

I ask him about moving the killers to the high security prison in Maputo. Ferrão promises to look into this though he says, somewhat glibly in my view, that we should have no concerns about the men escaping. Tête prison is also high security. I would shortly have bitter cause to remember his words.

Driving back home to Malawi, we are all overwhelmed by relief and despondency. We have had our day in court and it has gone as well as it possibly could have done. We are lucky. In the main we have been able to achieve a form of justice for Andrew and Caroline in just six months. That eluded the families of Helen Smith and Julie Ward, despite decades of determined battling by their fathers. But now we are left staring into the abyss.

We have all clasped the objective of justice – or was it a more complicated cocktail of justice and revenge? – so tightly to our hearts over the past months. Now that it is all over, we are left exhausted and bereft. Where do I put this terrible, jumbled mountain of events and emotions? Is there a box I can put it in and then firmly bolt down the lid? It doesn't seem possible that I can somehow incorporate it all into my life going forward. Will it leach out and affect, infect, every area of my life?

I anticipate that the psychologists would tell me that I need to look forward, to concentrate on building new hopes and dreams.

As Churchill's wartime secretary told him in his darker, brooding moments, 'Don't look back Winston. You're not going there.' But right now I have the distressing feeling that all this will continue to consume my waking moments and follow me well into the future. I am drifting on a featureless grey sea that stretches well beyond the distant horizon.

The inquest in the UK was held on the 3rd March 1998, nearly six months after the trial. It revealed nothing new. The Home Office pathologist confirmed that Caroline had been shot in the back twice and would have died immediately. Andrew had been shot once, the bullet severing a main artery, and he would have bled out quickly.

I have a personal theory based on the location of Andrew quite a number of metres from Caroline when we found them. That he had realised what was about to happen and had tried to make a run for cover and had been very unlucky that Quembo's bullet found an artery. A few millimetres, just a lion's whisker, one way or the other, and who knows...

The coroner heard that the three British detectives had flown out to Mozambique two months after the murders, combed the crime scene and found vital evidence missed by the Mozambican police. Recording verdicts of unlawful killing the coroner rightly praised the work of Detective Superintendent Brian Woodfield and his small team. 'I am sure without their assistance there would not have been the successful criminal proceedings,' he said.

Of that I have absolutely no doubt whatsoever. In fact Detective Superintendent Brian Woodfield had superbly negotiated a difficult and delicate path combining experience and determined detective work on the one hand with quiet but firm diplomacy on the other, always mindful that however inept and lackadaisical the Mozambican police might appear, he still needed their co-operation and could not afford to jeopardise the investigation by putting their noses out of joint.

CHAPTER 21

# CATCHING KILLERS

How do you catch a gang of killers? Let me rephrase that. How do you catch a gang of killers in southern East Africa, where the borders between all the various countries are totally porous? There's nothing resembling a Trump Wall here.

We were told later that the Mozambican police set an initial investigation in motion. I don't know what that investigation entailed, but it led nowhere. After our meeting and interviews at Mount Browne in late April, Detective Superintendent Woodfield had to exercise extreme patience. Weeks passed without any positive news and it became clear that the Mozambican investigation, such as it was, had stalled. Personally I have my doubts that it ever really got going at all. After pressure from the Foreign Office through the BHC in the Mozambican capital of Maputo, the Mozambican Ministry of the Interior was finally persuaded to accept the help of a three-man team of detectives from Surrey Police Headquarters. The suggestion, all couched very diplomatically, was that the Surrey Police were willing to fly over to assist. Rather than being seen as an admission of failure and a request for help, it should be seen as an agreement to pool resources and co-operate between fellow Commonwealth countries. A positive result would reflect well on such a collaboration and the parties involved. As a bonus, the Mozambicans might learn a thing or two about how the British police investigated and solved crimes, and the British would find out about the challenges faced by the Mozambican police. All this teamwork and networking could only be useful going forward. Especially for the lucky, chosen few in the Mozambican police who would be able to arrange a freebie reciprocal trip to the UK.

The Mozambicans had no hi-tech forensic facilities. In fact, I believe they had little in the way of low-tech equipment either. The British police team that flew in to Tête – Detective Superintendent Woodfield along with a Detective Inspector and a scenes-of-crime officer – brought everything they were likely to need with them. Despite the time that had elapsed, they quickly picked up fresh clues and pieced things together, liaising closely and building up a rapport with Andissene Silveira, the Provincial Police Commandant, and Artur Filipe, the Tête Chief Inspector of 'PIC', the Mozambican equivalent of the CID.

The British team commenced its investigations 196 kilometres from Tête, questioning the locals and combing the bush in the area of the hijacking. The locals were unable to provide any reliable descriptions of the bandits or even how many there were. Combing the bush at the scene, however, revealed vital evidence missed by the Mozambicans. In particular, two of the three bullet cartridges.

Moving on, they revisited the scene of the vehicle crash. There was nothing major to be found here except to get the villagers who had witnessed the crash (and had shortly afterwards surrendered Andrew's passport and Caroline's driving licence to the police) to confirm the details they had already given to the Mozambicans. Three people had scrambled out of the vehicle, leaving two AK47s behind, and run off. Two had been wearing army fatigues. Descriptions were sketchy and unreliable and essentially amounted to men of normal height and build.

The skeleton of the crashed vehicle had been towed to the police post at the town of Moatize some thirty kilometres east of Tête. Picked bare by the villagers, it was a depressing sight. A blunt and brutal testimonial to the crime and its aftermath.

With the British police team quietly but firmly steering operations, the Mozambican authorities considered the accumulated evidence and the manner of the killings and now had a very good idea of who they were looking for. Three individuals, probably soldiers or ex-soldiers. They could check for missing weapons at the army base in Tête. Talk to the commander and his soldiers. Who was friends with who? Who had left or deserted the army recently? Had weapons gone missing?

Following this trail, they came knocking at the door of the army. The commandant was highly embarrassed when it was discovered that the weapons had very probably been supplied by two of his own, based down the road at the army barracks in Moatize. Whilst I do not know for certain, my best guess is that behind the scenes a deal was now struck. The 'Moatize Two' would volunteer information in return for anonymity and a get out of jail free card. With the British police right on the spot there was absolutely no chance of anyone brushing this crime under the carpet, and the army commandant was probably very keen indeed to clear up his mess 'in house' and not have it broadcast. Corporal Ernesto Ferro, who had been stationed there and had recently left the army, is fingered. Armed with a name, enquiries of his family and acquaintances enabled them to quickly discover the likely identity of the other members of Ferro's gang. Suddenly they had the right numbers: a gang of three. As the judge stated in his summing up, enquiries confirmed that the three of them had been recently seen together in the cities of Beira and Tête and around the Angonia district, where they were implicated in a number of robberies.

It was now about casting the net wide and hauling them in. Africa may be populous, but the rural communities form a vast web of interconnectivity. A single person will be connected not only to his immediate family, but to a large extended family, friends and friends of friends, not only in his village but in many of the surrounding villages. Trying to disappear in a village was a non-starter, as the bush telegraph would soon 'out' them. Which left the towns.

The PIC made enquiries of their urban informants and made it clear that this was not routine. It was top priority. They wanted contact names and locations. Fast. There was a long, dark tunnel waiting for anyone caught harbouring the fugitives or withholding information about their whereabouts. The informants realised that this was not the time to hold out. The wanted men were seriously toxic. Better to chalk up some useful credits against a future rainy day and point the police in the right direction.

As their information was corroborated along their chain of contacts and informants, the PIC closed the net, concentrating on Beira on the east coast north of Maputo, and Harare, the capital of Zimbabwe. The police in Beira caught up with Ernesto Ferro on the 8th June. Joaquim Quembo managed to duck and dive for four days, but there was nowhere to hide. His luck ran out on the 12th June, around about the same time Paulino Nguaza was also arrested by the Zimbabwean police in Harare.

Despite the fact that the car was very highly compromised with the fingerprints of any number of people, the AK47s and the bullet cartridges were not. Matching the cartridges to one or both of the AK47s that had been abandoned at the vehicle crash sight, and then the prints on the AK47s and the cartridges to Ferro and/or Quembo would not have been difficult. In the event the three men decided – or more likely were persuaded – to come clean and confess.

Perhaps I have a suspicious nature. Although I don't think so. The identities of the Moatize Two were known to the police and the army, but despite Judge Charles' request when delivering his judgement, they were never arrested and charged. They were allowed to slip into obscurity. Would these two accomplices have arranged the supply of the fatigues and weapons and thus risked being compromised and caught up in such a crime just to be able to share the spoils? It's entirely possible, if they believed that it was highly unlikely that things would be traced back to them. What is clear is that this particular crime was very specific. It didn't fit the profile of the previous crimes committed by these men. It wasn't a clumsy, almost spontaneous, attempt at robbery. Certainly the carrying out of the crime was a bungled, tragic disaster, but to my mind these bandits were put up to it. As the judge commented, the crimes were 'planned and premeditated.' AK47s were secretly withdrawn from army stores, transported and stashed in the nearby village and then delivered to the bandits, probably by one of the Moatize Two. Army fatigues were supplied to complete the deception and ensure that they looked like the real deal. A bona fide military police stop. Then the location. Out in the bush where there were likely to be few if any witnesses and no genuine police. Waiting until they could pick a specific, soft target. Certainly they were acting on instructions. Perhaps one or both of the Moatize Two were former comrades in arms and guerrilla commanders.

What the Moatize Two did not envisage was that their stooges would completely lose the plot and panic. That Nquaza would drive in a blind panic, crash the stolen vehicle and they would all flee leaving behind the guns they had been supplied with. And in their wildest imaginations, they could not have envisaged a team of British police detectives landing on their doorstep and driving forward a proper investigation that would end not only in the capture of the bandits but would also implicate them.

CHAPTER 22

# THE SIDEWINDER AND THE SAVIOUR

The Namibian sidewinder snake is a highly successful ambush hunter. A small but highly venomous snake, generally less than a foot in length, it has developed a unique sidewinding motion to climb or descend sand dunes. This graceful, flowing movement also allows it to keep a good percentage of its body off the burning hot sand as it moves about. Unusually for snakes, the eyes are located on the top of the head. Its ambush technique is to bury itself in the sand with just the eyes and the tip of the tail visible. In his film 'Beautiful People,' the writer and director, Jamie Uys, shows footage of a sidewinder moving down a sand dune and burying itself in order to ambush a gecko. He narrates the action as follows:

'The sidewinder's favourite meal is the diamond gecko. But geckos play hard to get. So the sidewinder resorts to a very sneaky trick to catch his prey. First he buries himself in the sand until he is quite invisible. Then his tail comes up and pretends to be a blade of grass. Now geckos don't eat grass, but ants do, and geckos eat ants. At this point things happen very quickly. Ant goes for tail, gecko goes for ant and [the sidewinder goes for] the gecko.'

I was about to experience the Mozambican bureaucratic equivalent of such an ambush.

I visualise the dapper Cintura, Mr Fast Track, sitting in his cramped office in Lichinga. By the time John and I left him in September 2006 he had become not exactly chummy but certainly friendly. He had indicated that he was eager to help. He apparently has clout and will talk to the judge in Nacala and sort out the mess. The assurance is that we will soon be able to make plans to quietly take the *Pelican* home without the threat of AK47s.

It's the best part of a week after my return to Malawi before I am able to get hold of Cintura again. He says he has been in contact with the judge and is confident that he will be able to get back to us very shortly with some news.

A day later I receive a call from the Managing Director of Malawi Lake Services, Anton Botes. The pleasantries over, he offers his latest intelligence.

'Lamek, my captain on the *Ilala*, has just spoken to Cintura about the situation with the *Pelican*. Basically to ask if he can arrange to take her on tow back to Malawi.'

'That's great, Anton,' I say in an upbeat voice. Perhaps if I'm cheerful that will somehow translate into good news. 'I've just returned from Lichinga and we had meetings with Cintura. He has apparently spoken to the judge in Nacala about the *Pelican*. It all sounds very positive.'

There's a pause before Anton responds in an edgy voice. 'Ha. Well Ewen, as you know this is Mozambique we are talking about. Mozambique Customs. It's never a straight line to the finish, my friend.'

My heart sinks. 'I sense you're about to tell me something I don't want to hear?' I mutter tightly. Anton is Africaans and there's something that I really value about Afrikaners. They always play a straight bat, though I do wish they would occasionally sugar coat things just a little bit.

'Look, Customs don't actually have a beef with you. But the *Pelican* is – how can I say this – the tool to achieve their objectives. The means to an end.'

'I hear you, Anton, but I'm not sure I understand. What is the end they are after? A big fat payout?'

'Yes. And no. It's more complicated. You and the family are the owners of the *Pelican*. I know that. But the authorities in Metangula have only ever dealt with John Fleming. He's been cocky and bossy with them. Waving his high-end contacts and big projects and big wallet in their faces. Gave them the impression that he was in control of the *Pelican* and effectively the owner.'

'I do understand that John's had everyone jumping through hoops doing his bidding.'

'Precisely. And he's put a lot of noses out of joint. Really upset these guys.'

'So they're resentful and feeling used. Probably also feeling a bit stupid.'

'Yes. Yes, that's it. Exactly. He promised them all sorts of funding and it's never materialised. Suddenly he's just upped sticks and gone. Instead of a tasty pay out they've been left sucking on air.' I embellish his description with a feeble one of my own.

'Like a fish out of water.' There's a brief pause whilst Anton gets his head around this.

'Ha, Yes. But the point is the *Pelican* has become a lever to get at John. And you've got caught up in that.'

'So where is it all heading? Does Lamek think Cintura will help?'

'We don't think so. Look, from Cintura's point of view there are two things here. One is the story out of Metangula. They will have told him about John Fleming and his broken promises. Two is that if the judge in Nacala presses ahead and makes a ruling against you and imposes all sorts of Customs duties and penalties in relation to the *Pelican,* then everyone comes out of it very well. Cintura's seen to be doing his job and increasing revenue and supporting his colleagues. Those guys in Metangula will feel they've at least given John a bit of a bloody nose.'

'Except it's not John who will be inconvenienced and have to pay up.'

'They don't believe that. They think that in the end it is still John who will be left fighting to sort it all out and the fine will be coming from his pockets. Which, as we know, are actually not that deep.'

'Unfortunately what you're saying all makes sense,' I concede unhappily.

'I'm afraid that is Lamek's reading of things. And mine, my friend. You've got a battle on your hands if you want to hold onto that boat. It's one or the other. Either they get the boat or they get to see you – and by association John Fleming – squirm whilst they turn the knife and hammer you with duties and penalties. The fact that you've done nothing wrong is, as you can see, irrelevant.'

'DIA.' [Dis is Africa].

I see it all too clearly. Customs and the judge are the sidewinder. John is the gecko. And I'm the bait. The curious, ignorant little ant. It's a sneaky trick indeed and if Anton is correct I certainly never saw this coming. In the end they'll get the ant but not the gecko.

'Precisely. These guys have a grudge to settle.'

'We'll have to dig in for the long haul then,' I say with feeling.

'If you've got the energy for it.' Anton reinforces this statement. 'If you've got the energy for it.'

'It's a case of having come too far to give up now,' I say tightly.

'I've heard that before too.'

'Well, thanks for the info, Anton. Let's keep in touch.'

'I will. We want to see the *Pelican* back in Malawi. I've got ideas – projects – that she could be used for which will make you and the family a good income.'

Talk about deflated. I decide to ring Cintura immediately. To my surprise he answers straight away. He's official and unfriendly. Yes, he's been in contact with the judge and everything is now in the hands of the judge. No he can't, won't, give me any further information save to say that we must now liaise with the judge going forward. Ringing off, it's clear that Anton and Lamek are right. Sure enough, less than 24 hours later a five-page fax comes through setting out the judge's order, which is dated 12 September 2006. Cintura had confirmed that he had given the judge the sworn statement made by John and me. But he's done nothing to help clarify things and sort the mess out. Rather he's shaken the hornets' nest. Over on the coast, I visualise Judge Miagre Morgado sitting in an office with sea breezes and oceanic views looking at the papers emanating from tiny Metangula and Lichinga in the hinterland and deciding to have some fun. Let's not look too closely at the facts. Rather let's squeeze some money out of these rich boat owners. Not just for Nacala Provincial Customs and Cintura, but also for me personally.

After several pages of administrative waffle, and absolutely no reference along the way to the facts set out in our sworn statement, the judge imposes duties and a fine totalling MTn10,475,000. The 'n' is important. On 1$^{st}$ July 2006, less than two and a half months previously, Mozambique redenominated its currency, the metical, by removing three zeros. Between the beginning of July and the end of 2006 the country was in a transitional phase when both the old and the new meticais could be used. The new currency was abbreviated to MTn. Under the old currency MT1 million was roughly equivalent to $40 which would make the current duties and fine around $419. Using the new MTn however, the amount came to $419,000, many times the estimated value of the *Pelican*. Clearly a complete nonsense, and I'm told this level of fine cannot be imposed by a judge in a provincial Customs court. Clearly the judge is confused, along with everyone else in the country. The Mozambicans think that the metical has actually appreciated hugely against other currencies, so trade around the lake has become somewhat fraught as they try to charge these new inflated prices for timber and other commodities. They believe that their President is very clever and overnight they are all going to become mega millionaires. There must be a good book, a comedy of the absurd, in all this.

We have an intermediary called Wilfrid in Nacala. He tries but fails to get any sense out of the judge or the court. $419 we'll pay in a heartbeat, but I doubt very much that the judge intended letting us off so lightly. We can't wait until the judge comes to his senses. The Order is vague and says that we have '10 to 15 days' from the date of receipt to lodge an appeal. We ask Wilfrid to lodge an appeal and fax him a letter signed by John in which he confirms that he is no longer chartering the *Pelican* and has no financial or other interest in the boat. The hope is that this will help free us from the negativity associated with him and his Niassa Project.

Over nine months go by. We make no progress. The judge is playing the long game and it's like holding an eel by the tail and trying to get it to swim through a hoop. There's always a reason why he cannot deal with our appeal. He's in Maputo. He's sick. He's on vacation. He's got a busy court schedule and cannot fit our appeal in.

The family and I dig in. We refuse to give up. I think of Harrison Ford as the tormented Allie Fox in the film version of Paul Theroux's unsettling book, 'Mosquito Coast.' There are no comparisons at all on a factual level, but I am starting to wonder if my bloody-minded refusal to accept reality and head for an easier life is not too dissimilar to Allie Fox. Are we actually heading towards greater disaster by continuing to pursue things?

Just when I'm starting to believe that the murk is never ending, something unexpected happens.

Very occasionally in life you meet a truly outstanding human being. I've mentioned Severiano Molande from Help Age International, who acted as interpreter and friend to the Surrey Police team and later for all of us at the trial. He is one member of this elite company of delightful and exceptional human beings. Angelo is another.

In mid-2007 I asked a friend who headed up an international company if he had any good, reliable contacts in Mozambique. He promptly put me in contact with Angelo, a Portuguese agronomist based in Niassa Province. To this day I've never met Angelo face to face. I initially contacted him by phone when we spoke at length as I outlined the situation to him. I then emailed him and also copied wads of papers and couriered them over to him.

I first get an inkling that I am dealing with someone extraordinary when he comes back with questions. Really good questions that indicate he has listened and read through everything and thought about the unhappy state of affairs. He sympathises with us and understands our predicament. He seems affronted by the actions of all these officials, and he's prepared to take things on. He warns me that lengthy frustrations lie ahead and my best attribute during the trying months ahead will be patience. I'm going to need heaps of it. 'Do nothing.' That's actually a lot harder than one might think.

Angelo, it seems, is not fazed by having to drive for eight hours through pristine miombo woodland on lumpy dirt and broken tar roads to get to the harbour town of Nacala on the east coast. In 2007 this area was a magnificent, forested wilderness. As I write it is being ripped apart by illegal logging, hundreds of containers filled with hardwoods being shipped across the Indian Ocean to China.

Angelo makes several sorties to Nacala late in 2007 and I assume that he will stop in early 2008 once the rains are in full swing when the roads will change from bad to truly appalling. Not a bit of it. Angelo continues his trips to the Customs Court. At first he is ignored, brushed off and left kicking his heels. He is diplomatic and persistent and eventually the message gets through. He's one of their own and he's not going away. He forges a working relationship bordering on camaraderie with the court registrar, and in due course with the judge. Then he gets the story.

The judge acknowledges that the case should never have been brought to his court. We have actually done nothing wrong. We have all the paperwork that could be required of us. But he has been put under pressure by Customs in Niassa Province and as a result he made his order. He is not going to lose face and admit this by rescinding the order. He is not going to let us off scot-free. So the good news is that he will agree to the fine being paid calculated at the old currency rate. The 'n' could be treated as an administrative error, so we owe just $419. Happy days.

However, there's the inevitable sting in the tail. Not that onerous from a financial viewpoint but it leaves a bad taste in my mouth. To put his signature to the order releasing the *Pelican* the judge expects to receive $2,500. In cash. Directly. No government receipt.

I think about my stubborn refusal to grease palms. Perhaps I could have quietly offered a nice sweetener to Vilanculos in Metangula. 'What would you suggest is a suitable amount, Mr Vilanculos, for all your valuable time and effort?' But the reality was that even if I had been so inclined, there was no such opportunity. Vilanculos had left early on the day after our acrimonious meeting for Lichinga where he had then filed his 'report.' Now I had reached an impasse. If we ever wanted the *Pelican* back I had absolutely no choice but to pay off the judge.

In late March 2008 a reliable 'runner' is sent to Nacala with an envelope stuffed with American dollars. A few days later, on the 31 March, Angelo emails me.

'This is really the end!!!! LOL!!! Find attached the official docs I have received from Customs court in Nacala.'

I pick up Angelo's email, very appropriately on April Fools Day, and respond immediately.

'This is absolutely great – fantastic – news. Thank you so much! We are all go here and getting things together [in readiness to go to Metangula]. I actually cannot believe that after all this time you have succeeded!'

An hour later Angelo responds.

'I told [you] it was only a matter of time but time going by was the only thing you could see [when] we started this epic journey. The Gods at Olympus should be proud of us!!! You need to thank yourself for keeping cool on the most difficult moments because others would have given up!! ... Will keep in touch.'

It's been a long nine months. Angelo has plugged away at things with quiet but persistent diplomacy à la Kissinger, plying his way backwards and forwards. We have a long chat about a month later. I know he will be offended at an offer of money for his time and effort. I offer him something intangible and invaluable. The sincere and heartfelt thanks of the entire family. We extend our best wishes and hope he will come and visit us sometime. Anytime. Perhaps in due course a trip on the *Pelican*?

CHAPTER 23

# LIES

It's early December, 1997. Christmas is coming and everyone's confused. Who is going where and what shall we do? It seems indecent to celebrate Christmas after all this tragedy and no one is in the mood. We're dreading it. Understandably my parents cannot face the prospect of coming back to Africa. After the trauma of Jamie following on the back of Andrew and Caroline's deaths, Karen naturally wants to be around her family. I'm torn in different directions and basically it's a mess. And about to get messier.

Thursday, 11th December. The news comes through to me from Dad who has had a call from the Foreign Office in London. All three convicts have escaped from Tête prison. There are no details. The Mozambicans are being cagey about how it happened.

There's complete disbelief bordering on denial. It's a huge blow for the families. We'd all had a form of closure. In just six months the seemingly impossible had been achieved. The identification, capture, trial, sentencing and imprisonment of the three primary criminals. We had been so much 'luckier' than the families of Helen Smith and Julie Ward who had battled decades of government obfuscation, corruption and utter incompetence aimed at ensuring that any form of justice eluded them. And would for eternity.

A week passes. The Mozambicans release no details about the escape or their efforts to recapture the men. Dad writes to the Foreign Office with a suggested text for a local press release offering a reward of £5,000 for information leading to the recapture of any of the killers. The Surrey police team are rattled and upset. They put what pressure they can on their contacts in Tête – Andissene Silveira, the Provincial police commandant, and Artur Filipe, the PIC man. The escape makes a mockery of all that has gone before. The joint investigations, the capture of the killers and the well-staged trial. Coming less than two months after sentencing I'm convinced that someone has tipped them off about our request to have them relocated to Machava, the maximum security prison in Maputo. One or two escaping could be seen as highly suspicious. All three, and only these three, escaping at the same time, is a set up. Ex-civil war guerrillas are not ex-friends. Bonds formed fighting in a bloody bush war over many years don't simply evanesce overnight. There's an intricate and tight web of fighters who will want to do whatever they can to help their former comrades in arms by greasing palms and applying pressure in the right places. It just takes a prison guard to briefly leave his post unmanned and gates temporarily unlocked. Or perhaps it's simpler than that. Perhaps the plan throughout was to enable these men to escape. Probably after a suitable period of time when the dust had fully settled. My request to have them transferred has put a spanner in the works. It would be most unlikely that any ex-RENAMO fighter or sympathiser would have any clout to help the bandits if they are moved to Maputo.

In early 1998, a message comes through. The Commander in Chief of the Mozambican Police, no less, is proud and pleased to advise the local press that all three killers have been recaptured. Well that's certainly good news. Extremely good news. Problem solved. Except that to my ears, it sounds far too good to be true.

If you've lived in Africa long enough you learn to place a lot of trust in intuition and not believe everything that you are told. There's an endearing yet infuriating trait that oftentimes forms part of the African psyche. Or at least that seems to be the case in this corner of Africa. It is that they really want to please. If I ask the mechanic if the car is fixed, or the carpenter if he's finished the chair, he'll nod and reply amiably, probably with a big beam on his face, 'Inde.' Yes. He'll tell you what he thinks you want to hear. When the car grinds to a halt down the road with a seized engine, or you sit on the chair and it collapses under you, he won't laugh. In fact he'll be mortified and come rushing to your aid saying 'Pepani. Pepani. Pepani.' Sorry, sorry, sorry. When confronted, he'll simply shrug and make an excuse. Any old excuse will do. His affirmation of job done has nothing to do with the truth and everything to do with expectation. The response that 'the car isn't ready to drive because actually the seal on the oil filter is damaged' or 'I only had one screw left for the last chair leg instead of the required four' isn't likely to please, so it's the wrong answer. You learn quickly that it pays to be a little sceptical and to check.

Dad follows up the Police Chief's pronouncement with a letter to the Foreign Office asking what the position is regarding the now urgent transfer of the recaptured prisoners to Machava. He also asks what has happened about the capture of the Moatize Two who supplied the guns and fatigues. The message comes back in early March that the Mozambican Minister of the

Interior agrees that the prisoners should be transferred and he will take this up with the Justice Ministry. The police in Têle are apparently still searching for the two men accused of supplying the guns and ammunition, but we know this is nonsense. As my mole in Têle had confirmed a long time ago, one of the two men, the senior ranking army officer, had been moved from Têle to Maputo a long time ago.

We wait. Just over two months later, in mid-May 1998, dad receives a letter from the Africa Desk of the FCO to say that the Mozambican Director of Provincial Prisons has said that the prisoners would not be moved and he was not prepared to discuss the matter further. We should rest assured that the two guards involved in the original escape by the killers have been detained. Basically, everything is in order and we should now leave well alone.

Detective Superintendent Brian Woodfield, it seems clear to me, is a seriously good detective. He's a veteran who has witnessed deception, duplicity, and deceit and seen all the myriad ways that human beings carry out very nasty deeds on each other. You might think that it should make him rather cynical, although I have never seen anything resembling that in him. But he does have a highly developed, healthy sense of suspicion when it comes to believing certain storylines and statements. This is one. Even if it is offered by the Chief of the Mozambican Police.

His misgivings are backed up by the FCO. From his network of discreet contacts, the resident spook at the BHC in Maputo is hearing a different story about the recapture of the killers. They need someone reliable on the ground who can verify the situation. Brian arranges a trip to Têle to touch base with his Mozambican police contacts and with his interpreter, the thoroughly decent Severiano from Help Age International. Upon arrival on the ground, it takes him no time at all to find out that the Mozambicans having been lying. They have recaptured only one of the escapees, Ernesto Ferro, the ex-FADM corporal. Now we know why the Director of Provincial Prisons did not want to move the prisoners and instead had tried to draw a line in the sand. He couldn't move the prisoners because he didn't have them, at least two of them.

It's easy to pinpoint when all co-operation by the Mozambicans at all levels ceased. It was the day the great lie was found out. Rather than apologise, redouble their efforts, renew co-operation, they moved rapidly in the opposite direction and put up a big wall of silence. Reciprocity became a thing of the past. Dad's local MP, James Arbuthnot, put his best foot forward and wrote to the then Foreign Secretary, Robin Cook, who in turn asked the Minister for Foreign Affairs, Baroness Symons, to respond on his behalf. Baroness Symons said that the BHC in Maputo was raising the case regularly with the Mozambican Ministry of Foreign Affairs, the Minister of the Interior and the Minister of Justice, the Commissioner of Police and the Governor of Tête Province. Yet all these efforts at obtaining information were met with platitudes and promises from the Mozambican side. Even from a distance it seemed clear that the Mozambicans were doing a Pontius Pilate and trying to wash their hands of the whole affair.

Just before we close out the year, on the 29th December 1998, we get a message from the BHC in Maputo. They have received a short, tardy communication from the Governor of Tête to say that Ernesto Ferro died in hospital on 15 November 1998. My mole subsequently tells me that after being recaptured, Ferro had been savagely beaten by the prison guards, his bones broken, leaving him crippled. I wonder if his crime was escaping or allowing himself to be recaptured? I am closer to some form of acceptance, perhaps even forgiveness, for these murderers now that I have had the benefit of some time and distance to look at things from another viewpoint. Reflecting on that well-worn phrase about man's inhumanity to man, I find that I am sick to my stomach at all the lies and deceits. And this. The cruel and violent ending of another life. I surprise myself with some silent tears for this lowly corporal. And for a life so devastatingly wasted.

CHAPTER 24

# A MIRACLE

Friday, 28th April 2000. We have renewed hope. We have the expectation that a real miracle is going to take place. In the background, the lively, uplifting melodies from Vivaldi's 'Four Seasons' fill the room. There's a lot of green material. Hospital green.

Karen has spent three long months in the UK, mostly on her own in a small rented apartment. There's a limit to how much time you can fill ringing friends, staying with them, having lunch or coffee with them. A sizeable chunk of time has been spent visiting a pregnancy clinic and the hospital in Guildford for seemingly never-ending scans, tests and check-ups. Visits laden with apprehension and nervous smiles. Would she walk away in relief, in the clear for another week, or be whisked off to theatre to undergo an emergency caesarean? Today, though, all that waiting is over. Everything is going according to a plan, without trauma or undue anxiety.

The consultant obstetrician performing the caesarean

is a smiley woman in her early forties who positively radiates competence. How does she greet each day? I assume with a big smile as she brings life after life into the world. Around 11:30 in the morning, from behind the short-cropped curtain where I am sitting at the head of the bed quietly talking to Karen, I see her pass a small crumpled form to a theatre nurse. A few moments later Vivaldi is totally drowned out by a loud, strident bawling.

'It's a girl,' the consultant says as she lifts her mask away from her mouth and smiles. 'And sounds like a very healthy one!'

We already know our daughter by the name we have chosen for her: Kate. Despite the long build-up, the waiting and all the preparations, we're still taken by surprise, afraid to believe that this is really happening. After all the tragedy of the last few years, neither of us had dared hope, much less expect, something so extraordinarily wonderful to enter our lives. On this date three years ago we were saying goodbye to Andrew and Caroline and the world was crashing around us. It's certainly poignant, yet very fitting, that we are now celebrating new life, and renewed hope in the future, with the appearance of Kate. At least we certainly will be once her arrival has sunk in properly.

En famille

Mum and Dad in happier times - boat safari on the Zambezi River

Don and Anita after the investiture at Buckingham Palace, May 2004

With Karen

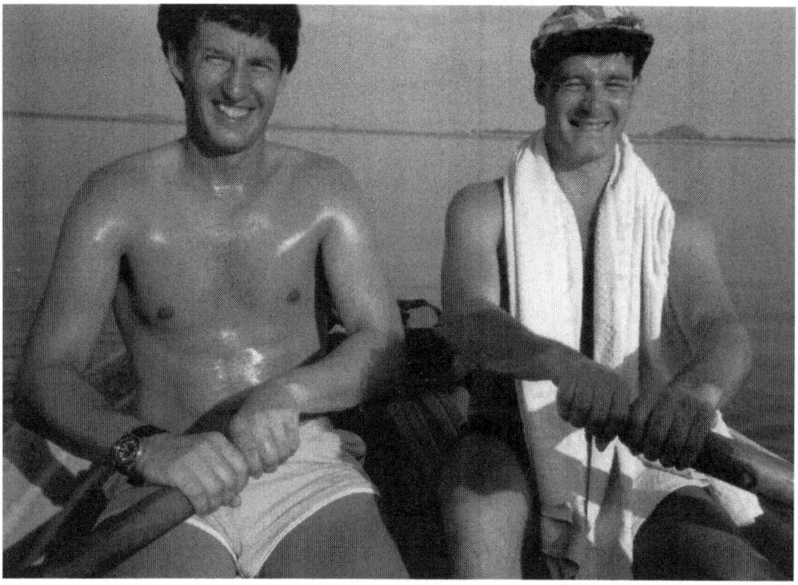

Rowing a boat on Lake Malawi. Something has raised a good laugh!

Karen

CHAPTER 25

# Dead ends

Dad has continued to press the FCO for information. He believes, rightly in my opinion, that the only way to get results now is through a reward offered in the local and regional newspapers and on the radio. He refers to the case of Jill Dando, the British TV personality and newsreader, whose family offered a reward for information leading to Jill's killer or killers. In this case we are a step ahead. We can post photographs of known killers. We just want to know where they are. Caroline's father, Edmund, adds his weight to things in November 1999 and his local MP, Tim Yeo, confirms that he has asked Robin Cook to "personally convey to the Mozambican Authorities as a matter of urgency, the concern of the British Government about their handling of the matter. If we do not get a satisfactory reply from the Foreign Office, I am prepared to raise this matter on the floor of the House of Commons on your behalf."

It appears that no amount of communication or pressure is going to persuade the Mozambicans to co-operate. Their police are unwilling to pursue any proposals for advertisements and radio announcements. They cite a flood of misinformation by people trying to turn in relatives and friends to claim the reward. How this could be the case, given that the identity of the killers is known, no one can fathom. It's a poor attempt at a red herring.

A year goes by. The MP for my parents' constituency, James Arbuthnot, adds his voice to that of Tim Yeo and also writes to the Foreign Secretary.

Less than two weeks after the birth of Kate, on the 9th May 2000, I am catapulted back into the fray. I now have these two conflicting sides to my life: the shining light for the future that is Kate, and the brooding shadows of the past that continually threaten to catch up and overwhelm me. A meeting is held in London with Baroness Patricia Scotland, the new Minister of Foreign Affairs. Dad, Edmund and I find ourselves in a room opposite the Houses of Parliament in Westminster. We sit around a large table with Baroness Scotland, her Permanent Secretary and a representative from the FCO. I'm surrounded by a surfeit of wood. A very large wooden table and chairs. Ancient wooden panelling and floor. Wooden beams. Perhaps all in the main provided courtesy of Henry VIII's oak forests. I don't know.

The concerns expressed by Edmund, my father and me revolve around the lack of communication and progress by the Mozambican authorities. Using the bush telegraph and the police's network of informants would surely help in locating the two missing prisoners – as it had in their original location and capture – but the reality is that these convicts have sympathisers and friends, blood brothers, and as a result the police are not motivated. Only pressure applied at the very highest level now is likely to render results. For me that means the President of Mozambique leaning hard on the Governor sitting in his pink mansion and so on down so that each level in the hierarchy can be made to understand that protecting the prisoners is not in their interests and they should use their contacts and redouble their efforts. Dad is convinced that reward advertisements will render results.

Baroness Scotland appears genuine in her concern and intimates that she has herself had to deal with personal tragedy, so she understands and sympathises with us. But the borders around Tête into Malawi, Zimbabwe and Zambia are very porous. The killers could be almost anywhere. It's like trying to find two needles in a monstrously large haystack. I take her point. However, it's already been done once, so surely it can be done again?

By the end of the meeting I am more despondent about locating the killers than I have ever been. Stripping away all the diplomacy, I know that in the nicest possible way we are being told that our chances of getting a good result are extremely slim and that we should think about moving on. Reading between the lines, the Mozambicans have lost interest and motivation and rekindling the hunt is going to be virtually impossible. Their Chief of Police has lost face, having been found out as a brazen liar. The loss of his integrity is reflected down the line.

The Baroness offers to send her vice consul in Maputo up to Tête to try to find out what is going on, and she is as good as her word. I can at least congratulate myself for being magnanimous in the face of my despair and deep frustration laced with a good dollop of bitterness. Writing to the Baroness a short while later, I thanked her for her 'involvement and commitment' and she had the good grace to write back to thank me for my kind words and reiterate that she would continue to press the Mozambican authorities. But I knew in my heart at this point in time that it was probably all over.

In August 2000 the vice consul duly met with Andissene, the

now elderly Provincial head of the Police in Tête and other senior police officers. He even met with the head of Army Intelligence in Southern Malawi. He spoke to border police and immigration and handed out photos everywhere he could think of. He basically tried to refresh memories and breathe new life into the hunt. The new police chief, Superintendent Banda in Tête, offers a single crumb of information. There was in fact only one guard responsible for the men's escape, and he was presently residing as an inmate of the prison. The vice consul made an offer of "whatever resources were needed to assist", which the new Governor, Senor Tomas Mandlate, curtly turned down saying that resources were not the issue and "the Mozambicans would provide whatever was necessary to pursue justice." Essentially a big fat nothing.

Dad does not want me to get involved. He worries, unnecessarily in my view, that living very nearby in Malawi and pressing for the remaining killers' recapture, Karen or I might somehow be a target for these men on the run. So whilst we liaise, the communications and pressure are seen to be coming from him. He also expresses his haunting, grief-stricken thoughts. 'You have a life still to live. Mine is nearly over. My wish is that I could have exchanged my life for Andrew's.' Parents shouldn't outlive their children, and he would never shake off the feelings of guilt at still being alive whilst his son and daughter in law's brief lives were over.

Over the next three years dad pushed doggedly on. He pressed the FCO for information. The FCO pursued the BHC in Maputo, who duly raised the matter with the incumbent Minister of the Interior, who in turn chased up the Head of Criminal Investigations in Tête. The standard response came back down the line. 'We are actively following leads, but nothing to report at this time.'

Dad still wanted to go down the reward advertisement route, and he brought this up again and again. He referred to the 2001 case of a torso wearing orange shorts found in the River Thames. A very young black male whom the Metropolitan Police call Adam. It turned out to be connected to trafficking and Nigerian voodoo. A big reward was offered and leads came in and were chased down. Even President Mandela put in a personal plea for information. We know now that a decade went by and the culprits were never identified.

The Mozambicans continued to steadfastly refuse to allow the posting of a reward for information. Dad and I gave consideration to posting our own private 'Wanted' ad offering a reward to any individual or individuals turning the killers in to the police, but we quickly realised that this could lead to all sorts of complications. Large numbers of the Mozambican police and army might become distracted from their real jobs. I imagined the region turning into a sort of Wild West with a vast, ragtag array of bounty hunters roaming the land. Whoever found the killers might struggle to keep their bounty or themselves alive long enough to claim the reward. One could hardly say 'Wanted, Dead or Alive.' Next up in court would be dad and I, for having effectively put up a reward for their murders.

In August 2004, nearly four years after our meeting with Baroness Scotland, I was racing against the clock to get back to the UK. Mum had rung to say that Dad was critically ill and on life support. He was alive when I arrived at the hospital, but in an induced coma. In his twenties Dad had served in the British Army in Burma where he contracted hepatitis which, it seemed, had now manifested itself in the form of cirrhosis of the liver, which in turn had led to complications including severe bleeding in his oesophagus and stomach. Mum and I knew that he had not been well for several years, but he had refused to seek help. It seemed he felt that whatever was coming could come and take him away. He was a gentleman, in both senses, and was heartbroken that Andrew and Caroline's lives should have been brought to such a senseless end. Death for a cause where one accepts the risks, say in the line of duty when serving in Northern Ireland or the Middle East, would have been tragic but more tolerable. He was a doting father, immeasurably proud of his younger son. For the light to be extinguished for the grubbiest motive of all – money – was simply more than he could bear. He had tried and tried so hard to smile and remember a jovial, happy young man with lots of plans for the future, but the pain and bitter sorrow of Andrew's loss constantly threatened to overwhelm him. The bleak reality is that the dead never leave us. We have to learn how to live both with and without them.

For forty-eight hours the doctors and surgeons pondered their options to save Dad, or at least bring him out of the induced coma, whilst the nurses worked around the clock. They were quite simply outstanding. Eventually they had to accept that there were no options left. The day before my birthday, on 21st August 2004, the life support machines were switched off and Dad slipped away. For the following months, at home with Karen, who was working overtime providing support and comfort, and a four-year-old daughter pulling me into her beautiful, uncomplicated world, where danger lay in the realms of imaginary witches and dragons, his loss nevertheless threatened to overwhelm me. Dad had known and understood me almost better than anyone and more than anything it was the fact of being deprived of the opportunity to say goodbye that ate me up inside. His stone marker on top of Andrew and Caroline's grave summed up his private, unvoiced wish: 'At peace with his son.' I would have liked to add the words 'No longer tormented by grief.' Some years later I was helping mum do a clear out. I opened a large drawer at the bottom of dad's work bureau and discovered it packed with files and A4 envelopes bursting with papers. Absolutely everything relating to the murders was stashed there, including the copious correspondence that Dad had embarked upon in a dogged but doomed endeavour to organise the recapture of the escaped killers.

Mum has done what mums the world over do: pressed on with Churchillian stoicism. But Andrew's ethereal presence, sometimes benign, sometimes overbearing, sits squarely on her shoulders, accompanying her everywhere.

CHAPTER 26

# PING-PONG

Monday, 7th April 2008. Early morning. Stephen is shaking me gently. I surface slowly, groggy and momentarily disorientated.

'Are we there?' I croak.

'I just popped my head out. The coast is closing fast. Perhaps another fifteen minutes.'

He heads up the steel ladder out of the hold, a stifling metal storage compartment that has been fitted out with bunk beds for the crew's quarters. I swing my legs off the bed and clamber up the ladder to join him on deck. The sun has just topped the approaching mountain peaks, catching our battered old tug steadily chugging along over a smooth, velvety sea. Amidships, Captain William Chamba fills his tiny wheelhouse, deep-set dark brown eyes under a battered captain's hat and the remains of a self-made rolled cigarette hanging from his mouth. He is the picture of an old sea dog, his leathery face creased with chiselled lines, his large, callused hands holding the wheel spokes with a light touch.

'Did you get any sleep?' I ask.

'Barely. It felt as though I woke up more or less as soon as I fell asleep.'

'We've probably managed about four hours. Not as bad as it feels.' I jiggle my arms and raise each knee to my chest to waken up my body.

'Are we ready for this? Is it going to be another battle?' Stephen asks almost rhetorically as he peers towards the approaching coastline.

'Who knows what Chirinsa and Customs will dream up?' I reply. My jaw spontaneously clenches and I voice my resolve. 'All I can say is that this time we're going to win. We are going to beat these buggers at their own game.'

'I'd drink to that if it weren't quite so early,' Stephen responds in his usual cheery manner.

I had last seen Chirinsa in September 2006 when I had driven to Lichinga to meet with John Fleming with the aim of enlisting Mr Fast Track Cintura's help in dealing with the Customs Court. Knowing that the *Pelican* had broken free of her anchorage in the main bay and that Chirinsa had flailed around organising a rescue, Drew and I had popped down to Metangula to check on the condition of her hull. We had had to pay Chirinsa 650 US dollars for rescuing the boat. Chirinsa had then sat and machinated. He had plenty of time to do this. We anticipated that he would perhaps be a little nervous about our arrival, but in the main his greedy fingers would be twitching. He had had the frustration of a valuable asset sitting in his jurisdiction and he would want to extract some more money from us. There was little to be gained from licences and inspections of the little wooden fishing vessels in his domain. If he tried his luck with the local fishermen they would either laugh at him or more probably fillet him alive.

I had spent the best part of the last twenty months being the model of patience. I had stayed super patient whilst Angelo had quietly worked his magic on the judge over in Nacala so that we could get the release order. But by June 2007, just ten months after the rescue, Chirinsa had concocted a new scheme. Reversing prior statements, he now asserted that because the *Pelican* was in his jurisdiction she was therefore his responsibility. He summarily dismissed our watchmen – whose main job had been to bail out the water from the leaking prop shaft in the engine compartment once a week – and took the keys off them. Then he sat back and waited to collect his fee for 'care and control.' For over six months the *Pelican* lay abandoned, the locals oblivious to the fact that she was floating lower and lower in the water. Then, in January 2008, she sank. Chirinsa's worst fears had been realised, and he had another panic. I imagine him tottering around like an African version of Poirot, except in his case totally clueless, flapping his arms aimlessly as he frantically tried to organise another rescue, this time the *Pelican's* resurrection from out of her watery grave. He commandeered pumps, pulleys, petrol and people. All without success.

It was Captain Lamek of the MV *Ilala* who had alerted me to the fact that the *Pelican* had sunk. At first I had been sceptical, as a previous similar claim had proven to be false. But Lamek had assured me that unfortunately this time it really was true. He had seen for himself.

From my point of view, there was no point in rushing over to initiate a rescue until we had sorted out the situation with the Customs Court in Nacala. If we failed to get the order impounding the *Pelican* reversed, then the bay would become her permanent grave. Only if we succeeded in getting the order reversed would we make the attempt to rescue her.

We had left the farm the day before, Sunday 6th April 2008,

nearly four years after the adventure with the Pelican first began. Calling in at the harbour at Monkey Bay on the drive north, we had picked up two employees from Malawi Lake Services, Captains Nyoka and Gella Anderson, together with an assortment of equipment which included a large red fire pump nicknamed 'Lady Godiva', which was to prove extremely fickle and temperamental.

Some two hundred and fifty kilometres and a further five hours further north we arrived at Nkhotakota, a small lakeside town just over a third of the way up the western lakeshore. In the second half of the nineteenth century this ancient town had been at the heart of the Arab slave trade in the region, until a Christian mission was established there. Around sixty kilometres from Nkhotakota on the far side of the lake lay our destination: Metangula and the *Pelican*. We had arranged to link up here with a tugboat, the *Thyolo*, which was on her way south to Monkey Bay to undergo repairs and maintenance. The idea was that she would do a quick excursion across the lake to tow the *Pelican* back. Assuming of course that we could re-float her. The *Thyolo* was actually an ancient fishing vessel which had sat on the lake bed at Monkey Bay for well over a decade. When the concession to run the harbours and associated large passenger and cargo vessels around the lake had passed out of the hands of the government to a new private entity, Malawi Lake Services, or MLS for short, the managing director of MLS had resurrected the old tub, renovated her and reassigned her to a new and somewhat precarious life pulling another refloated vessel, a thirty-ton barge, between the Malawi mainland and Likoma Island on the eastern side of the lake. It's a distance of some sixty-five kilometres over a very exposed part of the lake where the depth is often in excess of four hundred metres. The barge became a lifeline for the islanders, ferrying over passengers and an assortment of commodities such as fertilizer, maize, cement and building materials.

The lake is very shallow at Nkhotakota. so the *Thyolo* is anchored about two hundred metres offshore. She has no tender. To get to her we have to barter with the local fishermen to hire their small wooden boats. The transfer of the equipment is a nervy process, complicated because it has to be carried out in the dark as it is now gone seven in the evening. There's Lady Godiva and the sundry chains, suction pipes and equipment plus a 250-litre barrel of diesel – the fuel for the return trip across the lake. If any of this falls into the lake, our mission will be over before it has barely started.

Stephen and I leave the fishermen and crew of the *Thyolo* to manage the operation. adopting the 'que sera sera' approach. Frankly, we are mystified as to how some of these items are going to be hauled from a bobbing little fishing vessel up onto the deck of the tugboat. Across the water we can hear shouting and bashing, but more importantly, we never hear a splash.

With the equipment transfers completed, we get a ride across and wait. The lake crossing will take around five hours and there is no point arriving at Metangula in the middle of the night, so we lie on deck staring up at the stars, munching biscuits and chatting in muted tones. We're relieved that the *Thoylo* is on time for the rendezvous and the equipment transfers have been without mishap.

The lake is sleeping, a motionless and barren membrane of inky black nothingness stretching away into the immense African night. At this single moment in time I find myself amazed but content to be a part of it.

As we motor into the main 'Ilala Bay' at Metangula, it's unusually quiet. It's a National Holiday – Women's Day – and the locals are enjoying a slow start before putting on their glad rags for the forthcoming parade and speeches. We get our passports stamped at the immigration office and meet the newest head of Customs, Mr Inacio. He's mighty surprised to see us, as the original Court Order for the release of the *Pelican* arrived on his desk barely twenty-four hours earlier. He rings Chirinsa at the Marine Department, who drives down in a battered pickup truck. Stephen and I jump in the back and he takes us up to his offices, where we sit around a new addition to his office furniture, a large, square dining table. We all smile cordially at each other. Here we are again. Here we go again. I wonder, somewhat uneasily, what Chirinsa has dreamt up for us this time around.

'Good to see you again, Mr Chirinsa.' I give him a tight, polite smile which he acknowledges with his usual slow nod before responding.

'I was not expecting to see you so soon.'

'Now that the Order for the release of the Pelican has been made by the judge I'm sure you can understand that we are anxious to get the boat back to Malawi as soon as possible.'

'So you have come to make a plan. I regret that you are going to find the boat is not in a good situation.'

'I understand that she has now sunk.' I want to add 'thanks to your greed and incompetence' but that of course will not help our cause. I wait to see if Chirinsa is going to say anything about the sinking, but he merely stares at me and then slowly blinks like an owl before stating the obvious.

'You will need to bring a lot of equipment for the salvage. When are you expecting to come back for that operation?'

Stephen is getting impatient and now jumps in. 'We intend to start that operation immediately,' he says. 'We have brought equipment with us and a tug to tow the *Pelican* once she is afloat again.'

Chirinsa's brow furrows. This he had not anticipated.

'I'm concerned that the Marine Department will be held responsible if anything goes wrong with a private salvage operation in my jurisdiction. If someone is injured,' he ventures.

Like Stephen, I'm now losing patience. It is rapidly becoming clear that now that Customs' hands were tied and they had no option but to abide by the terms of the Release Order, Chirinsa saw this as his opportunity to be Mr Bad Guy and squeeze some money out of us. I suspect he is going to angle for the Marine Department to do the recovery and claim some salvage rights. He has no shame, and the fact that Chirinsa is responsible for the *Pelican* sinking in the first place will not deter him. My move.

'And I'm concerned for you and your department. If you get involved in this operation and something happens, then of course you will be held personally responsible.'

Chirinsa chews on this for a few seconds. 'I will have to contact the Naval Base Commander in order to obtain his consent to the salvage as the boat is in waters which fall under his jurisdiction.'

Chirinsa has unwittingly just pulled the rug from under himself by now declaring that the *Pelican* is not in fact in his jurisdiction. And it's absolute bunkum. We all know that the boat is well outside the naval base – there is a fence line going down to the water's edge marking the limits of the naval base. When we first proposed mooring the *Pelican* in the bay where she is now resting with just the superstructure poking above the surface of the water, Chirinsa himself had been at pains to point this boundary out and tell us that under no circumstances should we moor anywhere inside that fence line. I nod and turn to Inacio. Time to take control.

'Before Mr Chirinsa goes over to the naval base, I just need to be clear that so far as Customs are concerned you have no issues regarding the removal of the boat back to Malawi.'

Inacio grins. This is easy. He gets to be Mr Nice Guy.

'No problems. We have the court order. When you complete the salvage you are free to take the boat away.'

Chirinsa tootles off in his pickup with Inacio, ostensibly to find the Naval Base commander. I look out of the window at the beckoning lake and imagine the *Pelican* being towed across her glinting surface, breaking free of the sticky clutches of these greedy officials and disappearing towards that promising horizon. That is what we came to do and that is what I am determined we will do. I spot our mooring platform, complete with buoyancy drums. I must remember to ask Lamek to arrange for it to be taken down and loaded on the *Ilala* the next time she calls in to the bay.

The Naval Base is a good ten minutes' drive away around the other side of the bay and I'm unclear where Chirinsa has really gone, because he's back in less than ten minutes.

'The Commander has confirmed to me that you have his permission to enter the bay where the *Pelican* is located.'

Stephen cannot resist a little dig.

'That's good of him, Mr Chirinsa. Please convey our thanks. Perhaps we can arrange to meet and thank him in person?'

We head down to the *Thyolo* and chug off round the peninsula to go and see the extent of the job that confronts us. We find the *Pelican* lying with her bow hard down and canted alarmingly to port. Essentially the whole of the hull is underwater. The wheelhouse and main cabin are flooded. Of the superstructure, only the top deck is fully above the waterline. This is our first sighting since we found out that she had sunk. It's far worse than I had imagined, and looking at Stephen I can tell he's also shocked. How on earth do we refloat her?

There's a light blue glass fibre rowing boat half submerged in the sand on the shoreline. She's pretty decrepit, leaks badly and all the fittings are missing. After bailing her out we cut a long branch from a tree and punt inexpertly from the shore to the *Thyolo*. Later in the day we will use an old climbing rope to rig up lines from the shore to the *Pelican* and the *Thyolo,* and by pulling hand over hand whilst sitting in this little craft we will use these lines to pull ourselves backwards and forwards between the vessels and the shore.

Pulling on my shorty wetsuit, I drop a scuba diving tank and buoyancy control device into the water and jump in after it. Kitted up, I go down to do a recce. We need to be sure there's no new damage below the waterline, and to get a better understanding of the lake bed and the *Pelican's* position on it.

These aren't crystal clear waters. Visibility is just a few metres and I have to be very careful not to touch or disturb the thick layer of silt sitting on the bottom. If I do, the visibility will immediately reduce to zero and we'll have to wait half an hour for the silt to settle again. I move slowly, whenever possible pulling myself around on the boat's external fittings. It's actually a cold, murky world, the main sound being the rasp of air being released through the regulator as I draw breath followed by a gurgle of bubbles as I breathe out. I'm not a big fan of freshwater. For me it's a foreboding and sterile environment, lacking the colour and vibrancy of the ocean. There are very few varieties of underwater life apart from a few species of fish, large quantities of snails and huge, smooth rocks covered in an algae slime. Below around fifteen metres there's very little light, and from twenty metres you're engulfed in blackness. Perhaps part of my unease is due to the fact that I had lost a very good friend in a freshwater quarry. There was no explaining why he had left his diving buddy, but with only a few metres of visibility you can lose someone in a heartbeat if you're not using a buddy line. He was later found floating in the darkness as if he had momentarily fallen asleep.

The two skegs at the back which would normally house the

bottoms of the rudders are all twisted and buckled, and it seems clear that they have actually done a very good job of protecting the prop shafts after the *Pelican* broke free of her anchors back in August 2006. The hull has numerous dents, but nothing that looks new or terminal. In the end my main concern is how she is actually lying. The last few metres of the bow are hanging over an almost vertical drop off. I follow this down for a few metres, but there's no sign of the bottom in the increasing gloom and no need to explore further, so I head back to the surface. I know the drop off is quite deep because the *Thyolo* is moored some twenty metres further out in the bay and William had had to let out a very long anchor line. Later, when I ferret out our 1957 chart for the area, it indicates a drop off to ten metres and then after a few more metres it drops steeply down again to over twenty metres. What we now know is that we must ensure that at no stage during the salvage operation does the *Pelican* gain any forward momentum. She could reach this little abyss very quickly, glide down and disappear for good.

Back on shore I strip down to my shorts, put some beach sandals on and Stephen and I swim over to the *Pelican*. We manage to open the rear double doors and find the water in the main cabin reaches up to our chests. On the surface there's a stagnant, greasy brew of diesel and oil which has created a super slippery film over everything we come into contact with. The saving grace is that only the main wheelhouse window has shattered; the rest of the windows are unbroken. Bits of wood and a waterlogged cushion float around us. The floor is solid beneath my feet, confirming that the engine compartment hatches are all closed. We head up to the top deck, which from here on in will act as an island HQ where we can site the pumps and equipment and manage operations. As long as the *Pelican* doesn't turn turtle on us.

How do you float nearly nineteen tons of solid steel? Stephen and I don't have the answers. Our plans will be centred around the equipment we have with us, whereas normally salvage operators will recce a problem and then work out the specific equipment required for the job. We know that our knowledge base is small and our experience is sorely lacking. We have none, so we are going to have to be inventive and flexible.

Our old boat guards, Anachio and Kaleleto, whom Chirinsa had summarily sacked in June 2007, have heard we are back and they materialise out of the trees. We hire them on the spot and ask them to arrange a team to go and retrieve the eight 1,000 litre metal barrels belonging to the *Pelican's* mooring platform which are hiding behind Chirinsa's office.

It's late afternoon by the time the barrels have been collected and lined up on the shoreline. We arrange to meet everyone at seven the following the morning. Then we trek into town to grab some fish and chips laced with peri-peri sauce and a couple of beers.

'Ping pong balls,' I say casually.

Stephen takes a swig of his beer and gives me the eye, a puzzled frown on his face. But he humours me.

'What do ping pong balls have to do with the resurrection of the *Pelican*?' he inquires.

'Well, obviously one of the hardest parts of raising any boat is sealing it. Making it nice and watertight before you pump out water or pump in air. Agreed?'

'Absolutely. Whether you're going to pump air in to displace the water because your ship is well under the waterline, or it's near the surface like the *Pelican* and you're just pumping water out. In both cases you don't want water rushing back in. Or the air seeping out.'

I grin, because Stephen loves these engineering type puzzles.

He should. He's an engineer.

'You're totally with it. Well I saw a documentary once about raising a warship. She wasn't that deep but logistically it was impossible to make the holds fully airtight. So they used special ping-pong balls. Millions of them. Sealed the holds as best they could and then dropped the balls down a tube from the surface. Up she came.'

Stephen rubs his chin in thought. I can see he's envisaging the operation.

'That's great lateral thinking. Won't help us unless you know of a massive stash of ping-pong balls nearby. But really great.'

I shrug and smile neutrally.

'It's the idea. We could buy up all the footballs in Metangula,' I say.

'Magoo, I'm not sure if you are now being serious or you've truly lost your marbles.'

'I'm thinking we need to try to think laterally to help solve our problem.'

'You're not kidding! Except I'm guessing you're short of that one crucial lateral thought we need at this point in time?'

'At this point in time,' I concede.

'Well, we have the metal barrels. We can use them. Tie say two on each side of the *Pelican* to help provide stability,' Stephen suggests. 'If we can find a good anchor point we might be able to also use them to provide buoyancy.'

'Makes sense.'

'Probably more sense than ping pong balls,' he suggests with a grin.

And so begins our equivalent of Groundhog Day. We have no definitive plan. We clutch at our natural optimism and a belief that by embracing the challenge and being flexible, trying this and then that, eventually we will have an 'aha' moment and the problem will be elegantly solved.

We exist within this repetitive time warp for the next six days. We are fully in the moment and the moment is filled with a jumble of emotions – frustration, encouragement, despair, anticipation, anger, resignation, disbelief, boredom and excitement, to name a few. Small, humble victories follow dejecting failures. We doggedly hang on in there, constantly re-evaluating, batting ideas back and forth in our quest to find the key that will eventually release the *Pelican* from the lake's smothering embrace.

CHAPTER 27

# THE LONG HAUL

*Day 1 – Tuesday, 8th April*

We are up early while the world is still grey, a light mist rising off the water. Smoke on the water. There's already a steady parade of village girls chattering and laughing as they come down to the water's edge to fill plastic buckets with water for cooking. They hoist the full buckets onto their heads, lower both arms to their sides and sway and glide back along the paths leading up the hillside to the village, all without spilling a drop. It's an exhibition in posture and graceful movement which we watch with quiet admiration as we chomp down on a breakfast comprising rolls lathered in peanut butter and pilchards washed down with tea. There's certainly nothing pretty or elegant about that.

We start by floating the steel barrels over to the *Pelican* and tying four to each side. The idea is that they will help to act as stabilisers should the boat start to tilt excessively. Our two most senior men, captains Anderson and Nyoka, are missing. Their absence is irritating, as it's fiddly work which could do with as many hands as possible. By late morning we have managed to thread some steel cables through the small eyelets on the bobbing barrels and tie them off broadsides on to the railings, four barrels each side. Next we take several heavy-duty nylon lines and tie them from the boat's stern bollards to some nearby trees to ensure that the *Pelican* cannot slip forward. Lastly we take our chain pulley with a paltry three tons lifting capacity and also attach that from the stern to a nearby tree.

Anderson, and Nyoka, slink out of the trees and emerge on the shoreline. Anderson stands quietly, looking about uncertainly. I know he's wondering how to get over to the *Pelican*, his demeanour that of the sheepish and guilty man. Nyoka flops down in the sand, head between his knees. I use our semi-submersible rowing boat, now nicknamed *Bluebell*, to get back to shore. Anderson is full of apologies and I send him off in *Bluebell* to help on the *Pelican*. At which point Nyoka wakes from his stupor and starts waving his hands about, gabbling in broken and incomplete sentences about how we should be conducting the operation. He is well and truly drunk, and I tell him to disappear and not return until he has sobered up. He eventually staggers off into the undergrowth, where I expect he will collapse and sleep it off. Later Anderson tells me that Nyoka was out into the early hours at various drinking dens sampling innumerable cartons of gin and vodka, which are priced at barely more than the cost of a beer for the same volume.

It's mid-afternoon when we decide to try an experiment. How much does the best part of nineteen tons of submerged steel actually weigh? Ideally we need to know the volume and therefore the weight of the water displaced by the *Pelican*. I'm guessing it's not as much as I hope. The boat is basically constructed of 6mm steel plate, low volume but very heavy. One litre of water weighs one kilogram. How many litres of water have been displaced by the steel? We have no clue but it doesn't take a genius to understand that steel weighs many times the equivalent weight of water for the same volume. I suspect that the weight of water displaced will be around two to three tons, leaving the partially submerged boat still weighing well over fifteen tons in the water. Still, we can't help ourselves. It's like a kid throwing a balsa wood aeroplane to watch it fly. He knows it will only fly at best for a few seconds, and it may all end in disaster, but those few seconds are truly magical and worth all the risk. We don't expect magic, though we won't say no to anything vaguely positive. We want to see if the *Pelican* will actually move at all.

The cables attached via the boat's railings to the barrels are tightened up to help maximise lift and we put the pulley to work. Within barely a minute of hauling, the block chain connected to the stern of the boat snaps.

Suddenly I'm no longer in that singular moment of hope. Clearly we are going to have to work a lot harder for our miracle, and I'm only too aware that after the best part of a full working day we are barely any further forward. My muscles ache. I'm dirty, sweaty, tired and dehydrated. Up on the hillside I can see Chirinsa's spy, Agent Glum, sitting in the shade of a large tree, watching impassively, ready when we call it a day to head off to his master and relate the day's happenings. I'm crushed by the thought that Chirinsa will be celebrating our failure, probably with a few beers. He will, I'm sure, feel a lot better knowing that he isn't the only one to fail at this resurrection business.

Tomorrow's another day. Tomorrow the result will be different.

Time for Plan B.

*Day 2 – Wednesday*

Lazaro is the one and only mechanic in the area. He splits his time between repairing vehicles and the fishermen's outboard motors. A cheerful and friendly chap, when we finally catch up with him at a garage on the outskirts of Metangula he happily hires his 3-ton pulley to us.

Back at the bay, we pay out the mooring lines on the *Thyolo* so that she drifts backwards until her stern is stationed up against the bow of the *Pelican*. We attach our pulley to one of the *Thyolo's* sternposts and then thread a new chain onto it and down through the *Pelican's* anchor slide and back up. The plan is to use the *Thyolo* to provide extra buoyancy by using the pulley to lift the bow of the *Pelican*. Then we'll have another go at hauling the *Pelican* backwards towards the shoreline.

Once again it's late morning before Anderson and Nyoka put in an appearance. Anderson uses *Bluebell* to haul himself over to the *Pelican* and explains that Nyoka had turned up at their guest house in the early hours again and kept him awake drinking and shouting incoherently. Looking over to the shore at Nyoka's swaying form and drunken commentary, it seems as though he is now more drunk than the day before. We ignore him and his insistent yells for 'the ferry' to come back and collect him. Eventually he jumps in fully clothed and thrashes his way over to the *Pelican*, lurching his way up the ladder onto the canted top deck, where he spends the best part of half an hour staggering around in his soggy clothes issuing commands that are ignored. Eventually he sits down in a corner and spews forth a forlorn soliloquy on his vast experience as a captain, class II. His experience could save the day.

Finally he staggers to the bow and hauls himself up onto the *Thyolo,* where he tries unsuccessfully to pinch the crew's lunch before haranguing the captain, William. Which is a mistake. William is old school; he believes in respect being earned by hard work and staying sober when on a ship. He doesn't appreciate Nyoka's drunken insults and meanderings and is not afraid of him. He tells the forty-year-old Nyoka straight that he is behaving like 'a stupid numata' (youth). If there is one word in the dictionary guaranteed to hit home, it is the word 'stupid'. I've seen Africans go absolutely berserk when that word is mentioned. Nyoka, however, isn't up for a fight. He slinks off below decks to sleep things off.

Back on board the *Pelican*, things take a turn for the better. As we laboriously tighten the cables attached to the barrels the *Pelican* slowly turns. Instead of being canted to port she is suddenly sitting, beam-to-beam, level. It's a small triumph, but all we need to inject us with new energy.

Stephen and I head back to shore and arrange for our band of workers to haul in on Lazamo's pulley, which is now attached to the rear of the *Pelican*. We call a halt when it's as taut as we dare to make it. We don't want this chain to snap as well. We then spend the next few hours hauling in on the pulley at the stern of the *Thyolo* and tightening all the cables and lines on the barrels until by late afternoon we have raised the *Pelican's* bow a full metre and the bow rail is sitting just below the waterline. We still need the bow to rise substantially further in order to be in with a reasonable chance of sealing the main cabin and wheelhouse windows so that we can finally make an attempt to pump her out.

The sand skirting the bay gives way to thick mud within a couple of metres of entering the lake. The *Pelican* is resting in this mud bath. We can't know how strong the suction created by this mud is, but we think it must be considerable. Hopefully raising the bow has also helped break its cloying hold on the boat.

We've all seen the occasional large yacht or cruiser being trailered around the countryside. They look so much bigger out of the water because so much of the vessel is hidden below the waterline – just like icebergs. Having dived around the *Pelican* I'm only too aware of how much of the steel superstructure and hull is sitting underwater, and even with our small victories today at this point in time it seems to me as though we have taken on mission impossible.

We have enough in the way of problems to solve and we certainly don't need any unnecessary headaches and distractions. Stephen and I agree that we must cut Nyoka loose. We can't dismiss him because he is employed by Malawi Lake Services, so we call him up out of the hold of the *Thyolo* and Stephen gives him an ultimatum. We will give him a day's food allowance and enough cash to enable him to get a lift from Metangula to Lichinga and from there to the border with Malawi, where he can then get a minibus home to Monkey Bay. If he refuses, he will be barred from the *Pelican* and *Thyolo*, will get nothing at all and will be left to fend for himself. Nyoka refuses to make any decision and is holding out for more time and more money, so Stephen says he is going to ring his boss, Captain Lamek, to advise him of the situation.

With that statement hanging in the air we work our way to the rear of the *Pelican*, jump into *Bluebell* and ferry ourselves to shore. We need Nyoka to believe that we will carry through with the threat. although in reality it is doubtful if we will be able to get a mobile signal to enable us to ring Lamek, who is probably somewhere in the middle of the lake on the *Ilala*.

However we needn't have worried. William later tells us that the threat to call Lamek has an effect on Nyoka that is nothing short of electrifying. He disappears below decks, collects a carrier bag of belongings, screams for 'the ferry' and stumbles after us.

We pay him his allowance and travel cash and never see him in the bay again.

Later we receive reports from the crew that he is still around, arguing with street vendors, slumped in bars and ditches. When the *Ilala* calls in to the main bay at Metangula on the following Saturday we give a report to Lamek on our progress and the situation with Nyoka. Subsequently we find out that Nyoka had quietly slunk on board the *Ilala* to hitch a lift home. Lamek was furious and refused him any rations. When the ship reached Monkey Bay he was dismissed. It seems he had reverted to this drunken behaviour before when working for MLS up in Tanzania and the MD, Anton, had decided to give him a second chance, which he had now blown.

We decide to decamp from the *Thyolo* and move to the Bamboo Basket Guesthouse, where we stayed on our previous visit. This meant that we would not be taking berths from the crew and we could also have something of a respite by removing ourselves from 'the operational zone.' The same sombre, quiet cook, Fredrico, is managing the place and each morning, as before, we give him cash to go down to the market and buy the ingredients for our dinner. And, as before, dinner is invariably fish fillets or usipa with chips and salad. Along with a couple of beers, the sameness of the food and drink perpetuates the Groundhog Day feeling.

*Day 3 – Thursday*

Our new ally, the mechanic Lazaro, has found us a new recruit, a jovial and muscular man called Batista. He won't know that on the other side of the world, in America, his namesake is, on and off, the world heavyweight wrestling champion. Batista shares attributes with his namesake. He is powerful and seems to have an inexhaustible supply of energy. Now that Nyoka has gone, Anderson decides to also come to the party. He and Batista become friends and over the coming days they are never far from wherever the hardest work is to be found.

We are quickly becoming used to certain sights and sounds. There was the early morning parade of women and girls, which later would be followed by the mid-morning parade when they would all return to wash pots and pans and bathe in the water. Naked from the waist up, the girls' cavorting and shrieking became a little more exaggerated and enthusiastic as the days went by. Usually they had no audience, but our efforts to rescue the *Pelican* had provided them with one and they were enjoying the limelight, splashing and dashing around in the shallows, teasing and joking with any of the men who were able to multi-task enough to work, observe and engage in conversation. Later the girls would get braver, and some would come down to the bay in the afternoons, strip down to bra and panties and drape themselves in the water over one of the boat's life rings, idly flicking the water with their hands, slowly floating backwards and forwards and pirouetting around the *Pelican*.

We use a spare cable to tie off the bow of the *Pelican* to the *Thyolo* so that we can free up that pulley. A new heavy-duty chain has been blagged by Lazaro from the Marine Department at some unknown but no doubt extortionate rental price. It's so heavy that it has to be transported by pickup and then, for its final short journey down to the bay, hauled like some giant anaconda by a team of six men. This new chain is threaded into our pulley and both pulley blocks tied off to the same baobab tree. Two gangs of three men each now pull in tandem to draw the *Pelican* towards the shore. It's hard, back-wrenching work with the men having to dig their feet into the ground to anchor themselves and wrap cloths around their hands to help provide grip and avoid flaying the skin.

The ratings on both pulleys are for three tons lifting capacity. The chain is threaded between a steel outer casing and a cog with prongs. The casing ensures that the links are fully engaged on the prongs of the cog and cannot jump off. As the cog can turn in only one direction due to an internal ratchet, once a link of chain has been taken up on the cog it cannot slip back unless the ratchet breaks or it is released manually.

The morning wears on. Stephen and I step forward and offer to help. Work stops and the men stare at us. There's some quick banter in Chichewa followed by loud guffaws. Lazaro tries to keep a straight face as he thanks us but says it's not necessary. The guys won't hear of it. It's really hard, sustained physical work and we know that they don't believe we're up to it. They are probably right.

I become mesmerized by the sound of the clicking ratchets as, in fits and starts, the pulley wheels turn and the main chains attached to the stern of the *Pelican* increase their pull, drawing the boat towards us millimetre by millimetre. The men keep up a continual banter as they strain away and the sweat streams off them. Breaks for a rest and drink become more frequent.

Eventually my mesmeric state turns to alarm. The chains are now taut like violin strings. Stephen and I halt work and discuss the situation with Lazaro. We don't believe that the chains and pulleys can withstand much more tension. They are bound to snap at any moment. Lazaro merely smiles and chuckles. We need faith he says. Lots! The chains, he assures us, can withstand much more stress. His concerns lie with the ability of the men to continue to pull on them.

Over the course of the morning we have had to tighten the cables on the barrels to keep the *Pelican* sitting level in the water, and this is a clear indicator that the boat has moved towards the shore and into shallower water. At the start of the day we had taken a visual fix between a large rock and a prominent tree on the far side of the bay that were in direct line with the rear of the *Pelican*. Checking out these markers now there is no doubt that the she has reversed up around a metre. We need perhaps another metre. Then we would be in with a fighting chance of sealing up all those windows and doors to enable us to start pumping the water out. I take a mask and cautiously check out the stern. There is no doubt about the movement backwards. But we now have a fresh problem. As she has reversed up, the *Pelican* has gouged a short, deepening path into the lake bed. We are now trying to pull her as she digs herself in.

It's mid-afternoon when we call it a day. We'll start again early tomorrow when the crew will be fresh and rested and we have pondered where to go from here.

### *Day 4 – Friday*

The weather is on the change. The wind has got up in the night and as the day wears on, dark clouds bring the rumble of thunder and the flash of distant lightning to the south. It adds a degree of urgency.

We visit the state electricity company compound looking for blue gum poles. They have plenty lying around but are not prepared to part with any. A friend of Lazaro's locates some old, discarded fencing poles at the telephone exchange and we arrange for half a dozen to be brought down to the bay. Our objective is simple. Dig out the mud and stones under the skegs at the stern of the *Pelican*, slide poles under the skegs and use the poles as rollers to enable us to drag her back another metre. We know this will mean working by feel, because as soon as the mud and silt are stirred up visibility will reduce to zero. On the plus side, the depth involved is barely more than a metre. And everyone wants to have a go. The banter and advice given to each volunteer is good natured and incessant.

Eventually each 'free diver' nods as if he has taken in everyone's counsel, takes a deep breath, closes his eyes and pulls himself under. It seems to be more about who can hold his breath the longest. Anyone breaking the thirty-second barrier is good. As the seconds tick by the beach crowd issues forth with numerous 'Eeees' and 'Aaaahs.' It all turns out to be more about comic relief and team building.

After an hour I go down to inspect the work and discover that there is actually nothing to find. Reshaping the lake bed is not going to happen without a mechanical digger, and we had made enquiries about diggers and cranes at the very beginning and drawn a blank. We give up on our pole rollers idea.

Plastic is both wonderful and terrible stuff. It's shaped and benefited our world hugely. And polluted it massively. We have large quantities of black bin liners and this seems like the time to see if we can make use of them. Stephen and I work our way around the outside decking of the Pelican, pressing the plastic liners into every gap and crack we can find and then spreading more across doors and windows. By mid afternoon we are satisfied with our handiwork and we ferry Stephen's small petrol pump over and place it on the top deck with the suction pipe snaking down the stairs leading from the top deck to the wheelhouse and then down into the main galley.

The big red fire engine pump, Lady Godiva, is heavy and we are not prepared to risk transferring her from the *Thyolo* at this stage. She sits at the rear of the old tugboat with the suction pipe draped over the bow of the *Pelican,* then along and through the smashed wheelhouse window and down into the main galley. Over the next few days we will get to know Lady Godiva well. She often threw tantrums, but when working she could pump huge volumes of water. We were totally reliant on her and she seemed to know it. For all of us she became a living personality that we variously cajoled, begged and cursed, usually to no avail. Anderson took control of her, and with time and patience he learned more or less to manage her moods and idiosyncrasies though she never tired of teasing him and keeping him on his toes.

Eventually we get both pumps working together and the water level inside the *Pelican* drops a foot very quickly. Anderson is grinning and nodding at us from his stage on the rear deck of the *Thyolo*. The level drops another six inches or so, but then refuses to go down any further. We switch off, recheck suspect areas for water ingress, reinforce as we think necessary and get ready to give it another go.

Then an unexpected disaster strikes. The tubular metal framework onto which the shade awnings on the top deck are tied is at half-mast. Moving around, one has to constantly duck under the framework. Stephen, excited and exuberant, bends down to prime his pump. The brim of his hat obscures the framework and he heads it good and hard. Bellowing in pain, he slumps down onto the decking. There's a copious quantity of blood and lots of mutterings. I suspect that we will now have to get him ashore and off to the nearest medical centre for stitches.

I hold a clean rag to his forehead for a couple of minutes and then take a peek. I'm relieved and a little astonished. He has a nasty cut, but it won't need stitches. There's already a growing bump. He's going to have a nasty bruise and a stellar headache. I clean him up and bandage his head with a clean T-shirt torn into strips and he insists that although he's feeling distinctly woozy, he's ready to soldier on. Which he does, though he's clearly disorientated, staggering around and not making one hundred per cent sense. In retrospect I realise that he was quite badly concussed.

To avoid any further such accidents, we spend half an hour hammering out the awning frame and throwing it overboard to be dragged ashore later. Then the pumps are primed and we're off again. With exactly the same result. We simply cannot get past the previous low water level in the pumping process. We've hit a 'water wall' beyond which the pumps cannot take us. A sage psychologist I think is credited with saying something along the lines that madness consists in trying the same thing again and again and expecting a different result.

We call a halt and take stock. Perhaps what we are trying to do is crazy. But I feel a growing resolution and stubbornness. Perhaps a bit of madness creeping in. And yes, it smacks of Paul Theroux's Allie Fox and his refusal to accept defeat. 'Fighting the current' to the bitter end. We've come too far to give up without a fight. I just hope I can recognise the moment when it's time to walk away.

We ask Lazaro to find a good carpenter who can board up the wheelhouse doors and in short order he returns with a young Malawian who has relocated to Metangula in pursuit of a girl and a better life. We agree the job, the price and the timeframe. He must have the job completed by midday tomorrow. We then head into town for a cold beer and, in Stephen's case, paracetamol for his thumping head.

### *Day 5 – Saturday*

The carpenter pitches up with the boarding around nine in the morning and sets to work. The early morning parade has come and gone and Stephen and I are restless, unused to this idleness. In the end we opt to manhandle Lady Godiva across to the *Pelican* and get everything ready. As the carpenter nails the boards up we trail after him with black plastic, jamming and forcing it with screwdrivers into every crack and cranny.

By two in the afternoon we are ready to have another go at resurrecting our black plastic painted boat. The pumps are primed and started and we're off, water gushing in promising torrents from the two outlet pipes amidst a cacophony of noise and a steady plume of smoke from Lady Godiva. The water level drops fast and the nose of the *Pelican* rises as she cants to port. And there she sits with the water level stubbornly refusing to go down further. Once again we shut everything down.

Stephen and I sit on the deck and Anderson comes and slumps nearby. He starts to grill us and I realise that this mild-mannered man, who started his acquaintance with us so shakily, now truly has the bit between his teeth. There is a fierce determination about him. He doesn't accept my response that 'we're at a loss to know where the water is getting in.' We go through the possibilities yet again. The prop shafts may have a leak but it would never be big enough to allow the ingress of water in the volumes that we are pumping. The hatch on the bow deck is properly sealed. So are the windows and doors, even the engine exhausts so that water cannot flow into the exhausts and up through the engines. The only other possibility relates to the small windows of the main berth and the heads. There are four on each side, steel framed with reinforced glass set into the hull. Although they are a good two metres below the waterline, I checked them when doing my initial underwater inspection of the hull and they are intact and properly bolted shut.

'Boss, it must be in the front area. What about you putting your underwater clothes on and having a look? I'm sure you will find the problem then.'

I smile at his phrasing and appreciate his confidence in me, but I consider this option only briefly.

'I'm not happy to go diving around inside the front of the boat. Visibility will be virtually zero so I really don't think there's a lot I can achieve.'

I'm also thinking diving inside a sunken, unstable vessel is a recipe for a tragedy.

'What if you were to re-check those windows again from the outside?" suggests Stephen.

My first instinct is to shrug and say no, what's the point? Yet it's not an unreasonable suggestion. We are, after all, into eliminating possibilities. I heave myself upright.

'Okay, let's do it. But we should also start the pumps again. Then if water is getting in through any of those windows we'll know pretty quickly.'

Twenty minutes later the pumps have reached their predictable standstill in terms of pumping out, and I slip down the side of the hull with a clutch of black bin liners tucked into my weight belt. The liners are now our equipment of first and last resort. I test the first window, trying to push against it. There's no movement. It's shut tight. I put my hand up against the window but can't feel the pull of water being sucked in from around the sides of the frame. I'm about to give it up and move on to the next window when I think 'What the hell.' I pull a black bin liner from my weight belt and push it towards the window. To my amazement it's as if an invisible hand has taken hold of it. The liner pulls away and slips purposefully towards the window, where it is immediately sucked into the sides of the frame. I take out another bag and watch as it also gets sucked up. The third bag floats free and I grab it and move over a few feet to repeat the process on the next window. In less than ten minutes all eight windows have gobbled up my bin liners and are fully sealed. I'm completely astonished and elated. This is surely a game changer.

When I eventually surface and have hauled myself aboard, I find Stephen doing a jig and Anderson has a huge grin on his face. The water level is dropping fast. I want to join them, but though I can't keep what I'm sure is a totally inane grin off my face. I'm cautious. Surely it can't be this easy?

Over the next half hour the *Pelican* empties fast. The bow comes up, the stern down. She is like a sinking ship in reverse and looks as if she is trying to propel herself out of the lake.

What we don't know is that we are about to take a lesson in the swift and terrifying consequences resulting from 'the free water effect.'

On the first day of our rescue mission we had attached several lines on each side of the *Pelican*, taken them ashore and tied them off to large sturdy trees. These, along with the steel buoyance barrels that we had attached to the sides of the boat, were supposed to hold her level. Yet they were simply not man enough for that job. As the water level now drops. the *Pelican* starts to heel alarmingly to port. Anderson, Stephen, two crew and I find ourselves hurtling down the tilted top deck. The pumps join us, cascading down and crashing into the railings, which thankfully save all of us and the pumps from hurtling overboard into the lake. In a heartbeat the circumstances have changed. From cautious optimism we have been literally catapulted into a rather startling situation.

'Switch off the pumps!' Stephen bellows.

As the pumps splutter to a standstill, for a few seconds all is quiet and motionless. Then there are shouts from the shore, and turning I pick out Agent Glum, who has been sufficiently stimulated by the flurry of action to change from his usual position slumped down against a tree to standing and staring intently in our direction.

Self-preservation kicks in and the two crew are climbing

the deck railings. They jump overboard and splash towards the shore. I turn to Anderson, crouched down by the pumps. He looks ready to go down with them if necessary.

'Anderson, if the boat turns over you can't save the pumps. Best to get yourself off the boat now.'

He simply smiles and responds with a confidence I certainly don't share.

'The boat is not going over, boss. The stern is sitting on the bottom. She won't turn any further. We should keep pumping. She'll come level again. You'll see.'

He might be right. He might also be very wrong. I have never forgotten the pictures broadcast in relation to the MS *Herald of Free Enterprise* ferry disaster. She left Zeebrugge in Belgian on the evening of the 6th March 1987 bound for Dover on the English coast, a roll on/roll off vessel fully laden with cargo, vehicles, 459 passengers and 80 crew. Only ninety seconds after she left the calm waters of the harbour she had listed to port twice and capsized. 193 passengers and crew were lost, despite the fact that the ferry was barely a kilometre from the harbour. Basically the massive bow door had been left open and as she picked up speed seawater had rushed in. The resulting free water effect destroyed the ship's stability. She ended up beached on her side like a huge red whale, and the only reason she did not sink was because she capsized on a sandbar. It was extremely tragic, but also astonishing. The free water effect had been so profound and quick that a ship of nearly eight thousand gross tonnage had capsized in less than two minutes.

I heave myself up to the top of the canting deck, where Stephen joins me. We stare at the taut lines, three of them on this starboard side stretched very tightly now from the *Pelican's* railings to nearby trees.

'If those shorelines give way I doubt the barrels will be able to hold her. She'll turn turtle,' Stephen says gravely.

'Sayonara *Pelican*,' I mutter, turning back to Anderson. 'No, Anderson. We'll not risk it. It's late and everyone's tired. Let her fill up with water again and we'll have another go in the morning.'

He looks distraught. I know he thinks we are very close to victory. Stephen and I are not so sure. We might be close to total catastrophe. We scramble to the stern and take the *Bluebell* to shore. Captain William on the *Thyolo* will keep an eye on things and send someone if anything disastrous happens. For now it's in the lap of the gods. Ironically, what we really need to happen now is for the *Pelican* to sink quietly back down onto her bed of silt.

CHAPTER 28

# BREAKING FREE

*Day 6 – Sunday 13th April*

Stephen and I are up and out early. The grey clouds have disappeared to the north and been replaced by a bright blue sky. At the crown of the hill leading down to our little bay, tree canopies gently sway in the fresh, cool breeze. The *Pelican* has settled back onto the lake bed and she is thankfully more or less level. Ready to greet us. 'Okay folks. Here I am. Sitting pretty for you. Give it another go if you dare.'

Of course we dare! We spend the morning trussing her up like a turkey. Every spare inch of line we can find is used and soon we run out of anchor points on the shore. We resort to placing loops of line around huge boulders. There's an intensity and purpose to everyone's actions. We now know – or think we know – exactly what is needed to get the boat re-floated. Incredibly, it's two in the afternoon by the time we tie off the last line and slump down exhausted in the shade to admire our handiwork.

It's a source of great regret that I didn't take photographs of all our efforts throughout this week. My excuse is that we were all totally immersed in the moment and busy with whatever needed to be done. Somehow taking out a camera would have been an almost frivolous activity. Nowadays taking photographs on a smartphone is a simple, almost reflex action. People of all generations snap anything and everything that takes their fancy in pretty much any situation. Here's an interesting example of how ingrained, essentially second nature, smartphone photography has become.

I was told a story about a game guide who was leading a small party of visitors on a foot safari specifically to view some black rhinoceroses in a rhino sanctuary. Coming round a large termite mound, they startled themselves and a mother rhino with a young calf who were quietly chomping on the grass some thirty metres away. The guide told his guests to stand still while he moved off to distract the mother rhino, who had instantly become very alert and agitated.

To give some idea of what the guide was up against, consider the following. Your average fully-grown female black rhino generally weighs in at over a ton. They are browsers who like a quiet, solitary life and don't like to be surprised. They may not be the Ferraris of the animal kingdom, but they are surprisingly agile and quick. The fastest speed that Usain Bolt ever reached whilst breaking world records and winning gold medals was just under 28 mph. The black rhino rumbles over the ground at around 35 mph. In a race 'the Bolt' would have no chance. Strong senses of smell and hearing help compensate for poor eyesight – they have been known to charge odd-shaped trees and rocks.

One of the tour group decided to ignore the guide's order and to follow him. Goodness knows why. Perhaps she thought she might get a better view or simply didn't understand the danger.

The guide and his disobedient stalker probably ticked most threat boxes. Unfamiliar smell and shape, noise and movement close to her and her calf. Black rhinos are not wired to assess a threat; if startled, the aggression is instant. They lock on and charge, hell bent on total destruction.

This rhino mum charged the disobedient elderly guest and then things happened rather fast. The guide rushed back to save the guest, pushing her to the ground and then turning to run across the rhino's path to distract her. The agitated rhino instantly changed course and pursued the hapless guide as he attempted to leg it into the nearest bit of cover. With her large horn she caught him in the buttock and tossed him into the air before moving in to thoroughly trample and gore him. Very luckily for the guide, at this critical point the rhino mother found herself conflicted. Her calf had not moved and was now calling from some distance away. For long seconds she snorted, undecided. Eventually she opted to trot back to her calf, and after surveying the scene for a few more seconds, mother and calf turned and disappeared into the bush.

Blood is now pouring from the brave guide. On his stomach, he slowly hauls himself over the ground to where the guest is lying prone on the ground in order to check if she's all right. Which it turns out she is. When he next looks up at the rest of his party of safari guests he finds them obediently standing right where he left them. But none are coming to his aid or that of their colleague. These are the modern gunslingers; all of them have drawn their mobile phones and are absorbed in taking bloody photographs and videos of the action.

Lady Godiva is throwing one of her tantrums. She doesn't want to do any work this afternoon and Anderson and Stephen spend a precious half-hour checking her over, priming the fuel system and pulling on the starter cord until finally, with a loud bang, she emits a cloying black cloud of exhaust smoke and rattles into action.

The next half-hour is familiar. The water level drops and the bow comes up. Stephen's pump now splutters to a standstill. Then Lady Godiva starts to huff and puff at being left to do all the work and also throws in the towel. For a long, frustrating half-hour we tinker and clean and cajole until finally Stephen's pump starts up again. Another twenty minutes of pumping and then to our amazement we reach a point where the main hull of the *Pelican* – the front berths, the main cabin and the engine compartment – are more or less fully pumped out.

Our problems are not, however, over. The stern compartment that houses the steering gear is completely self-contained. The rear hatch that gives access to this compartment is located at the very stern on the starboard side. That compartment and the hatch remain underwater. We had hoped that there would be sufficient buoyancy once the main body of the *Pelican* had been pumped out to lift the stern just slightly up and off the lake bed, allowing us to then either pull the boat backwards towards the shore or for the hatch to rise above the waterline to enable us to then pump out the compartment.

We decide that we now have to do what we have spent the whole morning working to guard against: very carefully loosen the lines on the starboard side so that the *Pelican* tilts to port. By dropping the port side and raising the starboard side, we might just be able to bring the stern hatch above the waterline. It's a slow, nerve-racking job which increases the strain on the starboard lines considerably. I agonize that we are about to lose the *Pelican* just when victory is within our grasp. We face one or more crux points in many of life's enterprises. Climbing mountains, giving birth, passing a chemistry exam. And in this case, marine salvage.

We hold our nerve, releasing the lines until we are within a centimetre or two of bringing a section of the hatch above the waterline. The *Pelican* makes an odd and disturbing site with the bow pointing skywards and the vessel skewed to port. Decorated as she is with strips of black plastic, in the world of the weird and wonderful she looks like a shipwreck that has finally thrown off the shackles of Davy Jones' locker and is frozen at the point of bursting back into the land of the living.

I grab some offcuts of plywood and more of our trusty black bin liners and wrap them around the collar of the hatch, then tie everything tightly in place with nylon line. We have our extra centimetre of height and it's just enough!

It's nearly six o clock in the evening and the daylight is disappearing fast. We work feverishly, bringing Stephen's pump down onto the stern deck and perching it on some planks that we have run between the railings. The suction pipe is thrust down into the hold and with Stephen holding the pump in situ, Anderson starts her up. The water level drops rapidly and the free water becomes concentrated on the port side, further increasing the Pelican's crazy angle in the water. She's heeling to port at around thirty degrees, and the stern is still refusing to lift off the lake bed. We are working with torches now but cannot get the suction pipe past all the steering gear into the far side of the compartment. Frustrated, we switch off the pump.

We need someone to drop down inside and thread the pipe into the far corners of the hold. We need someone very brave and probably a little cooked in the head. If the starboard lines give way there is absolutely no doubt in my mind that at the very least the *Pelican* will flip onto her side.

Calisto, one of the former guards on the boat, is standing with us and he has picked up on what is being said. He immediately volunteers. He's always been dependable and I know he's very upset at what has happened to the *Pelican*. He's made it well known that he thinks Chirinsa is a bad and greedy man.

I'm fretting like the proverbial old woman and insist that we spend precious minutes trying our best to explain to Calisto what is needed, and most of all, the dangers. I take my head torch, position it on his head and switch it on. For such a large man he lowers himself surprisingly quickly into the compartment. Anderson hands him the end of the suction pipe and he disappears with it. Less than thirty seconds later he shouts. 'Okay!'

The pump is primed and we cross our fingers. Our luck holds and the pump rumbles straight into life. For the next twenty minutes Calisto moves the suction pipe around inside the compartment, chasing down the remaining free water. Frequently we have to briefly stop and then reprime and restart the pump as Calisto lifts and resites the pipe.

The twilight drama has lots of onlookers. Not only our workers, but it seems as if the entire nearby village is strung out around the shoreline of the little bay, the girls from the morning parade standing silently with the adults, all waiting and watching expectantly. The portside lean of the *Pelican* has increased yet further and is now so severe that Stephen and Anderson are struggling to keep themselves and the pump in place. I have Stephen's torch, flicking the beam between the pump, the hatch and the mooring lines, nervously looking for any signs of trouble, ready to shout out a warning if any of the lines snap.

Surely there could not be much water left in the rear compartment? I am beginning to doubt that the silted lake bed will ever release the *Pelican* from its cloying embrace when we feel an almost imperceptible shift in the decking. Then, in slow motion, the *Pelican* rolls to starboard and levels out as the stern rises out of the water. In unison Stephen and I roar 'Yeeees!' We shut the pump down, and from out of the twilight come shouts of jubilation and we can see shadows in motion, the morning parade cavorting and splashing around, hollering out the universal high-pitched African yodel. Calisto's head appears at the hatch, the light from his head torch jumping across our faces and revealing huge grins all round.

We close the stern hatch before anyone can fall into it in the dark and place the pump onto the decking. Then we pull away the plastic and boarding, open up the rear double doors that lead into the main cabin and enter the boat. The floors are treacherously slippery from grease, oil and algae, so we skate and slide along like drunkards, clutching at any fittings that come to hand. I lower myself carefully down into the engine compartment, my head torch lighting up a dripping cavern, the immutable engine blocks black and glistening. Crawling to the stern, I fix the prop shafts squarely in the torch beam and stare for long seconds. There's nothing to see other than the expected very slow drip of water from the starboard shaft seal, unhurried teardrops, which are certainly no cause for concern. Back in the main cabin we check out the forward areas and then return to inspect the steering compartment. I breathe a big sigh of relief. There's no sign of water ingress anywhere.

Captain William arranges for his crew to take shifts keeping an eye on the *Pelican* throughout the night. Although I was now certain the *Pelican* was essentially watertight, one of them would come up to the Bamboo Basket if there were any problems. We were totally elated but also all in. The day had been a roller coaster and had chewed up our last reserves of physical and nervous energy.

*Day 7 – Monday*

'Before you can leave Metangula with the *Pelican* you will require a Certificate of Departure issued by the Marine Department,' Chirinsa declares primly.

He has left us hanging around for an hour outside his office this morning. His way of telling us that whilst we might have a Court Order, he's still the guy in charge around this neck of the woods. We have been summoned, and clearly he's intent on causing problems. He looks and sounds truculent. I sigh inwardly and take a deep breath. We all know where this is heading. It's a question of how much. Equation. Take the higher figure for what Chirinsa thinks he should be able to squeeze out of us and add it to what we are hoping to 'get away with' and divide by two. Except of course we have no clue what amount Chirinsa is hoping to fleece us for.

Now we know what Chirinsa's ace in the hole is. Or one of them at any rate. Stephen and I have discussed what his next play might be. All we could be sure of was that he would lob one or more obstacles into our path. No graceful acceptance of our success in raising the *Pelican,* no 'go in peace with my blessing', from this man.

'This is basically a departure authorisation?' Stephen enquires. Chirinsa merely nods.

'Can you issue that now?' I ask, knowing that Chirinsa is at least one move ahead of us and will have a list of reasons why not. Which will certainly include the little matter of a fee.

'In order to issue this certificate I need to carry out an inspection to be sure about the seaworthiness of the *Pelican*. I also need to be sure that the crew for both the *Thyolo* and the *Pelican* are properly qualified. You do not appear to have a qualified captain.'

'Mr Chirinsa,' I say with exaggerated slowness. I'm barely holding my composure, but whatever else I don't want to give Chirinsa the satisfaction of seeing me loose my cool. 'We have three qualified captains. Anderson, William the captain of the tugboat, and myself.'

'The ship's manifest states that the captain is Nyoka. All others are simply skippers or crew. They do not have the correct qualifications.'

As Chirinsa knows only too well, Nyoka has left in disgrace on the *Ilala*.

'William Chamba is the captain of the *Thyolo*. Anderson is also fully qualified to captain a boat up to 50 tons. Nyoka was included in the crew only because he had experience with salvage work. However, as you know, he was of little help to us.'

'I need verification. Bring me Chamba's captain's certificate and we should ring Captain Mponda of the *Ilala* so that he can verify Anderson's qualifications.'

We play cat and mouse for the rest of the day. Captain Chamba's certificate is produced. We cannot get hold of Lamek Mponda to verify Anderson's qualifications and Chirinsa remains adamant that we cannot leave without a departure authorisation which he won't issue until he is satisfied that both boats have a qualified captain and he's done his seaworthiness inspection. I'm also kicking myself. I didn't think to bring my qualification certificate. With three other captains in the rescue party I had thought my certificate would be entirely surplus to requirements.

It's mid afternoon when Chirinsa tells us what we owe him for his 'help.' He dresses up his bribe as a rental fee for the loan of an old water pump he had thrust upon us earlier in the week (and which, as he must have known, would never work as it was missing several vital parts) and the heavy link chain, which had been very useful. Lazamo had told us it didn't actually belong to the Marine Department. It is apparently the property of the Naval Base, which would make sense given its size. If a fisherman tried to load it onto his wooden fishing craft it would almost certainly sink. I'm sure it was one of the items Chirinsa purloined when he was desperately trying to salvage the *Pelican* back in June 2007.

The rental fee requested is $808 and we settle on $500, paying this over to Chirinsa in cash on the back of his promise that Agent Glum would come down to the bay with the relevant receipt later in the day. Chirinsa takes the opportunity to sternly remind us that under no circumstances are we to leave until he is in a position to issue a Certificate of Departure.

'If we see you are preparing to leave the penalties will be most severe.'

Well he's undoubtedly giving it his best shot at scaring us into obedience. Stephen and I know it's best to play meek and compliant roles. Deadpan, we just nod.

Although sceptical, to our great surprise just before five in the evening Agent Glum appears with our receipt. It reads:

'Despesas de operacao de salvamento da embarcacao *Pelican*.' *Pelican boat salvage operation expenses.*

Having been directly and solely responsible for the sinking of the *Pelican*, Chirinsa is now minded to ensure that if this receipt ever actually finds its way into the official logs, his superiors will know only that he has been directly responsible for her successful salvage. Agent Glum has instructions to repeat Chirinsa's warning about not leaving, which he does, using Lazaro as his translator.

Everyone who has helped has been paid off with good bonuses and we've splashed out on beer and cokes and arranged some goat's meat and bread. Of all people, Inacio, the Customs chief, appears and promptly sets about cooking the meat on a metal grill he has magicked up. He's on good form, smiling and joking with everyone. It's a monumental turn around in terms of the Customs department. We make speeches of heartfelt thanks to all our sweaty, friendly and almost always cheerful band of brothers who have made it all possible. It's been a special week that I will always treasure and wouldn't swap for anything.

Up on the hillside I spot Agent Glum, who has retreated to his post under the large baobab, impassively watching and listening as always. I wonder which parts he will report back to his master. Suddenly I feel that this is a time when we should be inclusive and generous, and I turn to Stephen.

'We should ask Agent Glum to join us. He's been part of this, Chirinsa's spy on the hill. You could even say he helped make us even more determined to succeed.'

Stephen waves his beer bottle in genial agreement and swivels around, his eyes searching the hillside.

'Yes, absolutely. Bring him down. The more the merrier.' He peers harder, searching around. 'Where is Agent Glum?'

I look back up the hillside. Agent Glum has vanished.

*Day 8 – Tuesday*

It's a short night at the guesthouse. Midnight, and time to execute our simple – and we hope sweet – plan. Stephen and I grab our bags and head down to the bay using head torches to light our way, feet crunching loudly on the dirt road. With the exception of the distant yap of a dog, Metangula is fast asleep. On the ridgeline an occasional puff of wind is the first hint that a change in the weather may be underway. Somewhere over my right shoulder the black night merges with the vast, slumbering lake.

There's movement and hushed voices aboard the *Thyolo*. After the beach party we had given William instructions to wait until midnight and then release all of the *Pelican's* mooring lines and attach a short towline. We do our final short punt across to the *Thyolo* in *Bluebell* and shove her off towards the beach as we climb aboard. William is waiting for us on deck and he reports without any preamble.

'Anderson has checked the *Pelican*. There are no problems, so we should go.'

He is clearly just as anxious to get away as Stephen and me.

'Who is going to stay on board the *Pelican* during the tow?' I ask.

'Anderson. He's on board now.'

'Okay, Captain William. Heave up the anchor and let's go.' I move to the stern, where I can just make out a dark shape moving about in the *Pelican's* wheelhouse. I wave and beckon. Anderson appears at the bow grinning.

'Morning boss,' he murmurs softly.

It's an incongruous pleasantry in the circumstances, but I reciprocate in kind.

'Morning Anderson. William tells me you've volunteered to stay on board the *Pelican*.' I hand him my head-torch. 'Take this. It will last longer than your handheld torch. You understand how important it is that you check the engine compartment and the rest of the ship for water leakage very regularly? I don't want to look back and see you disappearing down into the lake!'

He chuckles. 'Don't worry. I'll check – but there will be no problem.'

'Well, just in case. Flash the torch on and off if you have any difficulties. Anything at all that is worrying you. Okay?'

'No problem,' he repeats mechanically. He thinks I'm worrying over nothing and he's probably correct in that. I have a new motto: 'Plan for the worst because that's probably what's heading your way'.

'Right then. Let's get this show on the road.'

Bang on cue William starts the engine, which quickly settles into a gentle thrum. The last few metres of the anchor chain start to clatter noisily up the anchor slide onto the winch drum, and suddenly we are moving dead slow ahead. I look at my watch. Just before one in the morning. I half expect to hear someone, probably Agent Glum, shout out of the darkness. *'Stop! Come back! You have no departure certificate. We'll send the navy after you. They'll shoot you out of the water!'*

William steers a course down the middle of the channel and close to a long string of lights running parallel to the far shore: fishermen in their small wooden pirogues catching usipa, those tasty little fish which, unfortunately for them, are attracted to the surface by the light. For half an hour we head slowly up this perfectly still stretch of water and onto a gently bobbing sea. The lights of Metangula appear around the headland and then slowly start to recede. With the cloak of darkness, the steady vibration of the engine and our hushed voices, it really does feel as if we are escaping, slipping away from a hostile shore.

My overactive imagination is working overtime. I glance astern, expecting to see the angry silver trails of the Mozambican Navy launches racing in pursuit and the arc of red and green tracer bullets. However John Fleming once told me that their motor gunboats look pretty and the engines are diligently cleaned and polished until they gleam, but they rarely run them due to a lack of diesel.

After an hour, when we are well out on the open lake and the lights of Metangula have faded away, William puts the engine into neutral and we replace the short towline with a longer fifty-metre one. As the tow is taken up again, Stephen and I watch the white silhouette of the *Pelican* slip back and become swallowed up in the darkness. There's a member of the *Thyolo's* crew posted at the stern rail watching for any signal from Anderson. Just in case. There's nothing for either of us to usefully do, so we decide to head down below to get some shuteye. It will be a long, slow crossing.

I'm jolted out of my sleep. The *Thyolo* has rolled hard to starboard and nearly thrown me from my berth. Another roll in the reverse direction and I'm pressed against the side of the hull. A few seconds later the whole ship judders. Gripping the ladder tightly, I climb up and out of the hold. Pre-dawn, a weak, ashen light reveals washed-out lines and half-shadows, the grey sea merging with the leaden sky in every direction. A fine drizzle is sweeping in and the lake is in a lumpy, ugly mood with big, heavy swells and crashing rollers. Our old tug is tracking a course almost parallel to this running sea, her long thin beam causing her to roll and pitch in an exaggerated fashion. She's definitely not designed for this.

Turning to stern I can make out the pale and ghostly shape of the *Pelican,* which appears to be coping much better, bobbing on top of the waves and riding them like a cork.

I join Stephen, who is holding onto the beam rails amidships by the little wheelhouse. I look at my watch. It's just past five in the morning.

'Are we halfway across yet?' I shout.

William nods. 'Yes. About half way. But the lake is angry now. Another five hours to Nkhotakota,' he replies.

'Well the *Pelican* looks very stable. No concerns there at least,' I say endeavouring to be positive.

Stephen leans in to speak into my ear.

'Perhaps not, but there are concerns here,' he says sombrely. 'The battery alternator has packed up, so the batteries are no longer being charged. The engineer has just been up to say that the water-cooling pump has also now packed up.'

I frown, digesting this information. The fact that the batteries are not charging should not be a major issue as long as the engine does not need to be restarted. Which it shouldn't in normal circumstances. The water-cooling pump is another matter. If the engine overheats, gaskets and parts could fail or the engine could seize up. Then we'll be floating helplessly at the mercy of a wild, open sea. Somehow it's the fact that it's so deep in this part of the lake – often well over a hundred and fifty metres – that I find most disconcerting. It adds to the sense of being a tiny blip surrounded by a universe of water, even though it would make precious little difference if the *Thyolo* went down in just ten metres of water.

'That's a bit of a bummer,' is all I can think to say.

'William says that this is not the first time the water pump has given up on him. Normally he wouldn't be worried. The old girl can manage without it as long as the engine is not pushed hard. The problem for him right now is that he's battling a nasty sea and also has the *Pelican* on tow. It's putting a lot of strain on the engine.'

I consider that. After all we've been through, is William about to say that he wants to cut the *Pelican* loose? It doesn't bear thinking about so close to our destination.

The engine note changes, dropping down to an idle, and William pokes his head out of the wheelhouse. He plucks the remains of a flattened cigarette from his mouth.

'Engine needs to cool down. Maybe fifteen or twenty minutes we stay in neutral. Then pick up again.'

He surveys the sea over our heads as if noticing it for the first time. Then he grins, his sea dog eyes alight. 'No need to worry. This tug very strong. Gonna make it!'

He sounds convincing, which is certainly comforting. The tug wallows and sits obstinately parallel to the oncoming rollers, soaking up the full force of the increasing wind and breaking waves, rocking like a metronome on her journey from trough to crest and back down again. Released from the pull on the towline, I note that the Pelican has automatically turned bow into the wind and is meeting the waves head on, pitching up and down but in no distress at all. I can make out Anderson standing at the stern of the top deck. I'm sure he's looking at us and thinking that he's very happy to be where he is at this moment.

For the next few hours the tug battles bravely on. Half an hour under way, fifteen minutes or so idling to let the engine cool. The light gradually improves, pushing down through the heavy clouds to illuminate our little drama below. By nine o'clock the wind has driven the clouds away to the north and suddenly we are thrown into a fresh, bright new world.

At eleven in the morning, ten hours after we set off from Metangula, we drop anchor just off the beach at Nkhotakota. Quite suddenly and unexpectedly, we are at the finish line. We have broken out of this hallucinogenic bubble which seemed to be controlled by some invisible and capricious sibylline hand, holding the *Pelican* and us in its grasp for four long years. Our Groundhog Days are over, immediately whizzing at improbable, lightning speeds into the past as we look with intense and bright expectations towards a new horizon.

We say effusive thanks and goodbyes to William and his crew, and to Anderson, whose own newfound exuberance has got the better of him. He has leapt off the top deck into the water and swum vigorously across to the *Thyolo*. The crew will continue the journey, pulling the *Pelican* all the way back on a friendly shoreline to Monkey Bay, where she will finally be put on a trolley and taken out of the water. Then we can all gawp and briefly relive the adventure that is the written in that dented, battered hull. And make plans about her future and how best to restore her back to her former glory.

Stephen is wearing a grin as bright and big as a sunflower as he marches up to me and slaps me on the shoulder.

'Well, Captain Magoo. Where too next? What new worlds are we going to explore?'

'Just beam me to shore, Stevie. A cold green or two awaits us.'

A fishing boat ferries us across. Stepping off the little wooden craft onto the beach where tiny sparkling wavelets gently slap the shore, the exhilaration of the journey and the relief at its conclusion come together and bubble up. We stand for photographs with Captain William and his crew. Beaming. Euphoric. Perhaps a picture really can tell a thousand words.

CHAPTER 29

# Releasing the Line

Under a bright blue sky in pretty woodland, three muddled men, driven by greed and devoid of empathy after years of war, executed two young people in a senseless act of violence. Like a big stone thrown into a pond, the ripples resulting from their brutal actions fanned out seemingly interminably, catching up family, friends and a whole army of acquaintances and strangers. I cannot begin to comprehend the raging ocean waves created by people impacted by wars and genocides.

I do have pangs of guilt that two of the three killers were never recaptured to serve their sentences. That at least two others, the crime facilitators and probably the primary schemers, were never even brought before a judge, the Mozambican authorities surreptitiously allowing them to quietly slip away. Perhaps I should have chosen to follow the example of the father of Helen Smith, who doggedly pursued the matter to his grave. Or Julie Ward's father, who is still bravely pursuing justice over thirty years later. I suspect that keeping these bandits behind bars in the face of the intricate web of post-war allegiances, and the hostile indifference exhibited by the various offices of the Mozambican State, would have been like chasing the wind. And continuing the fight for justice and essentially saying 'I cannot be happy again until they are recaptured' would be to end up in my own personal prison, built from endless disappointments and stresses, and an end to any quality of life. In effect the bandits would have claimed me – and my family – as further victims. I am sure that what I do have in common with Ron Smith and John Ward is an ongoing anger and frustration. A measured, quieter anger now with those perpetrators still at large. A more hostile frustration and outrage with the authorities for their duplicity, lies and cover-ups.

In those early days following the murders it seemed to me that justice and revenge could somehow be eloquently combined. In my mind's eye there were fuzzy images of retribution involving the killers being on the receiving end of lots of bullets. My rage and grief were so intense and all-consuming that I was convinced that if someone had given me a gun and put me in a room with the bandits, I would have shot them all out of hand Vin Diesel style and felt all the better for it. Maybe for a year. Or a month. Even a day. Most likely just a couple of minutes.

In the years that followed I grappled almost interminably with concepts of justice. Which in a sense was a truly odd thing to do, given that sentencing had taken place, one killer was dead and the others at large and unlikely to be recaptured. What if, I speculated, when sentencing these bandits back in October 1997, Judge Charles had had more sentencing options available to him? What then would have been the correct punishment?

At university I wrote a jurisprudence paper examining theories of justice. Under Islamic law the concept of retribution may be applied in circumstances where the perpetrator deliberately kills the victim, meaning the perpetrator is also killed. The sentence mirrors the crime and is severe enough to discourage such crimes. Crucially, as the legal case is between the victim and the accused (as opposed to the State and the accused) the punishment is considered the right of the victim or the victim's family, who can decide whether the punishment should be carried out. And if so, the victim, or a member of the victim's family in the case of a capital crime, may carry out the sentence. However, especially where the accused shows genuine repentance, pardoning is encouraged with the sweetener of the promise of a reward in the hereafter.

In many African cultures tribal or customary law (generally meaning the law applied prior to colonialism) emphasised the duty of an individual to act in the common good, rather than the Western world's primary emphasis on preserving the rights of the individual. Again and again there is reference to people acquiring and being of good character and leading moral lives. A bad person is often described as having 'no character'. Among the Igbo people of eastern Nigeria the deliberate killing of another person could result in all property and belongings of the murderer being destroyed, and the killer would be expected to voluntarily hang himself or else take the option to run away, in which case he would add the moral crime of cowardice to that of murder. The requirement of death by hanging would remain – forgive the pun – hanging over him wherever he fled into permanent exile. Given that the community is an integral part of one's life force, being banished from family and community was regarded as a very severe punishment. The option of punishment by imposing a term of imprisonment simply did not exist.

The British philosopher and Nobel laureate Bertrand Russell proposed the popular and exhaustively debated theory of the greatest good of the greatest number. Would it serve society, the community, better and be in the interests of the greater number to remove these killers completely? Does the very real likelihood of a few miscarriages of justice justify not imposing the death penalty? Should we acknowledge these killers as individuals with inalienable rights and show them the empathy and compassion that they singularly failed to display with Andrew and Caroline?

In the end, what I came to recognise was how intensely personal justice is. Whichever approach you adopt, justice remains a treacherous concept to grasp on both the theoretical and the practical levels. You cannot forgive yourself if you haven't done all in your power to get this thing called justice for those you love, which essentially translates to getting the appropriate punishment meted out to the perpetrators of the crime. What is the correct outcome by the victim, the villain and those left behind to suffer? In the real world people die from a single bullet and those left suffering in the aftermath certainly won't feel better after spraying bullets at everything vaguely bad, because in the real world people have to live with the consequences of their actions for a lot longer than a ninety-minute Hollywood film. If justice crosses some invisible line and becomes centred on revenge, the result will in all probability be brutal and bitter, and certainly no panacea. In all likelihood it will compound the effects of all those damaging, swirling emotions. As Socrates said twenty-five hundred years ago, when we take revenge we damage our soul, and if we damage our soul we also damage our chances for a fulfilling and happy life.

I came to accept that justice would be imperfect and that for some occurrences there can never be closure. Nothing could bring Andrew and Caroline back. The best that justice could offer was simply and only that the criminals served their sentences. Time for their crimes. The Mozambican Authorities had made a mockery of even that by allowing the killers to escape and others to evade judgment.

Andrew and I had natural ups and downs in our relationship as brothers, but ultimately we were tuned into each other, the sibling bonds of love, respect and always having each other's backs strong and unshakeable. Yet there came a point, around the same time that the British High Commission ran out of energy to pursue matters, when I knew that I must, in the words of a Zen proverb, 'let go or be dragged'.

You lose a large chunk of yourself whenever a loved person dies or a meaningful relationship fails. I don't subscribe to the often-promulgated idea that you have to forgive a killer in order to move on. I'd go so far as to say that is nonsense. I don't have the prerogative or power to forgive. Only the victims, Andrew and Caroline, could have done that. The killers need to work out how, and if, they can forgive themselves. I can and do choose to move forward, to make space and time to remember Andrew and Caroline in life rather than concentrate on their loss and that brief moment when they crossed the bar. It's an ongoing passage of the mind and spirit. I'm pretty sure I can hear Andrew's laconic agreement: 'Absolutely right. Move on. Pursue your dreams and make lots of those vignettes you always talk about. Just remember us with a smile from time to time.'

Similar sentiments had been expressed to me by my father in a telephone conversation we had had just a few weeks before he died. That you have to let go eventually or else you will drown in the tears of the past.

After dad's passing in 2004 I never heard from the FCO or the Mozambicans again. I will never know the fate of the bandits who are at large. Whether they have been forced to remain far from their communities in exile. Whether they have committed further terrible crimes. Whether they remain of no character, or have turned a new leaf and tried to lead good lives.

# Epilogue

July 2008. Three months since the *Pelican* was towed into Monkey Bay and pulled out of the lake on a trolley. Karen, Philip and I are staring up at the battered hull and twisted skegs. It seems incredible that the prop shafts have somehow escaped undamaged. The *Pelican* is now an empty shell, all the fittings stripped out including both engines, which after three months underwater need to be dismantled, cleaned up and rebuilt. They are very salvageable and one day will roar back into life.

'Well,' says Philip in his thoughtful voice, 'If it was my decision I would sell her to someone who wants to take on a project. A major project.'

He's uttered what I, and I suspect Karen, have been thinking but have been afraid to voice, but the prospect of saying goodbye to this beaten-up hunk of metal and handing her future care and control to someone else is distressing and actually feels disloyal. She's become a personality around which has been woven a part of the fabric of our lives for so many years.

'Let's ask Dad what he thinks,' says Karen.

A day later Don is looking at us with those penetrating, no-nonsense blue eyes, though his demeanour is kindly.

'Don't hold on to her for my sake,' he says in that extra-gruff voice of his, which those who know him recognise as the voice he uses when he's grappling with his emotions. 'The *Pelican* was my creation, my dream, and we've had some great times on board with family and friends. You've done an incredible job bringing her home. But now the best thing you can do is let her go.'

Sadly we know he's right. If we hold on to her we'll become beholden to this boat through misguided sentimentality. And she'll become a millstone rather than an inspiration to action. I ask for final confirmation. Perhaps also a sort of absolution.

'So we should find a buyer?'

'Absolutely. I have only one request. Check out the buyer. I don't want the *Pelican* cut up for scrap. We should be as sure as possible that whoever buys her is actually going to renovate her and put her back on the lake. That's more important, I think, than holding out for the best price.'

So that's what we did. Within a very short time of the word going out a good purchaser came forward and the *Pelican* as a solid, tangible entity disappeared from our lives.

Less than six months later we were all gathered on the farm to say goodbye and pay our last respects to my father-in-law, Edwin Donald Pyman, MBE. He had finally succumbed to cancer, courageous and dignified to the very end. It's a perfect spot for him to be buried – a spot he chose himself – on a small rise where on a clear day you can look out over the tops of the trees at another lake, Lake Chirwa, with the smoky outline of mountains in the far distance. Too many Malawians to count have come to say goodbye to 'our father.'

Don certainly lived life on his own terms, and he took on life's journey with very few regrets, at one with himself and comfortable and sincere in his deep, uncluttered love for his wife Anita, his family, the farm he carefully crafted out of the land and the Malawians he came to understand and love. The citation for his MBE states that it was awarded 'for services to agriculture, the community and the environment.' It was so richly deserved and nicely encapsulated his passions and beliefs.

It's only after the coffin has been lowered and the soil is being piled on top that we realise that it's the wrong way round. Don isn't facing towards the view. It shouldn't really matter, but it did bother me for quite a while. I heard this gruff, scolding voice in my head: 'For goodness sake, couldn't one of you at least have got that right!'

Sometimes it's good not to have too great an imagination, or too many expectations. The *Pelican's* odyssey began as a short adventure, a jaunt that spiralled into something much bigger. Life often does that to you. It turns small things into big ones, order into confusion, leaving you struggling to make sense of it all, to remember what is important and why. I could never have dreamt up the piecemeal and often quirky patchwork of events that eventually evolved into something much more than a story about a small steel-hulled boat. It took on a deeply personal vibrancy and momentum, a roller coaster until the *Pelican* became an unexpected flagship for something altogether subtler. Delivering her to Metangula had been a simple struggle against the elements and mechanical breakdowns. But the moment that the drunken Customs chief, Vilanculos, uttered the words 'You are going to die with this fine,' something inside me snapped. Everything changed. From that instant it became a slightly crazy, exasperating and at times comical struggle to reclaim and bring her home. A twisting story about claiming victory in the face of the amoral and perfidious abuse of power. And on another level it was the antithesis of Andrew and Caroline, because with the *Pelican*, the possibility always existed that we just might be able to resurrect and save her.

Here's the dichotomy. Whatever its problems, which abound, you end up both loving and fearing Africa. She mesmerises and seduces you with her vast horizons and the lush and seemingly inexhaustible store of breath-taking landscapes and magnificent wildlife. Very soon you fall profoundly in love with the intense vibrancy of life under her limitless skies. Yet the sheer rawness and the unremitting reminders of the fragility of existence there both grab and crush you. The rural people of Malawi smile, laugh and sing spontaneously and often. They are the have-nots who remain stoical and dignified in the face of grinding poverty as they struggle along in the immediate present without any window of opportunity into the future. In the villages they will happily invite you to cheza – chat – and take tea with them, instinctively offering whatever they have to eat. Is there any act more humbling or beautiful than this unconditional generosity of the very poor? Many know real, basic fear. The fear of starvation and of the sickness that often follows fast on its heels or in the wake of a multitude of killer diseases, chief among them malungo: malaria. It's a fear that the whole world has suddenly had thrust upon it and become familiar with in the wake of Covid-19.

Some experiences we choose to take on, whilst others come rattling towards us. Terrifying. Unbidden. Unwelcome. It is a real comfort to know that Andrew and Caroline were fully immersed and absorbed in the 'busyness of living' before their lives were brutally cut short. Their objective, proclaimed by example, was to make the most of every minute of every day because there are not and never can be any guarantees on longevity. To aim, if not for the stars, as far as they could get to them.

I do have an unease about the future. That we will lose that raw, immediacy of life – the impulse to take risks and push ourselves out of our comfort zones in order to chase hopes and dreams and those sublime or nerve-racking adrenalin-infused moments which, most crucially of all, enable us to discover who we actually are. Perhaps we are being programmed to be more and more willing to accept governmental chains implemented in the name of safety and security whilst we live more and more vicariously through various forms of media, the courage we are born with being inexorably squeezed out of us. Just existing. Then I remember that, old or young, there are still many voyagers out there who don't want to live with regrets. Without creating a memorable collage of life's offerings. They crave adventure, that iridescent sparkle. For most, not quite at the extremes of Captains Cook and Kirk. I've climbed mountains and dived into the shimmering blue world of the oceans. Carefully planned experiences, but nonetheless full of excitement and discovery. And whilst there were failures and failings aplenty, I wouldn't exchange for anything the vivid immediacy that lit up the eclectic kaleidoscope of challenges and escapades presented by the voyage of the *Pelican*.

I think of the brightest light in my life and Karen's: our daughter, Kate. As a child, like all children, brimming with energy and curiosity, a free spirit constantly busy heading off to explore the strange, wonderful world around her. Getting into scrapes as she tested and worked out where the boundaries lay. Letting her imagination work overtime. Whenever we asked where she was going she would simply say, 'On an adventure.' And perhaps the simplest answer as to why Dad and I were so doggedly determined to try to bring all the murderers to justice, and why I couldn't abandon the *Pelican*, is the same reply often given by those adventurers who struggle up mountains or are busy criss-crossing oceans in rowing boats. Which is the same as the self-evident retort of a child heading off to explore: 'Because I must.'

Printed in Great Britain
by Amazon

32238096R00198